Alternative Attitudes Toward Suicide and Its Survivors

Alternative Attitudes Toward Suicide and Its Survivors

Contesting the Darkness of Conventional Stigmas

Edited by Gordon Brubacher, Nicolae Roddy &
Christopher J. Krall, S.J.

t&tclark
NEW YORK • LONDON • OXFORD • NEW DELHI • SYDNEY

T&T CLARK
Bloomsbury Publishing Inc, 1359 Broadway, New York, NY 10018, USA
Bloomsbury Publishing Plc, 50 Bedford Square, London, WC1B 3DP, UK
Bloomsbury Publishing Ireland, 29 Earlsfort Terrace, Dublin 2, D02 AY28, Ireland

First published in the United States of America 2026

Library of Congress Cataloging-in-Publication Data

Names: Brubacher, Gordon Paul editor | Roddy, Nicolae, 1954- editor |
Krall, Christopher J., S.J. editor
Title: Alternative attitudes toward suicide and its survivors : contesting the darkness of conventional stigmas / edited by Gordon Brubacher, Nicolae Roddy & Christopher J. Krall, S.J.
Description: New York : T&T Clark, 2026. | Includes bibliographical references. | Summary: "To better understand and address the needs of suicide loss survivors and those at risk of suicide, this volume offers a multifaceted, multidisciplinary approach based on the natural and social sciences, but with the personal and spiritual needs of this vulnerable population in mind"– Provided by publisher.
Identifiers: LCCN 2025034062 (print) | LCCN 2025034063 (ebook) | ISBN 9781666977547 HB | ISBN 9780567726889 PB | ISBN 9798216251064 ePDF | ISBN 9781978767218 ebook
Subjects: LCSH: Church work with bereaved persons | Loss (Psychology)–Religious aspects–Christianity | Suicide–Religious aspects–Christianity | Suicide–Psychological aspects | Suicide victims | Christian ethics
Classification: LCC BV4330 .A48 2026 (print) | LCC BV4330 (ebook)
LC record available at https://lccn.loc.gov/2025034062
LC ebook record available at https://lccn.loc.gov/2025034063

ISBN: HB: 978-1-6669-7754-7
ebook: 978-1-9787-6721-8
ePDF: 979-8-2162-5106-4

Typeset by Deanta Global Publishing Services, Chennai, India

For David
For TJ
And for Dad

If you or someone you know is struggling or in crisis, help is available. Call or text 988 or chat 988lifeline.org to reach the 988 Suicide & Crisis Lifeline (U.S. and Canada only).

Contents

Foreword

His Grace Bishop Dolan, Diocese of Phoenix

As a survivor of suicide loss, I have come to understand both the deep pain and the complex questions that follow in the wake of such tragedy. Suicide is not only a personal and familial crisis but also a profound pastoral and societal challenge—one that calls for a response rooted in compassion, understanding, and truth. In this book, you will find an interdisciplinary approach that brings together the insights of psychology, neuroscience, scripture, and pastoral care. These perspectives, far from being at odds, ultimately converge toward the same end: the God of salvation and restoration.

I have often spoken about the essential harmony between faith and science. When working together, they offer a path toward healing and wholeness. When one moves too far ahead of the other, however, the result can be confusion, neglect, or even harm—especially for those who have already suffered the devastating loss of a loved one to suicide. It is for this reason that I have made it my mission to foster a mental health ministry in the Diocese of Phoenix, one that integrates proper education in psychology and spirituality, provides accompaniment to survivors of suicide loss, and advocates for increased access to trained counselors both locally and abroad. The Church must stand as a beacon of hope, ensuring that no one suffers in isolation.

This book is a gift to those who seek to understand and accompany others through the complexities of suicide loss. It offers not only knowledge but also consolation. It provides hope for those who struggle with despair and guidance for those—pastors, caregivers, family members, and friends—who wish to walk alongside them. My prayer is that this volume will serve as a source of healing and encouragement, helping all who read it to become instruments of God's mercy in a world that so desperately needs it.

Bishop John Dolan, Diocese of Phoenix

Introduction

Awareness of the need for this volume arose from a hallway conversation between two Creighton University Theology Department colleagues, both of whom experienced loss to suicide of immediate family members—in one instance a father, the other a beloved son, David. The dialogue, which began in the immediate aftermath of David's death, lamented the theologically misguided and insensitive language often heard from well-intentioned friends attempting to offer consolation to grieving suicide loss survivors—comments that often add heft to the burden of grief and despair they already bear. This disconnect between intention and effect is rooted in the fact that suicide is a disconcerting topic—taboo for some—and devastating for many suicide loss survivors. At the very least, proximity to suicide stirs up feelings of dread, evoking the *mysterium tremendum et fascinans*—that is, the numinous mystery that at once threatens to destroy yet attracts with the promise of some sort of fulfillment (Otto 1917; Eliade 1987). In other words, "Suicide is the stuff of religion" (Wasserman 2021, 3).

To better understand and address the needs of suicide loss survivors and those at risk of suicide, this volume offers a multifaceted, multidisciplinary approach based on the natural and social sciences, but with the personal and spiritual needs of this vulnerable population in mind. The project is ecumenical in that the interlocutors mentioned above—an Eastern Orthodox and a Protestant (Mennonite) Christian—added as coeditor a Roman Catholic (Jesuit) priest working at the intersection of theology and neuroscience. The volume's twelve chapters are organized in a phased threefold way that attempts to demythologize suicide, dealing first with the general thrust of the volume's intended purpose, then addressing suicidal ideology specifically among marginalized populations and cultures, and concluding with varied theological resources for further reflection on suicide.

Almost immediately, this volume began taking on a life of its own as thoughtful scholars from many backgrounds and disciplines stepped up to address the topic from their own perspectives and disciplines. The editors and contributors understand that words are seldom effective and often detrimental for attending to a person stricken with unfathomable grief and confusion. They realize that suicide loss survivors share an unspeakably wretched place of despair, but each bear their own deep and distinctive personal torment. To be sure, suicide deaths are grieved differently from natural, planned, or even unexpected accidental death. For this reason, the pondering, anguish, despair, pain, and profound sense of loss suffered by survivors is addressed in multiple ways, both scientifically and pastorally, with a hope that hope itself will be strengthened in contesting the ominous shadow that looms over the subject of suicide.

While the primary interest here is suicide loss, the volume presents a wider-ranging exploration of suicide in different social, psychological, and literary contexts as well. One will not find dispassionate articles limited to suicide proper, such as Durkheim's social capital model (Durkheim 1951), nor does this volume address suicide as presented in literature of the classical, neoclassical, or Romantic periods, which often describe suicide as tragically heroic (Faubert 2018). Instead, suicide is treated here with a combination of scientific objectivity and theological (pastoral) sensitivity.

The volume leads off with Elizabeth Antus's astute analysis of secular and Christian responses to suicide. This strikes at the very raison d'être of the book as envisioned in the hallway conversation mentioned above, namely, the complexities and potential dangers involved in how we respond to suicide in our communities. With this concern in mind, Antus reflects upon the disruptive as well as the reparative elements of Johann Baptist Metz's notion of "dangerous memory" to discern the best ways to honor those who have died by suicide and those who live with suicidality.

Next, Amy Badura-Brack and Ryan Fabry approach suicide loss through the lens of psychology, focusing on diagnostic and therapeutic considerations for those experiencing suicide loss-related grief. It begins by discussing the symptoms of psychological disorders that may present following suicide loss, including adjustment disorder, prolonged grief disorder, post-traumatic stress disorder (PTSD), major depressive disorder, and substance use disorder. It then addresses special therapeutic concerns for suicide loss survivors, which may include emerging or worsening psychological symptoms or elevated risk of the suicide loss survivor's own feelings of suicidality; so, too, grief therapy tailored to suicide loss survivors who may be experiencing feelings of guilt, isolation, rejection, or trauma. Badura-Brack and Fabry hope that an awareness of these diagnostic and therapeutic concerns will help suicide loss survivors and therapists pursue the full spectrum of treatments warranted in the wake of this special type of traumatic loss.

Shifting the balance toward the theological side of things, Gordon Brubacher offers bold reflections on voluntary death from the Older Testament for suicide loss survivors. He begins by pointing out the fact that the Hebrew Bible/Older Testament (hereafter, OT) contains no prohibitions on voluntary death and no moral guidance on the matter. He critiques traditional (mis)use of the OT by various theologians from Lactantius (*c.* 240–320) onward, which produced a harshly judgmental view of suicide as the worst and most unpardonable of sins, generating traditional prohibitions and harmful stigmas for Christian teaching and practice generally. The heart of this chapter contests the darkness of that teaching, presenting instead the major OT theme of a caring God; a highly relational God committed to well-being for all, known for reliability and characterized by faithfulness; and a mothering, compassionate God who is incomparably forgiving and delights in showing an enduring steadfast love.

Nicolae Roddy continues this line of argument by addressing readers who may feel burdened by theological concerns over the personal salvation of a loved one lost to suicide, drawing together a variety of historical and current perspectives on the topic of universal salvation. Unlike many theological approaches to the topic of the afterlife, Roddy's contribution does not presume to know the mind of God. The intent is not to argue in favor of universal salvation; instead, the article presents the historical and doctrinal complexity of the topic in a way that offers the grieving survivor a wider platform for hope in respect to the soul of the loved one who had experienced such utter hopelessness at a crucial moment that yielding their earthly lives back to God seemed to offer the only relief.

Moving now to the effects of suicide among marginalized populations, Todd Salzman and Michael Lawler focus on Catholic Church teachings that potentially traumatize LGBTQ+ people. They discuss the reality of suicide among LGBTQ+ youth and its origin in the social and ecclesial stigma, discrimination, and violence to which they are subjected. Together they argue that two Catholic realities that lie at the root of this trauma are in serious and immediate need of correction. The first is the teaching of the church about same-sex acts, which are taught to be "intrinsically disordered and can in no case be approved." The second is the list of reasons supporting this teaching: the nature of the human person, the constant teaching of the magisterium, and the moral sense of the Christian people, all three of which are theoretically wrong and cannot rightly be used for the purpose of sustaining any practical prohibitions against LGBTQ+ people and same-sex sexual acts. The hope is that this proposal for reform in Catholic sexual teaching will reduce the ecclesial stigma, discrimination, and violence to which members of the LGBTQ+ community are subjected and promote full inclusion in the Catholic community.

Christina Jones Davis examines the intersection of the "trauma revolution" of the past three decades and the advent of social media platforms that amplify trauma-related content, including the killing of Black lives by law enforcement. Davis, a pastoral theologian and a marriage and family therapist, explores how broadcasting Black trauma raises the collective consciousness of this trauma. Davis then investigates the potential interrelationship of racial trauma with the staggering increase in suicide-related outcomes for Black Americans, offering clinically integrated strategies for racially contextualized care in the assessment, prevention, and intervention of what may be considered one of racism's direst of consequences for Black lives—death by suicide.

Next, LaRyssa D. Herrington convincingly argues that the prevention of suicide by Black women begins with an awareness of the sociopolitical structures, presently and historically, which contribute to the persistence of Black suffering. To this end, the pervasiveness of suicidality in Black women can be approached through the healing dimensions present in ritual, helping the participants to recontextualize their experience of suffering within the light of God's grace. Herrington asserts that engagement with the testimonies of Black women achieves the following: first, when one's experience of suffering is united to Christ's own within the depths of the Paschal mystery, they are able to achieve wholeness and restoration to their damaged mind-body holism; second, the testimonies of Black women are prophetically calling all who bear witness to their stories of trauma and survival into penitent acts of confession and contrition, revealing the places within our own lives still in need of God's grace and mercy.

Jamall A. Calloway's chapter offers unique exploration of the pervasive nature of oppression and how it can cause one to, as he calls it, "acquiesce" to suicide. Focusing on two famous tragedies from 2014—the suicides of Sandra Bland in Waller County, Texas, and Rohith Vemula in Hyderabad, India—Calloway draws historical parallels between racism and caste oppression to emphasize the need for international dialogue and solidarity. He believes that international coalition building can help eradicate the oppressions that lead one to believe that suicide is the only solution.

Transitioning to varied resources that invite further reflection on suicide, ethicist Julia Fleming explores an opportunity for Catholic social teaching to better serve the needs of people with suicidal ideation and those affected by the loss of a loved one to suicide. Fleming observes that Catholic social teaching generally focuses on assisted suicide as illustrated in St. Pope John Paul II's *Evangelium Vitae* (1995), but that those who take their lives in other contexts and those left behind to suffer such devastating loss are largely excluded from consideration. Fleming proposes revisiting the opening lines of Vatican II's Pastoral Constitution *Gaudium et Spes* (1965) as a resource for support for this large and largely underserved population.

Next, building upon several years of experience as a feminist theological ethicist and pastor, Kimberly Penner addresses suicide and "medical assistance in dying" (MAID) in relation to the broad theological concept of sin. Understanding sin as injustice (both individual and social), Penner encourages Christian communities to respond to MAID and suicide contextually with a commitment to systemic justice and liberation from inequality and oppression, including supportive culturally appropriate and accessible health care. She concludes by offering suggestions for how to form supportive faith communities focused on healing and justice, which are less likely to cause theological or spiritual trauma.

Christopher J. Krall, S.J., builds upon Simone Weil's concept of *malheur* to describe the intensity of the "affliction" of inevitability and doom that contemplators of suicide may face. Examining the neuroscience of prayer and social neuroscience as complementary aspects of personhood, Krall argues that the hopelessness and loss of agency magnified in *malheur* can be transformed through relationality in connection with God and others.

Rounding out the collection, Tabea Pelzmann provides a fascinating and brilliantly nuanced interpretation of the life, death, and literary afterlife of Judas Iscariot, the disciple who betrays Jesus and eventually regrets his decision. The evangelist Matthew goes further in narrating the consequences of Judas' actions in terms of the betrayer's despair and suicide (Mt. 27:1-10). This in-depth analysis of Matthew's portrayal of Judas and the perspectives of early Christian witnesses such as the *Acts of Peter* and the recently discovered *Gospel of Judas* challenge the traditional interpretation of Judas as the embodiment of evil and his death as a result of divine justice.

In the end, the contributors and the editors unite in a fervent hope that readers will find something of value to equip them in the ongoing struggle to push back against the darkness and despair of suicide loss. And if you are experiencing suicidal thoughts or feelings and live in the United States or Canada, please seek support immediately by dialing 988, the National Suicide and Crisis Prevention Lifeline.

–The Editors

Bibliography

Durkheim, Émile. 1951. *Suicide: A Study in Sociology*. Translated by J. A. Spaulding and G. Simpson. Free Press.

Eliade, Mircea. 1987. *The Sacred and the Profane*. University of Chicago Press.

Faubert, Michelle. 2018. "Introduction to 'Suicidal Romanticism: Origins and Influences.'" *Studies in the Literary Imagination* 51 (1): i–iv. https://doi.org/10.1353/sli.2018.0000.

Otto, Rudolf. 1958. *The Idea of the Holy*. Translated by John W. Harvey. Oxford University Press. Originally published as *Das Heilige*. Breslau, 1917.

Wasserman, Camilla. 2021. "Religion, More than Just Protective." In *Oxford Textbook of Suicidology and Suicide Prevention*, edited by Danuta Wasserman, 3–7 Oxford University Press.

1

Practicing Dangerous Memories, Honoring Suicide Victims, and Building a Liveable World

Elizabeth Antus

When I taught at a different Catholic university some years ago, a student majoring in theology died by suicide in the middle of the semester.[1] The campus and the department were stunned. Though I knew I would soon be teaching a unit in my core class on suicidality, I lamented that the material would be so relevant for my students, many of whom had known the decedent (though I had not).[2] Shortly after finding out the news, I became curious about possible guidelines for faculty wishing to address the death with our students. I did not personally feel flummoxed as an instructor. Rather, I needed to know how the university and the department would be present in this moment. So, I approached our generally well-informed department administrator and asked what she knew about all that. She paused, leaned forward, and lowered her voice: "The president does not want us to talk about it. He said to me, 'We don't want to glorify it.'" For our department, this sentiment was soon translated into the directive to hear the students out if they mentioned the suicide, but not to broach the topic with them otherwise.

I brought it up with my students later that day in class. Most of them already knew. Having written and taught about suicide for years and having lived as a suicide loss survivor myself for most of my life, I was already familiar with best practices for suicide postvention at universities. I knew that addressing it carefully but directly was the correct course of action, particularly given that people were already talking. I asked them if any of them had anything they wanted to say briefly about their fallen fellow student, I answered their questions about suicide from a psychological angle (no, there was not one simple cause, etc.), and I spoke about the relevant theological issues at play (no, he was not in hell, and, yes, that older teaching was offensive, etc.). I spent the most time discussing various campus resources for processing their own grief and possible mental health distress. It was most important for me to normalize their questions and their grief and to let them know that they did not have to bear their agonies alone. Some of them thanked me afterward.

The university president's desire to hide a student's suicide under the cloak of silence is perhaps not surprising, but it perpetuates harm nevertheless. In the first section of this chapter, I use the category of "dangerous memory" from the German Catholic political theologian Johann Baptist Metz (1928–2019) in order to articulate why: when somebody dies by suicide, the surrounding community must accept and keep alive the dangerous memory of this person. Specifically, as Metz would have it, the community has the responsibility to remember that person in their full humanity and subjectivity, to confront the depth of their anguish, and to have its own falsely serene status quo disrupted because of its confrontation with this anguish. Furthermore, this difficult remembering-in-solidarity allows the community to provide a space of recognition for its current members who are not only grieving but who may also be suffering from similar emotional pain, isolation, and mental health conditions as the person who died. These conversations may reveal seismic shifts that need to occur so that the community may become more supportive of people who are suffering, but this disorientation is in service of a kind of *care*, not only of the memory of the person who died, but also of people who are currently suicidal and suffering in relative isolation. Secrecy silences the decedent as well as the people who see themselves in the decedent's agony, and dangerous remembering helps honor the decedent and the pain of those still trying to stay alive.

However, as the second section of this chapter explores, offering the concept of dangerous memory for suicide victims and surrounding communities must not be confused for focusing exclusively or perseverating upon the most violent or deeply upsetting aspects of a particular suicide. While not speaking about suicide is damaging, *speaking badly* about suicide is also noxious. The hazard of bad speech reveals the half-truth in the university president's reluctance to foster honest conversation. As best practices for journalists, media, and schools currently suggest when it comes to public messaging about a suicide, certain unfortunately commonplace ways of speaking must be avoided, importantly so as to prevent a documented phenomenon called "suicide contagion" or "suicide clustering." I focus here on two examples of poor discourse. First, lurid depictions are verboten, largely because they can enable other emotionally vulnerable people to visualize the steps involved in suicide and therefore move closer toward it. Even apart from the particularly tragic possibility of a cluster, it is also evident that focusing on the most shockingly violent content in a suicide constitutes a dehumanizing sensationalism that betrays the suicide victim, the suicide loss survivors, and the broader community.

Second, best practices for discussing a suicide also forbid framing it fatalistically as the inevitable or effective response to any one life stressor, setback, or loss. This framing simplistically flattens out the complexity of the decedent's life and inadvertently implies that nobody else who is struggling could ever get help and go on to have a full life. Such language is a denial of both the victim's multifaceted subjectivity as a sufferer and as a human *and* of a framework of healing and hope for others who are struggling to stay alive. Although Metz promotes a disruptive element to remembering those who suffer, his work also demands that this remembering not occur in a shallow way making for easy commodification and consumption. Metz would have us remember dangerously in a way that re-complexifies, rehumanizes, and holds tenderly the person who is gone while also offering support for those who continue to suffer in this life. In this other way, then, dangerous memory is healing and gentle.

Ultimately, I argue that if communities seek to become more ethically attuned to suicidal misery and death, Metz's concept of dangerous memory helps illuminate promising pathways forward for proper discussions of suicide, especially after a suicide loss. Specifically, to honor all the dimensions of dangerous remembering, communities must thread the needle between, on the one hand, recognizing the torment of the suicide decedent and of others who struggle similarly, and, on the other, embracing such people with proper respect for their complexity and supportive hope for their healing (whether in this life or only eschatologically). Only through this careful attention will communities avoid both an apathetic amnesia and an objectifying exploitation of those who suffer. Dangerous memory requires not only remembering those who suffer, but *remembering them well.*

Metz, Suicide Decedents, and Suicidal Suffering as Dangerous Memory

Metz does not speak about suicide, but unjust death and deep anguish have shaped his theology in a manner that should inform theological approaches to this topic. When Metz was a teenager during the Second World War, he was conscripted into the German military. One night, he was sent out on an errand, and, when he returned the next morning, his entire company had been bombed, and all his fellow soldiers—also teenagers—killed. Metz speaks of the "wordless cry" that he felt upon making this discovery (Ashley 1998, 35). Nothing could be the same for him, and, as he developed over time as a theologian, he became increasingly convinced that theology's fundamental task was to disrupt the faux-serene systems of thought and bourgeois mores of modernity that beckon to us to forget others' pain.

Specifically, Metz comes to feel that the theological task fundamentally centers around what he calls dangerous memories: those memories that we as a community should hold for those who have agonized and died, the unfathomably large group he calls "the dead and the vanquished" (Metz 2007, 67). All suffering concerns Metz, but he is especially focused on the anguish and death of those who are not the victors of history, those who are not remembered for posterity's sake, those who are crushed by others (Metz 1998, 134). He often speaks of this group as those who have been robbed of their subjectivity. While Metz maintains that all persons have innate human dignity, to be a subject more specifically means having the agency and freedom that enables one to stand as oneself before God and to support all others in solidarity to do the same (Metz 2007, 71, 78). Subjectivity for Metz, then, is not that of the radically self-making modern individual, but rather, that of the person who remembers their collective past with others, who hopes with others for a future in which all will be free, and who strives to narrate these stories truthfully (Ashley 1998, 153; Stetler 2013, 304). Specifically, he is notably concerned about the persecution of the Jews during the Shoah, which animates him to insist that we must understand ourselves as doing theology using the metonymic phrase "after Auschwitz," namely, after the massive injustice that has thwarted arrogant illusions of historical progress and theological adequacy (Metz 1998, 54–6).

In a broader sense, his purview applies to any victims of injustice, especially groups who are systematically oppressed around the globe (Metz 2007, 134–5). He declares:

> What I have in mind here is that suffering which makes people fall dumb in "worldly grief" . . . Who would dare contest the fact that there is suffering like this, especially looking in the countries of the southern hemisphere . . . And who would dare deny that this is not a matter of some extreme individual cases, some extreme private affliction, but rather a situation of suffering that has collectively overshadowed whole peoples or groups. . .? (Metz 2007, 134–5)

In fact, Metz views the heart of Christian faith as oriented toward the dangerous memory of Jesus, who suffered and died as a fellow victim of history, a criminalized and crushed person within his own society (Metz 2007, 182–7). Though Jesus' resurrection offers to others who suffer and die the promise of healing within God, that promise remains eschatologically distant and, as yet, unfulfilled (Metz 2007, 182). So many people have been trounced in death, and Christians can only hope that their subjectivity will be granted by God eschatologically (Stetler 2013, 303). In the meantime, their unfulfilled subjectivity and stymied vindication are deeply lodged splinters of grief within collective Christian consciousness. Although Christians can hope that God will justify Godself at the end of history in response to the question of theodicy—of why such massive torment has occurred and robbed so many—this question remains unresolved. As a matter of justice, theologians must keep this question open. The resurrection must not be used to cover over Jesus' cries on the Cross (Metz 1998, 42).

I am fascinated here by the notion of danger that Metz attaches to this remembering. At one level, this connotation seems counter-intuitive: this remembering is of those who are gone, who can no longer do anything, who maybe were never allowed to do anything to begin with. What could be threatening? However, Metz knows the visceral power of remembering history's victims, in part because their suffering is troubling to contemplate in any detail. He muses, "Could it be that there is too much singing and not enough crying out in our Christianity? Too much jubilation and too little mourning, too much approval and too little sense for what is absent. . .?" (Metz 1998, 125). Here, Metz needles his readers about their likely reluctance to make mental and spiritual space for others' affliction.

At another level, such a connection to these victims foments uncomfortable, inconvenient, and costly change in the present. This is what Metz means when he states, "It is dangerous to be close to Jesus" (Metz 1998, 47). True discipleship to Jesus requires identification with the poor and the oppressed in one's midst now. If we who are alive today let our consciences be pricked by the unresolved agonies of those fatally wounded by history, then that necessarily leads us to confront the changes that still need to be made in the present, to see who is still being crushed under the wheels of history in a way that reveals our apathy, if not our complicity. Dangerous memories spark action, because, as Metz explains, a society that does not care about its dead will not be able to sustain any sort of care for its living (Metz 2007, 80). The injustice of the world is not acceptable or inevitable, and we are all called to change the world as much as possible so that fewer people are trampled and forgotten (Metz 2007, 78–81).[3]

Metz's account of dangerous memory applies in a fruitful way to our erasure of suicide decedents and our poor treatment of suicidal people who are currently struggling. For one, suicidal people live with a specific kind of agony. They are characteristically convinced that they are burdens, that they do not belong, and that everybody would be better off if they were gone (Joiner 2010, 6–7). Palpable self-loathing is common in all of this. For example, one suicidal teenager wrote in her journal two weeks before she died, "I don't want to live. I have had nothing bad happen to me except my own doing. I don't deserve happiness" (Bering 2018, 122). This anguish is not surprising given that suicidal people are often still vilified in the public sphere and in religious contexts as selfish, cowardly, careless, ungrateful, defiant, and rageful (Joiner 2010, 12–110). This cruel, but common, vituperation creates stigma and therefore isolation around people who are struggling with suicidality, which compounds their self-hatred and frustration with themselves as they struggle to find a way to want to stay alive. For those who have died by suicide, Catholic theologian and priest Ronald Rolheiser correctly observes that these attitudes serve as "the antithesis of a canonization" (Rolheiser 2018, 56). Despite this opprobrium, however, suicidal people are living or have lived lives diminished by an ongoing emotional torment that the suicidologist Edwin Shneidman has termed *psychache*, which may push them beyond what they can handle (Shneidman 1996, 4).

There has been some complaint that the aforementioned dichotomy Metz draws between collective suffering regarding oppression centered around racism, poverty, and anti-Semitism, on the one hand, and "extreme private affliction," on the other, suggests that he trivializes the affliction associated with mental health distress (Stetler 2013, 307–9). Reading Metz more generously, however, I see him laboring with that distinction primarily to follow the insights of Latin American liberation theology and to emphasize the collective scope and social predictability of so much torment in the world. But if he *had* explicitly considered suicidality and mental health distress, I contend that he would have included the people who bear these burdens within his scope of concern. This is especially the case given the global prevalence of suicidal suffering within every population: around the world, suicide accounts for upward of a million deaths per year, and, in the United States, it is the eleventh leading cause of death, with approximately 50,000 people dying by suicide annually (Joiner 2010, 11; American Foundation for Suicide Prevention 2024). Suicide is tragic, but it cannot be written off as a purely individual tragedy. It is also a public health threat of massive scope, something Metz easily could have considered and at least theoretically accounts for with his insistence that there is no suffering in the world that does not concern him (Metz 1998, 134).

Even further, although it is still a hackneyed trope to treat mental health distress and suicidality as private, individual phenomena, critical suicide studies increasingly highlight the political dimensionality of so much suicidal feeling and behavior. The people who are intimately acquainted with suicidality in their lives are victims not only of acute mental health distress as such, but also of the stigma, misunderstanding, and distance wrought upon them specifically as "suicidal people" by so many around them (American Association of Suicidology 2023). To be suicidal is to inhabit an identity as an undesirable "other," a tainted malefactor from whom people distance themselves. Even further, suicidality is often wrapped up in other social issues such as economic precarity, sexual violence, homophobia, transphobia, and the enduring legacy of settler colonialism. Although suicidality is not always strictly caused by experiencing oppression within one's life, higher rates of suicidality are associated with being the victim of violence or living within a community targeted historically and intergenerationally by violence. Importantly, certain groups have been especially targeted by violence in a socially predictable manner that reinforces white supremacist heteropatriarchal imperialism.[4]

For example, over a third of LGBTQ youth—and almost half of trans and nonbinary youth—considered attempting suicide in 2024, though these rates drop when LGBTQ people are supported and affirmed within their communities (Nath et al. 2024). Similarly, many indigenous communities throughout North America have suffered significantly higher suicide rates than the general population, and this is the direct result of years of white supremacist colonial intervention and disruption within their economies and cultures (Kral and Idlout 2016, 229–33). Again, these rates decrease when these communities are supported and funded to create collective intergenerational spaces together where elders may share the ways of their tribal cultures with each other, especially with the younger generations (Kral and Idlout 2016, 233–7). Lastly, white men also have relatively high suicide rates, and even though this fact may seem to belie the notion that suicidality is tied to injustice given that white men are not oppressed along race or gender axes, it reinforces this point indirectly. White men's suicidality cannot be separated from the disproportionately high rates of firearms ownership and reluctance to use mental health care services that characterize this population (Anestis 2018, 33–59). White men are statistically more likely to internalize the pressure to subscribe to harmful notions of masculinity as dominance, control, and violence, and this pressure reveals itself at different points in white men's suicidal feeling and behavior. In sum, then, suicide is intimately woven into the tapestry of human anguish at every level, which means that it fits squarely within Metz's purview.

It is time to turn back to the death of the student mentioned at the outset. Taking my cue from Metz, I can recognize that this student provides a dangerous memory for me as I write this chapter. In fact, it is the responsibility of all Christians to grapple with the dangerous memories of all those who have died by suicide. Though I will soon discuss the legitimate concern about suicide clustering when communities are communicating about a suicide, my university president's command to keep quiet about a student's suicide unwittingly dovetails with a dehumanizing amnesia. At one level, this command ignores the place of this student in the community leading up to his death. Before he died, he lived as a member of the university. He was a friend and a classmate. He played the tuba and sang in the choir. In the midst of his complicated mental health struggles, he wanted to do well in his classes and be a good friend. He donated blood regularly.[5] Discouraging the students and faculty from speaking of this person in the recent wake of his death is a way of erasing him and what he would have meant to people. To put this in Metzian terms, the pressure for silence erodes this student's subjectivity as a complicated person who had been tending to his own life story as best he could in his community. Rolheiser describes well this pressure for amnesia regarding suicide decedents, writing:

> [S]uicide not only takes our loved ones away from us, but it also takes away our true memory of them. The gift that they brought into our lives is now no longer celebrated. We never again speak with pride about their lives. Their pictures come off the wall, photos of them get buried deep inside drawers that we never open again, their names are less and less mentioned in conversation, and of the manner of their death we rarely speak. (Rolheiser 2018, 9)

Because suicide is such a distressing way for somebody to die, suicide loss survivors and the community at large already struggle not to reduce a well-rounded and complicated person to their suicide. Therefore, the injunction to keep quiet is all the more repressive and toxic.

The pressure not to discuss a student's suicide contributes to a forgetting of the person entirely. My university would ultimately go on to tell students about the funeral so that they might attend if they wished, so I do not claim that the university needed to communicate every possible memorializing sentiment about this student in the days following his death. There were many different places and times to speak of this person, so any one context or communication should not be expected to say everything. Rather, my claim is that there was no point at which the students should have been given the message, even implicitly, that speaking of their fallen classmate was wrong, especially in the days immediately following his death. Although the university president said that faculty could respond to students who brought up the topic, this point was offered as an anxious concession that still reinforced a sense of silence and reluctance. It set a tone that could pass from faculty to students and that might be interpreted in the following manner, which would come across as callous for people devastated by this new absence: if you can't help yourself but fixate on it, we will acknowledge that somebody is now missing from your classes and clubs, but, otherwise, we'd like to get on with the day.

At another level, the command of silence asks us to avoid looking too hard specifically at this student's struggle, to push it away, to refuse to become unmanageably troubled. Many people have a discomfort specifically around recognizing the deep emotional torment of others, even when it has claimed their lives. It is here where Metz's emphasis on dangerous memories as memories specifically of the *suffering* of others comes into focus. This lens clarifies that, when possible, we must not allow ourselves to turn away from the undeniable loneliness and despair that so many suicide decedents have borne. This may feel unbearable for the rest of us living outside that experience, but it is wrong to uphold a culture in which we shut out other people's pain from our consciousness simply because it creates secondary pain for us.[6] Although one factor contributing to a university's discretion about a student's death being a suicide may be the desire of the student's family for privacy, this was not my university president's rationale for his skittishness (more on that rationale soon). Families of suicide decedents would also experience less pressure to hide the suicide if the world were not already so deeply stigmatizing of this reality in the first place. Understandably, families may fear that they themselves or their loved one will be judged, that the good memory of their loved one cannot be preserved if people know about their deep mental health distress.

Pushing further into this specific case, I note that my university president was Catholic, so it is reasonable to hypothesize that his anxiety was informed by the long-standing theological tradition of viewing suicide as a grave sin for which one could not repent and which landed one in hell (Antus 2020, 395). Painting suicide decedents as singularly sinful for all eternity is an effective way of eclipsing their misery, which then enables a specious demarcation according to which we are good and they are unholy. Unlike the rest of us who would never flirt with something so wicked as self-destruction (so the thinking goes), these wrongdoers suffer only as punishment for their selfishness. Though I do not promote a Catholic view of suicide that would normalize or romanticize it, this doctrinal shaming of suicide decedents does more than simply discourage suicide. It also enables us to harden our hearts against the cries of the dead and to refuse their dangerous memories.

Even if the university president were aware of the newer, more compassionate Catholic teaching that emphasizes the duress and lack of freedom involved in suicidality and the love that God always carries for suicide decedents (Catechism of the Catholic Church 1994, 2282–3), it is possible that this teaching lay precariously atop the deeper, older formation within his consciousness. This is not unusual. Rolheiser names well the tangle of these contradicting beliefs within the psyche, declaring,

> In the not-too-distant past, churches used to refuse to bury on blessed ground someone who died by suicide. The churches have changed their attitudes and their practice on this, but, truth be told, many people still struggle in their gut to accord a blessed, peaceful farewell to someone who has died by suicide. The stigma still remains. Someone who dies in this manner is still seen as somehow accursed, as dying outside the family of life and the circle of grace. (Rolheiser 2018, 35–6)

Here, Rolheiser invokes the Catholic prohibition against suicide decedents receiving funeral rites or being buried in Catholic cemeteries. This prohibition was lifted toward the end of the twentieth century (Antus 2020, 395–7). However, the centuries of teaching that provided the conceptual, legal, and cultural scaffolding for the condemnation of suicide decedents do not simply disappear after a mere change in canon law. Without active confrontation and struggle for re-education, the stigma remains. This is why even when individuals do not have harmful intentions, their reluctance to address a suicide directly within a community can reinforce harmful social pressures for silence and for the mere patina of resilience.

As dangerous memories, our memories of suicide decedents—their complex humanity and their suffering—must also prick our conscience toward action for the living, for those struggling with suicidality in the here and now. When somebody dies by suicide and the community falls silent about it, this silence can inadvertently send the message that the community either does not care about the loss of this person, or, even more strongly, that it rejects this person as an outcast never to be mentioned again. This messaging can be devastating for suicide loss survivors grieving the death of their friend, loved one, or classmate, and for those who may also be struggling with suicidality themselves. For example, a suicide cluster occurred at Herriman High in Utah between 2017 and 2018, and the school administration refused to identify the first few deaths as suicides or to acknowledge the particular wounds inflicted upon the community that happen in the wake of a suicide. Because of this failure of leadership, many of the students ended up feeling as if the adults did not really care about their grief (Lovett 2019).

Furthermore, many students articulated the chronic pressures they were feeling within their context: the pressure to be a "good Mormon," the pressure to conform in their appearance to certain narrow standards, the pressure to be heterosexual, and so on (Lovett 2019). Some of the research on teen suicide clusters suggests that contexts that promote rigid standards of acceptability can create punitive binaries around what is good or bad, which can leave teenagers feeling inadequate and alone. It is telling that this particular suicide cluster stopped at Herriman High only when the community brought in suicide prevention experts, named the problem explicitly, made space for students to speak their grief into words, and started engaging the students in ongoing conversations about mental health, belonging, and malignant perfectionism (Lovett 2019). There was no way out for this community except to let itself be confronted by the anguish of the dead and its own failures toward its teenagers, many of whom were struggling in ways similar to those who had died by suicide. Metz is undoubtedly correct, then, to claim that communities that do not care about the dead cannot really care about the living, and that this is why a dangerous memory is one that "badgers the present" (Metz 2007, 89). This disruption may be agonizing, but the dead and the living deserve better than the alternative, which is a collective amnesia that dooms us to repeat our atrocities throughout history.

Naming Dangerous Memories as Reparative

Though the disruptive potential of anamnestic speech that honors the humanity and the pain of suicide decedents is deeply important, I have also become increasingly attuned to the potential harms involved in speaking pointedly but incautiously about suicidality, even when people have good intentions. Disruptive but truthful speech about suicide should not be at odds with a gentleness that helps attend to people struggling with their own vulnerabilities around suicide and grief. However, over the past few years as I have tracked the coverage of suicide in the news, in entertainment, and even among fellow professors contemplating their responsibilities around this topic in the classroom, I have worried that some people want to cast off the suffocating cloak of silence by offering maximally shocking and bleak conversations about suicide. But even though silence is the incorrect response to suicide, swinging the pendulum wildly in the opposite direction is also hazardous, both to decedents and to people who are currently struggling with suicidality. In light of this concern, I can empathize with my university president's desire not to discuss the student's suicide, even if he was still generally wrong.

In this section, I will discuss concrete examples of this bad speech, which works against well-known best practices around covering and discussing suicide. It is not enough to say that we must discuss suicide. We must discuss it *well*. In making this point, I am not critiquing Metz's notion of dangerous memory so much as highlighting what I see as the reparative carefulness of it, which can be easy to overlook in his thought. While Metz's work on dangerous memory underscores the value of disrupting the unethical amnesia of the status quo guarded by the victors of history, it does not fetishize disruption for its own sake. Rather, proper dangerous memories are always in service of practicing solidarity with those who suffer in history so as to respect and nurture their subjectivity (in this life and eschatologically). This means that whatever speech and corresponding action best honor people who have died by suicide and who are currently vulnerable to suicidality should be the norm for limning the concept of dangerous memory in relation to suicide.

My concerns center around approaches to suicide that are, first, shockingly graphic or harmfully detailed, and, second, fatalistic in their suggestion that suicide is the inevitable or beneficial terminus for certain people. We can see both issues arising with the popular American teen drama *13 Reasons Why* that aired on Netflix from 2017 to 2020. This show focuses on the story of a young woman who had died by suicide and who had left behind cassette recordings about her (thirteen) reasons for doing so, ranging from unreliable friends to bullies to sexual predators. A young man who had loved her is the one playing the tapes. As he does so, the first season includes flashbacks guided by her voiceover, so she always feels narratively present, even after her death. Significantly, one of the episodes in the first season graphically depicts her suicide (which I will not describe, except to say that it occurs mostly in silence for three minutes).

Regarding the first problem, the tendency toward the lurid, it seems that the show's creators labored under the misapprehension that the most graphic or shocking discussions of mental health distress and suicide are the best way to shake the general public into awareness and prevention. After the first season aired and mental health experts expressed concern over its depiction of suicide, one of the show's executive producers, Nic Sheff, wrote in an opinion column for *Vanity Fair*, "It seemed to me the perfect opportunity to show what an actual suicide really looks like—to dispel the myth of the quiet drifting off, and to make viewers face the reality of what happens when you jump from a burning building into something much, much worse" (Sheff 2017). In the same piece, Sheff also discusses his own previous suicide attempt, which had been interrupted by his memory of the story of a suicide attempt offered by a woman at his rehab years earlier. This woman's story was violent, bloody, and shocking. The hideousness halted Sheff's own suicidal process, and he managed to stay alive with help. He clearly wanted to replicate this dynamic with the show and its audience.

I detect a similar line of thinking in the work of the philosopher Clancy Martin, especially in his pedagogical choices around the topic of suicide. In his 2023 memoir *How Not to Kill Yourself: A Portrait of the Suicidal Mind*, Martin discusses his own recurrent suicidality with candor, and, as part of this narrative, he recounts one session of his nineteenth-century philosophy course with his undergraduate students from 2013. They had been reading Schopenhauer's essay "On Suicide," and they had caught wind of a recent double suicide on the news. Martin writes, "I used this event as an occasion to get us all talking openly about our thoughts on killing oneself" (Martin 2023, 14). Martin then makes space for the students to debate whether suicidality is more of an individual or a generational phenomenon. Within this discussion, a student brings up his own suicide attempts and narrates his first one in detail. Martin asks him some clarifying questions along the way and then tells the class in detail about *his* own first suicide attempt as a child. Noting how this story is landing, Martin observes, "My students looked faintly shocked, and a few looked confused" (Martin 2023, 17). As the narrator, Martin then moves onto other areas of reflection, leaving the reader to conclude that this part of the class conversation has ended. Nothing in the story indicates that these specific students experienced greater suicidality as a result of this conversation, and Martin tells this story with the explicit intention of de-stigmatizing suicidality and contributing to suicide prevention.

Overall, then, Martin's pedagogical choices do not seem malevolent. Rather, they slot into what I call the "O Captain! My Captain!" paradigm of teaching: shake the students up with raw honesty about life, and become the teacher they will always remember.[7]

The half-truth contained within Sheff's and Martin's rip-off-the-Band-Aid approach is that suicide is horrifyingly real and that it does not serve our society to cover over this fact. Indeed, Sheff's own story suggests that encountering the sour realities of suicidality up close can create a preventative aversion to suicide. In his own context, Martin seems to have wanted to create a frank environment where at least some of his students could feel seen and perhaps less alone. For this reason, one can easily concede that Sheff's and Martin's intentions are ethical: they wish to draw attention to the issue of deep mental distress in all its unvarnished truth. This desire fits well with Metz's concept of dangerous memory and its emphasis upon disrupting our monstrous refusal to see other people's suffering. Sheff states later in the column, "It overwhelmingly seems to me that the most irresponsible thing we could've done would have been not to show the death at all. . . . [S]uicide is not a relief at all—it's a screaming, agonizing, horror" (Sheff 2017). In Sheff's mind, depicting the main character's suicide in all its graphic detail is *supposed* to upset viewers, produce a repugnance to suicide, and help lead to a world with less suicide. Relatedly, at the outset of his memoir, Martin argues that we as a society do not empathize with suicide decedents and that we therefore have a "dishonorable" relationship with suicide: we try to hide it and curate our own oblivion (Martin 2023, 11–13). Understandably, then, Martin sees himself as trying to puncture this falsely rosy consciousness and help build a more honest and empathetic culture for suicidal people.

Before evaluating how well that line of thought holds up, I will add in the second problem: fatalistic messaging around suicide. This is an accidental but surprisingly common byproduct of incautiousness around the topic. It may seem redundant to call certain discussions of suicide fatalistic, but this label is warranted for particular approaches to suicide that imply it is inevitable or appealing. While very few would claim outright that suicide is the most desirable solution to profound distress, this implication may nevertheless seep in despite good intentions. For one, approaches to suicide that suggest it has one simple cause or set of causes such as a job loss or breakup can inadvertently draw a deterministic connection: if you are struggling in this way, you might die by suicide, and that would make sense because people in your situation do that (Reporting on Suicide 2020). Relatedly, the supposed inevitability of suicide becomes more appealing if it is presented as a successful resolution to a person's troubles (Reporting on Suicide 2020). Further, that determinism can become even more powerful if it occurs in the absence of consistent messaging promoting the resources and supports available to people as they navigate suicidality and work to find reasons to live (Reporting on Suicide 2020). Lastly, memorializing a suicide decedent in a particularly emotionally charged and even glamorous way can signal that suicide is the best method for garnering the attention and belonging that a person felt they lacked in life (AFSP 2018, 26–31).

From the genuinely noble desire to shed light on the utter agony of suicidality, a person may inadvertently fall into these fatalistic tropes. We see this with *13 Reasons Why*: for one, the idea that a person could provide the definite reasons (even thirteen of them!) that they would die by suicide shades into subtle determinism: If I am treated this way, what else could anybody expect (Jo 2020)? This sentiment is then reinforced by the show's disinterest in examining the character's distress from an informed mental health perspective, which underscores the idea that her pain is entirely externally caused in a somewhat simplistic way (Jo 2020). There is also nothing in the show to suggest that somebody struggling with suicidality could receive help and go on to live their life (Jo 2020). Similarly, Martin's choice to have his students speak in detail about their suicide attempts without providing resources and messaging for living well even after being suicidal could inadvertently suggest a sort of fatalism: if you suffer with suicidality, there is no way out, and many of us exist within its clutches (and look at all these options for dying, graphically narrated in the middle of this philosophy class).

Relatedly, because the show frames the character's suicide as the result of the immoral actions of others, it inadvertently suggests that her suicide may be a satisfying form of revenge or punishment (Jo 2020). One writer correctly complains, "In the end, the first season of the show turns out to be a laundry list of why she had to die. For the viewers, Hannah's life, despite its richness and complexities, is watered down as a moral lesson, as if to say that niceness is humanity's saving grace" (Jo 2020). Suicide is portrayed as a potent form of instruction. Lastly, the show fosters a morbidly memorializing aesthetic: using this character's voice on the cassette tapes, combined with flashbacks of her, sends the message that this character is not really dead, that she is still somehow in control and present (Arshad 2022). This creates a fascinating mystique around this intelligent and beautiful sufferer, dead yet haunting. Ultimately, as with the choice to be obscenely graphic about suicide, this choice to be heavy-handed about its inevitability or merit is intended to underscore the gravity of suicidal distress. This choice is also born of an understandable frustration with those who may make this affliction worse along the way. For these reasons, I can see how this tack might align with a Metzian concern to allow the suffering of others to disrupt the numbing narratives of a society that does not want to bear witness to this pain and instead compounds it through violence and callousness.

However, the impact of *13 Reasons Why* illuminates the damage done when we invite the lurid and the fatalistic into our approach to this topic. As mental health experts had already complained before Sheff's writing of his column, his beliefs about the preventative power of graphically depicting suicide in a teen drama were dramatically wrong-headed. In 2019, an NIH-backed study concluded that the airing of the show was associated with a 28.9 percent increase in suicide among US youth ages 10–17 in April 2017, after the first season's release (National Institute of Mental Health 2019). There are likely a variety of reasons that the show may have caused this spike, but many agree that the show commits a cardinal sin: depicting the exact manner of suicide. Notably, two months after the release of this 2019 study, Netflix removed this scene (Marshall 2019). I view this decision as "too little, too late," because, across the board, every researcher of suicide I have encountered emphatically maintains that media should not depict or divulge the method or location of a suicide to the public (Reporting on Suicide 2020). This point is unambiguous and has been for decades.

Even before the study came out, mental health experts had attempted to explain the predictability of this kind of increase: for decades, scientists have studied what they call suicide contagion or clustering, a phenomenon in which there is a spike in the number of suicides following one suicide. Significantly, this phenomenon is backed by a substantial amount of research that has been known for decades, and Sheff should have paid heed. In fact, suicide clustering was labeled the "Werther effect" by the American sociologist David Phillips in 1974 to explain the spike in suicides after the reporting of celebrity suicides in the *New York Times* (Domaradzki 2021). This phrase is a reference to Goethe's 1774 novel *The Sorrows of Young Werther*, which depicts a protagonist who dresses in a very particular way and ends up shooting himself. After the publication of this novel, there were reports of young men dressed similarly to Werther—and in possession of the novel—who killed themselves in the same way (Bering 2018, 147). Since then, experts have detected many cases of suicide clustering after it becomes known that a celebrity or somebody in a particular community has died by suicide (Joiner 2010, 130–47). This occurs because enough people in the population are struggling with suicidality that a reckless discussion or depiction can tip a certain number toward death at any particular point.

As one suicide expert explains, "When *vulnerable* people are exposed to a *noxious* stimulus, untoward things may result. Talking about suicide in a way that makes it seem romantic, spiritual, or glorious is a noxious stimulus, and if such talk appears in a newspaper with a large circulation, it will inevitably be read by vulnerable people" (Joiner 2010, 139). Importantly, even though Sheff's intention with *13 Reasons Why* was to depict suicide with gritty and horrifying realism, the scene of the character's suicide makes death by that method seem more achievable. Further, the show still peddles a certain romanticism by attaching this graphic scene to a character with whom many young viewers identify and for whom suicide is portrayed as an effective revenge plan for others' mistreatment and as the logical response to the emotional anguish caused by this mistreatment. Ultimately, then, Sheff's intention to disrupt a culture that regularly torpefies itself to emotional misery backfired. In a similar fashion, even if Martin's decision to center first-person stories of suicide attempts in his class did not directly cause destruction, it is certainly out of touch with well-known wisdom. We can hope that the fact that Martin was alive as he was telling his students about his past suicide attempts conveyed that one can live through suicidality and come out the other side, but this seems to have been a conclusion that Martin left for his students to draw on their own, if at all. Overall, good intentions cannot be trusted to outweigh the power of these macabre images and story beats.

Upon first blush, these willful missteps might suggest that Metz's concept of dangerous memory is indeed too dangerous when it comes to bringing the topic of suicide into the light, but this is not so. I would argue that, for Metz, if one's approach to suffering directly leads to more of the same kind of suffering, and in a socially predictable manner, then this is not a mode of remembrance that honors the dead and the vanquished. At best, it is a mistake born of ignorance that is inexcusable for those who have any sort of platform in the twenty-first century. At worst, it is an act of exploitation in service of other motives: perhaps the desire to be entertaining and profitable by appealing to people's base curiosity (in the case of a television show), or perhaps the desire to provoke one's students with scandalous content and therefore feel efficacious (in the case of a professor).[8] As the phenomenon of suicide clustering demonstrates, these dynamics are often injurious for people struggling with suicidality.

But, as Metz can also help us see, these dynamics are also disrespectful of people who have already died by suicide. To remember suicide decedents appropriately, Metz would have us be educated about their misery, in a manner that will likely agonize rather than entertain. He would also have us contextualize their affliction within an appreciation for who they were as complex, multifaceted subjects with personalities, hobbies, talents, insights, eccentricities, peccadillos, histories, and communities. Ultimately, regardless of the various motives that we may have when we approach this topic, Metz would ask that we educate ourselves about the impact of our speech and adjust as much as possible to avoid harm. If we find ourselves resisting this type of discipline, Metz would prod us to interrogate the other motives we might be prioritizing ahead of honoring the suffering of the vulnerable. Do we honestly want to remember those who have suffered so as to cherish them and spark social change now, or do we want to consume their pain for our own pleasure, whether that pleasure be diversion, praise, or profit? While Metz's concept of dangerous memory nudges us toward disruption, it also steers us away from commodification and consumption.[9] Threading this needle is paramount in a society that regularly exploits the news of others' suffering (On Canada Project, n.d.).

One other significant theme to emerge from the fund of best practices for approaching the topic of suicide is the importance of hope, and Metz can illuminate this as well. Dangerous memories lead us to the hard work of changing the world now, and I see this sentiment reflected in the emphasis upon communicating to vulnerable people that they are loved and that they have resources that will meet them in their pain and help guide them to a more livable emotional space. Some efforts to this end include consistently highlighting mental health resources such as counselors, support groups, and lifelines, as well as emphasizing that communities are there to support each other on a regular basis and see each other through times of sadness and despair. For example, some colleges have begun implementing QPR training for faculty and staff, which helps them recognize potential signs of mental distress in students and then employ the method of "question, persuade, and refer" to help connect them to the right support (QPR Institute, n.d.). The aim is not to suppress discussion of suicide altogether, but rather, to speak of it in an informed, honest, and tender manner for people who are struggling and need reparative attention. There is some evidence to suggest that doing this not only does not spike suicidality but actually reduces it for vulnerable people (Dazzi et al. 2014, 3362).

More recently, research has tentatively suggested the opposite of the Werther effect, namely, the potentially positive, life-saving effect that media can have when it showcases examples of people navigating suicidality and finding a way to receive support, keep going, and discover glimmers of joy in their lives. This phenomenon was termed the "Papageno effect" in 2010 by the suicide researcher Thomas Niederkrotenthaler, after a character in Mozart's opera *The Magic Flute* who lives through a bout of suicidality after discussing his despair with three spirits (Domaradzki 2021). Though the literature on this positive effect is still emerging, these early findings suggest that humans are hungry for care and attention and therefore surprisingly receptive to exemplars of hope that show them a way through the hurt. This type of engagement disrupts the stifling silence that would deny suicidal torment, but it does so in service of those who struggle to keep existing and to live into their subjectivity. To me, this is the work of dangerous memory encouraged by Metz.

But, as a suicide loss survivor and as somebody who frequently ponders the student mentioned at this chapter's outset, I must ask: What does hope mean for suicide decedents, for those who are already gone from us? The hope to keep living is no longer available to this group, so constructing hope narrowly around this aim would be cruel, the exact type of forgetting that Metz has warned us against. At one level, then, I follow newer theological insights here and say that hope for suicide decedents must be redefined and expanded to take on an eschatological dimension. We cannot hope for them to keep living here, but we *can* hope that they live eternally within God, that God gives them the space to be healed and to come into their subjectivity as a member of the communion of saints, never lost and always loved (Antus 2020, 410–12). This is a hope that is worthy of God and worthy of our fallen friends, loved ones, and community members. At another level, however, I follow Metz here by insisting that we cannot entirely redefine hope for suicide decedents in a manner that resolves their suffering. We will not find a satisfying existential or theological framework that explains why they suffered, and we cannot undo it anyway. For this reason, our hope will always be tinged by lament, and we must find a way to live with these wounds and this sense of inadequacy: these interruptions. We must remember not that they failed, but rather that they *were failed*. This, too, is the work of dangerous memory.

Conclusion

In this chapter, I have focused on direct messaging around suicide, whether that be a television character dying by suicide, the journalistic choices that go into framing the news coverage of a suicide, or the postvention plans that colleges need to implement when a student dies by suicide. I remain haunted by the university student who died years ago, not only by the agony I know he bore for a long time, but also by my university's failure to honor him and other vulnerable students. From this discussion, the significance of Metz's concept of dangerous memory has emerged: we must push ourselves to bear the sadness of holding suicide decedents within our hearts, but we must do so in a way that respects their subjectivity and creates the possibility of new life for those currently struggling with suicidality. Metz helps us clarify that this work is not about disruption for its own sake, but rather, for the sake of reparative solidarity with the dead and the vanquished, and for those who are like them in the here and now.

Ultimately, though, for these points to land with full force, Metz prods us to see that we must take a broader view beyond explicit messaging around suicide as such. We must do the ongoing, inconvenient work of rooting out injustice in all sectors of society. This transformation would involve the eradication of wealth inequality, poverty, racism, colonialism, ableism, compulsory heterosexuality, and sexual violence (Bryan 2022, 179–98), as well as the dismantling of the culture of toxic productivity that harms so many of our students in higher education. The difficulty of achieving these ends does not make them optional. This is what we owe to the people whose lives have been shaped by suicidality. If we are building a world that is loving, then we can strive not only to keep people from dying. We can also accompany them in living.

Notes

1 Although the student's parents have been public about the death being a suicide, I withhold his name in order to be considerate of his family and their privacy. My concern with this story is about what it reveals regarding broader cultural and theological mores around suicide. Ultimately, I hope that readers will think compassionately about this person—and about the many others who are like him—as they read this piece.

2 Though one could object that the word "decedent" is legalistic, I choose to use it here specifically to refer to people who have died by suicide. This group is distinct from another about whom I am also concerned, namely, those among the living who struggle with suicidal thoughts, feelings, and behaviors.

3 Metz does not think we can create a utopia. Such a vision would indeed be a cruel, false narrative of absolute progress. At the same time, Metz thinks suffering and oppression are not natural aspects of life, and that we can indeed create a world where fewer people are crushed, displaced, and ignored.

4 Though it has become a truism to state that 90 percent of people who die by suicide have a mental illness, many researchers have questioned this statistic. Without litigating that debate, I am content to say that the possibility that mental illness is involved in many suicides must not be taken to ignore the many other social factors typically in play. Suicidal people are always embedded within particular contexts as they negotiate the social scripts that have formed their sense of identity and their feeling of not belonging, so it is important to use a capacious biopsychosocial model for thinking about suicidality (Bryan 2022, 25–48).

5 I learned these details from my students' comments in class, the announcement for his funeral, and a public interview his parents gave.

6 People must tend to their mental health, which may involve limiting the number of instances of others' suffering that they can absorb at any given moment. But judiciously tending to one's mental health needs is not the same as collectively maintaining a culture of careless amnesia around the agony of the dead and the suppressed.

7 This is the title of the 1865 poem by Walt Whitman about the death of Abraham Lincoln. I invoke it here because of the 1989 film *Dead Poets Society*. In this film, the boarding school teacher John Keating (played iconically by Robin Williams) inspires his male students through poetry. Partly as a result of feeling so artistically inspired but ultimately unsupported by his pragmatic martinet of a father, one of Keating's students dies by suicide. After this, Keating is blamed by the school and fired. As he exits the classroom, some of his students stand on their desks and recite, "O Captain! My Captain!" It is a triumphant final note. Overall, I would argue that the suicide is inappropriately minimized and subordinated to the romanticized lionization of Keating in the film.

8 I have asked some fellow professors in theology to stop issuing (or to rework significantly) a popular assignment in which students plan their own funeral, including their own eulogy. This assignment is meant to help students reflect upon their values and their mortality (i.e., it is an act of *ars moriendi*), but this assignment is a predictably treacherous exercise for somebody who is already struggling with suicidality, coming to terms with their own death, and imagining, perhaps with a comforting fondness, how sad everybody will be when they are gone. One junior high instructor told me she had discontinued the assignment years ago after a student used it to prepare for her own suicide (which she then attempted but survived).

9 My analysis parallels what some have identified as "trauma porn," which describes the public consumption of dehumanizing images and stories of violence against a group of oppressed people, especially Black people, as a form of entertainment (On Canada Project, n.d.).

Bibliography

American Association of Suicidology. 2023. "Stigma and Suicide." Posted January 19. https://suicidology.org/stigma-and-suicide/.

American Foundation for Suicide Prevention. 2024. "Suicide Statistics." Accessed May 11, 2025. https://afsp.org/suicide-statistics/.

American Foundation for Suicide Prevention and Suicide Prevention Resource Center. 2018. *After a Suicide: A Toolkit for Schools*. 2nd ed. Education Development Center. https://sprc.org/wp-content/uploads/2022/12/AfteraSuicideToolkitforSchools-3.pdf.

Anestis, Michael D. 2018. *Guns and Suicide: An American Epidemic*. Oxford University Press.

Antus, Elizabeth. 2020. "'The Silence of the Dead': Remembering Suicide Victims and Reimagining the Communion of Saints." *Theological Studies* 81 (2): 394–413. https://doi.org/10.1177/0040563920929653.

Arshad, Muskaan. 2022. "A Poorly Taped Show: Mental Health in '13 Reasons Why.'" *Harvard Political Review*, July 26. https://harvardpolitics.com/a-poorly-taped-show-mental-health-in-13-reasons-why/.

Ashley, James Matthew. 1998. *Interruptions: Mysticism, Politics, and Theology in the Work of Johann Baptist Metz*. University of Notre Dame Press.

Bering, Jesse. 2018. *Suicidal: Why We Kill Ourselves*. University of Chicago Press.

Bryan, Craig J. 2022. *Rethinking Suicide: Why Prevention Fails, and How We Can Do Better*. Oxford University Press.

Catechism of the Catholic Church. 1994. Translated by the United States Conference of Catholic Bishops. https://www.usccb.org/sites/default/files/flipbooks/catechism/VI/.

Dazzi, T., R. Gribble, S. Wessely, and N. T. Fear. 2014. "Does Asking about Suicide and Related Behaviours Induce Suicidal Ideation? What Is the Evidence?" *Psychological Medicine* 44 (16): 3361–3. https://doi.org/10.1017/S0033291714001299.

Domaradzki, Jan. 2021. "The Werther Effect, the Papageno Effect or No Effect? A Literature Review." *International Journal of Environmental Research and Public Health* 18: 2396. https://doi.org/10.3390/ijerph18052396.

Jo, Elyra. 2020. "What Pop Culture Gets Wrong about Suicide." *Medium*, September 27. https://mediacommoner.medium.com/what-pop-culture-gets-wrong-about-suicide-ae1fcb57f7ef.

Joiner, Thomas. 2010. *Myths about Suicide*. Harvard University Press.

Kral, Michael J., and Lori Idlout. 2016. "Indigenous Best Practices: Community-Based Suicide Prevention in Nunavut, Canada." In *Critical Suicidology: Transforming Suicide Research and Prevention for the 21st Century*, edited by Jennifer White, Ian Marsh, Michael J. Kral, and Jonathan Morris, 229–43. UBC Press.

Lovett, Ian. 2019. "One Teenager Killed Himself, Then Six More Followed—A Cluster of Youth Suicides Vexes One Utah Community." *The Wall Street Journal*, April 13. https://www.wsj.com/articles/one-teenager-killed-himself-six-more-followed-11555061402.

Marshall, Alex. 2019. "Netflix Deletes '13 Reasons Why' Suicide Scene." *The New York Times*, July 16. https://www.nytimes.com/2019/07/16/arts/television/netflix-deleted-13-reasons-why-suicide-scene.html.

Martin, Clancy. 2023. *How Not to Kill Yourself: A Portrait of the Suicidal Mind*. Pantheon Books.

Metz, Johann Baptist. 1998. *A Passion for God: The Mystical-Political Dimension of Christianity*. Translated by J. Matthew Ashley. Paulist Press.

Metz, Johann Baptist. 2007. *Faith in History and Society: Toward a Practical Fundamental Theology*. Translated by J. Matthew Ashley. Crossroad Publishing.

Nath, R., et al. 2024. "2024 U.S. National Survey on the Mental Health of LGBTQ+ Young People." *The Trevor Project*. Accessed February 14, 2025. www.thetrevorproject.org/survey-2024.

National Institute of Mental Health. 2019. "Release of '13 Reasons Why' Associated with Increase in Youth Suicide Rates." April 29. https://www.nimh.nih.gov/news/science-updates/2019/release-of-13-reasons-why-associated-with-increase-in-youth-suicide-rates#:~:text=The%20Netflix%20show%20%E2%80%9C13%20Reasons,Academy%20of%20Child%20and%20Adolescent.

On Canada Project. n.d. "Seeing Violent Acts Should Not Be a Prerequisite to Giving a Fuck." Group Project Initiatives. Accessed February 9, 2025. https://oncanadaproject.ca/blog/trauma-porn.

QPR Institute. n.d. "Question, Persuade, Refer." Accessed February 9, 2025. https://qprinstitute.com/.

Reporting on Suicide. 2020. "Best Practices and Recommendations for Reporting on Suicide." Accessed February 16, 2025. https://reportingonsuicide.org/recommendations/.

Rolheiser, Ronald. 2018. *Bruised and Wounded: Struggling to Understand Suicide*. Paraclete Press.

Sheff, Nic. 2017. "*13 Reasons Why* Writer: Why We Didn't Shy Away from Hannah's Suicide." *Vanity Fair*, April 19. https://www.vanityfair.com/hollywood/2017/04/13-reasons-why-suicide-controversy-nic-sheff-writer.

Shneidman, Edwin S. 1996. *The Suicidal Mind*. Oxford University Press.

Stetler, Emily. 2013. "Narrating Suffering, Remembering Hope: Metz's Theology as Paradigm for Examining Mental Illness and Disability Theology." *Journal of Religion, Disability, & Health* 17 (3): 301–16. https://doi.org/10.1080/15228967.2013.809886.

2

Mental Health Considerations for Suicide Loss Survivors

Amy Badura-Brack and Ryan Fabry

Suicide is inextricably related to psychological duress. Most people are fully aware that the psychological pain experienced by people suffering from mental illness may contribute to them contemplating the act of taking their own life. Estimates suggest that 90 percent of all people who complete suicide were experiencing a psychological disorder prior to their death (Cavanagh et al. 2003, 399). Mental health conditions including but not limited to addiction, post-traumatic stress disorder, and psychosis are associated with elevated levels of suicidal risk. Major depressive and borderline personality disorders list suicidality as a specific symptom in their diagnostic checklists (American Psychiatric Association 2022, 183, 752).

It is commonplace that experiencing mental illness is an important etiological factor associated with suicidal ideation and action. We begin this chapter by recognizing that those contemplating suicide, or attempting and surviving a suicide attempt, need intensive support and professional mental health care that aims to instill hope for the future.[1] However, it is with a heavy heart that we also recognize, despite the best efforts of friends, family, and professionals, sometimes those we care about do take their own lives and that loss carries its own mental health concerns. This chapter is not geared directly toward those struggling with their own suicidality but focuses instead on the psychological difficulties experienced by the family and friends of people who have lost a loved one to suicide, or suicide loss survivors.

All those who live will one day die, and those who love them will mourn the loss. As members of families and communities, experiencing the death of a loved one is one of life's most stressful events (Wallace et al. 2023, 15), and people usually experience multiple significant losses throughout their lives. The death of a loved one due to any cause—expected or sudden, natural or unnatural, peaceful or violent—is accompanied by intense feelings of loss and grief among those left behind. Distress, sadness, and missing the deceased are all expected and normative reactions following any loss. World religions have rituals to support the bereaved; hospitals and secular organizations take special care in assisting families as they cope with loss; and various communities reach out to the bereaved with outpourings of support in the forms of thoughts, prayers, food, and flowers. Despite the ubiquity of death and the readiness of support systems for those dealing with loss, bereaved people often experience grief reactions that require more intensive support through counseling even when those deaths are natural, gentle, and expected. The need for more formal services following the trauma of suicide is intensified. Bereavement following suicide causes severe psychiatric symptoms and more likely presentation for treatment than bereavement due to other mortality causes (Pitman et al. 2014, 87–90). Therefore, those bereaved by suicide deserve and need their own dedicated attention, understanding, and appropriate opportunities for intervention.

Young and colleagues write, "Losing a loved one to suicide is one of life's most painful experiences. The feelings of loss, sadness, and loneliness experienced after any death of a loved one are often magnified in suicide survivors by feelings of guilt, confusion, rejection, shame, anger, and the effects of stigma and trauma" (Young et al. 2012, 177). Suicide loss is often complicated by a myriad of emotions beyond common grief reactions, and suicide loss survivors may be less likely to receive the unconditional community support typically offered to people in mourning. Even though acts of suicide are often muted and sometimes treated as taboo, population level surveys suggest that more than half of us have been directly affected by suicide, and a full third of us may be directly bereaved by suicide (Feigelman et al. 2018, 227). Take a moment to be mindful of these numbers. Losing a loved one to suicide is not an uncommon experience. Moving forward, this chapter is dedicated to increasing awareness of the mental health considerations and needs of suicide loss survivors, with the hope that we come to better understand and address the complexities of this special type of grief.

Mental Health Diagnoses Relevant to Suicide Loss

Counselors are often called upon to help the living process their grief through formal channels such as pastoral, individual, or group counseling. Because they encounter grief on an everyday basis, the interventions they provide often proceed without any formal diagnosis. There may be the presumption that because grief reactions are difficult, but also normal and appropriate, no special diagnoses or therapeutic techniques beyond supportive listening are necessary. However, in addition to supportive listening, grief-specific therapy and interventions directed by formal diagnoses may be required. The next section discusses psychological diagnoses that bereaved individuals may qualify for with special attention to how these diagnoses are affected by suicide loss. Recognizing the presence of a mental health condition is powerful, because it can offer a framework for conceptualizing one's own symptoms, direct therapists in the provision of treatment, and allow for formal interventions and services to be billed to insurance.

Adjustment Disorder

The first formal diagnosis appropriate for consideration in grief reactions is an adjustment disorder. Adjustment disorders may be diagnosed when a person has experienced a difficult life situation such as a death, and the individual has a hard time coping with that event such that they have noteworthy changes in mood, anxiety, or behavior according to the *Diagnostic and Statistical Manual of Mental Disorders* 5, Text Revision, (*DSM*-5-TR: American Psychiatric Association, APA 2022, 319–22). Adjustment disorders are usually regarded as the least severe of all psychiatric disorders, but they are commonly seen in clinical practice. An adjustment disorder is a simple diagnostic option that allows for therapeutic services to be billed to insurance, which is a practical reason to apply a formal diagnosis when a person is reasonably struggling with a stressful life event. But interestingly and awkwardly, the *DSM-5-TR* includes an exclusion statement that the adjustment disorder symptoms "do not represent normal bereavement," but if applicable to grief, "the bereavement is judged to be out of proportion to what would be expected or significantly impairs self-care and interpersonal relations" (APA 2022, 322). The authors of this book share your confusion about what exactly normal bereavement is and what the out of proportion statement means because everyone grieves differently in intensity and duration. With that said, we are comfortable with the diagnostic conceptualization that grief is often intense and results in impairment in daily life, such as negatively impacting the ability to complete chores, study, work, and that grief often disrupts the social relationships we so clearly need during stressful times.

Despite the awkwardness of some of those diagnostic statements, many clinicians do assign an adjustment disorder diagnosis related to bereavement. In fact, a population study found that about 18 percent of bereaved people qualify for an adjustment disorder diagnosis following any type of death (Killikelly et al. 2019, 310), and rates of mental health disorders are even higher after sudden, violent deaths (Kristensen, Weisæth, and Heir 2012, 80)—including suicide. Moreover, those bereaved after sudden or violent deaths tend to have a slower recovery from psychological symptoms than those grieving a natural death (Kristensen, Weisæth, and Heir 2012, 87). Therefore, compared to bereavement in general, bereavement following suicide may indeed be of a more disruptive magnitude.

Prolonged Grief Disorder

Adjustment disorders reflect changes in general anxiety, mood, or behavior. More specifically, when the bereaved person's emotional struggles are ongoing and are punctuated by deep feelings of loss and preoccupied by memories of the deceased, the proper diagnostic consideration may move toward a grief-specific diagnosis. Different diagnostic terms have been applied for this type of grief that does not diminish in intensity or allow a return to daily functioning over the years, including complicated grief (Horowitz et al. 2003, 909) and persistent complex bereavement disorder (American Psychiatric Association 2013, 789–92). Recently these symptoms are reflected in the diagnosis of prolonged grief disorder which has been well described by both the *DSM*-5-TR (American Psychiatric Association 2022, 322–7) and the *International Classification of Diseases*, 11th edition, *ICD-11*; World Health Organization 2018, 6B42). Prolonged grief disorder is marked by ongoing symptoms of intense *yearning* or *longing* for the deceased person and/or a *preoccupation* with the deceased person.

These feelings of yearning, longing, and preoccupation are the hallmark symptoms of prolonged grief disorder, and, if present, suggest that prolonged grief disorder may be the best description of the symptom picture. Additionally, prolonged grief disorder includes other difficulties such as ongoing disbelief, avoidance, numbness, sorrow, loneliness, anger, loss of meaning in life, and difficulty engaging in social, educational, or occupational activities. It is worth noting that prolonged grief disorder has faced some criticism as potentially pathologizing a normal grief reaction, especially because it may be diagnosed as early as twelve months for adults and six months for children and adolescents after a close loss. The authors of this chapter want to emphasize that we all grieve differently and there is no time limit on grief. With that said, prolonged grief disorder is probably best understood as representing the most severe end of a grief continuum. Only about 10 percent of adults experience a prolonged grief disorder following a nonviolent loss of a loved one (Lundorff et al. 2017, 144), but a staggering 49 percent of people who lost a loved one to unnatural causes developed prolonged grief (Djelantik et al. 2020, 149). In other words, the bereavement of friends and families who have lost their loved one to an unnatural cause, including suicide, is dramatically more likely to result in severe and long-lasting grief reactions. In fact, suicide loss survivors who are closely related to the deceased experience complicated grief reactions approximately 50–80 percent of the time (Mitchell et al. 2004, 15). Losing a loved one to suicide is verifiably more difficult to cope with than most other causes of death, and we expect that more than half of suicide loss survivors would qualify for this useful diagnosis that directs grief-specific treatments.

Post-Traumatic Stress Disorder

Our next diagnostic consideration, post-traumatic stress disorder, may coexist with prolonged grief disorder discussed above or may be present independently. A key distinction is that feelings of longing/yearning and preoccupation with the deceased are not primary symptoms in post-traumatic stress disorder (PTSD) as they are in prolonged grief. PTSD is a diagnosis that applies more specifically in response to a violent and unnatural death such as a suicide than the other disorders discussed above. Many of us are most familiar with PTSD associated with the human-made violence and death associated with war, and although combat is a qualifying trauma, most PTSD develops in response to civilian traumas with similar horrifying and fear-provoking qualities. PTSD is the rare psychiatric diagnosis that includes its direct cause as a required symptom. We like that requirement because it erases some of the unintended pathologizing that some may perceive as accompanying a formal diagnosis. Put simply, given a bad enough trauma, everyone would develop PTSD.

One of the traumas regarded as severe enough to qualify a person for a PTSD diagnosis is being exposed to actual or threatened death. In the case of suicide, PTSD may ensue if the suicide survivor witnesses the suicidal act itself or comes upon its immediate aftermath such as if they discover or view the deceased body.

Even if one was not present for the act or directly encountered its devastating scene, learning about the violent death of a family member or friend, such as a suicide counts as a qualifying trauma according to the *DSM-5-TR* (APA 2022, 301). We want to clarify that PTSD separates deaths due to causes such as suicide, homicide, or war from other types of death, as specifically likely to result in psychological symptoms. Although it is difficult—albeit potentially beautiful—to bear witness to a loved one's death, expected or gradual death due to a disease process or old age is not a qualifying trauma for PTSD. Only violent or accidental deaths fulfill this criterion, emphasizing that surviving suicide loss may well be more challenging than many types of bereavement. Other required symptoms for a PTSD diagnosis include intrusion or reexperiencing symptoms related to the trauma, avoidance of trauma-related stimuli, negative changes in mood or thinking, and physiological reactivity (APA, 301–4).

Prolonged grief disorder shares some symptoms with PTSD such as preoccupation and avoidance; however, in prolonged grief those feelings are related to missing the person and avoiding reminders of shared experiences with the deceased, while in PTSD the intrusive thoughts and avoidance are specifically related to the traumatic event itself—in this case the suicide. Both disorders could be diagnosed in the same individual. However, if a survivor's symptoms are serious enough to fulfill the diagnostic criteria for PTSD, a PTSD diagnosis would supersede an adjustment disorder diagnosis. One final diagnostic consideration in these stress and trauma-related disorders is an acute stress disorder diagnosis which is very similar to PTSD except the symptoms last less than one month (APA 2022, 313–19). It is very possible that a suicide loss survivor experiences post-traumatic symptoms immediately after their loved one's death and qualifies for an acute stress disorder diagnosis for up to a month after the trauma, and then if symptoms persist past the one-month mark, the correct diagnosis becomes PTSD, which has no time limits and may even develop many months or years after the causal traumatic event. Thankfully, an acute stress or PTSD diagnosis directs mental health professionals to well-supported treatments that help ameliorate the very real symptoms of this stress response.

Major Depressive Disorder

Although not focused on general or suicide-specific bereavement, depressive symptoms including major depressive disorder well may be experienced after a loss. Major depression is marked by depressed mood and loss of interest or pleasure in almost all activities for at least two weeks (APA 2022, 183). Other symptoms of depression may include changes in eating, sleeping, motor movement, cognitive symptoms, feelings of worthlessness, and even suicidal thoughts, plans, and attempts (APA 2022, 183–5). If major depression fits the symptom picture, this diagnosis would be given over adjustment disorder, and independently or alongside prolonged grief disorder or PTSD. The main difference between general depression and the mood symptoms associated with other disorders discussed in this chapter is that in depression the sadness itself is generalized, steady, and not dependent upon thoughts of the lost loved one. Depression is pervasive and does not come in waves in the way that grief-related sadness is often described. Reasonably, the closer the bereaved person was related to the deceased, the higher the likelihood of depressive and anxious symptoms (Mitchell et al. 2008, 6–7). Interestingly, losing a loved one to suicide does not seem to result in more depression or anxiety than grieving another type of death (Sveen and Walby 2008, 15), so we mention this here as a more general effect of grief to be aware of, highlighting that depression is often precipitated by a loss and is therefore an important diagnostic consideration.

Mental health conditions such as adjustment, prolonged grief, post-traumatic stress, and major depressive disorders carry their own risk for suicidality. Experiencing psychological symptoms, as well as the risk of genetic suicide susceptibility (Brent and Mann 2005, 17) and the possibility for community contagion of suicidal thoughts and behaviors (Abrutyn and Mueller 2014, 219–22) lead us to encourage suicide loss survivors to be forthcoming about any of their own suicidal thinking. Mental health care providers should take care to conduct, document, and act upon suicide risk assessments with their suicide bereaved clients. Research has shown that among suicide loss survivors, those who have more severe depressive symptoms—especially those with strong feelings of hopelessness—were more likely to experience suicidal ideation themselves during their grief process (Grafiadeli et al. 2021, 186–7). Additionally, survivors who feel a sense of isolation and thwarted belongingness have significantly more suicidal ideation than those who feel more connected and integrated into their communities (Yossi and Aisenberg 2021, 1032).

Substance Use Disorder

Finally, and again not specific to survivors of suicide, many people may attempt to minimize the pain associated with a loss by numbing it with alcohol or other drugs, so we wanted to include substance use disorder in this chapter, although we suspect that readers are familiar with this set of problem behaviors. One interesting comment though is that while PTSD and depression occur at higher rates in the general population among women, men have a greater lifetime risk for developing substance abuse (McGrath et al. 2023, 672). Even though rates of depression in women double the rates of depression in men, depression still ranks high on the list of mental health conditions that men experience (McGrath et al. 2023, 672). Tying together depression and substance usage, even though it's not a conclusive finding, various theories consider that men may attempt to mask negative feelings such as grief and depressive symptoms with behaviors such as substance abuse (Addis 2008, 157–8), so this possibility should be considered and more adaptive coping strategies encouraged when coping with grief.

Special Therapeutic Concerns of Suicide Loss Survivors

In addition to new symptoms that may first present in the wake of a loved one's suicide, many people have preexisting mental health issues that may be exacerbated by traumatic life events. Over the course of a lifetime, half of all people qualify for a psychiatric diagnosis (McGrath et al. 2023, 670), so being aware of this issue is essential. People with preexisting mental health concerns are at risk for more complicated grief and more difficulty coping with the stress and loss that accompany surviving a loved one's suicide. While we have focused on some suitable diagnoses in the previous section, we do not mean to exclude the potential that a suicide loss survivor may experience any other psychiatric condition in the aftermath of a loved one's suicide, given that stress is a major risk factor for all psychopathologies. Regarding psychopathology in general, people who have experienced these difficulties prior to the additional stressor of grieving a lost loved one are at risk for a resurgence of these symptoms in the aftermath of a loved one's suicide.

Being aware of the full spectrum of mental health symptoms experienced by suicide loss survivors is essential to understanding your own experience and to directing mental health care providers to the most appropriate and full spectrum of therapeutic offerings. We know that more than two-thirds of suicide loss survivors seek individual therapy in the aftermath of their loss (Sanford et al. 2016, 551); however, we also know that loss survivors tend to receive supportive and grief-based therapies when they present for treatment. General grief therapy is necessary but not necessarily sufficient on its own to address the full spectrum of mental health needs, even for the common symptoms we discussed above. Research suggests that people presenting for therapy following their loved one's suicide may not be assessed for or assigned appropriate diagnoses such as PTSD, which means that they are unlikely to be offered the most appropriate treatment methodologies (Sanford et al. 2016, 555). A large research literature documents that certain treatments are effective for specific conditions. Readers can see the following review articles if interested in learning about the efficacy of key treatment approaches. For example, exposure therapy is the quintessential and most effective treatment for PTSD (McLean et al. 2022). Medication, cognitive behavioral, and psychodynamic therapy are all well supported for depression (Hofmann et al. 2012). Substance use disorder needs behavioral interventions (Prendergast et al. 2006) and benefits from self-help groups such as Alcoholics Anonymous (Kelly, Humphreys, and Ferri 2020). Optimal treatment for friends and family grieving a suicide loss should address any newly developing mental health conditions and/or exacerbations of existing psychopathology as discussed above, in addition to the specific grief and suicide bereavement issues discussed in the next section.

Grief-Specific Considerations for Suicide Loss Survivors

Whether or not a suicide loss survivor qualifies for a psychiatric diagnosis such as those discussed above, grieving a loved one lost to suicide requires special consideration and would likely benefit from interventions including individual therapy, group therapy, a bereavement support group, and family therapy if applicable. Jordan (2008, 681–2) summarizes four key themes that are likely to be especially salient for survivors of suicide loss: (1) Why? (did my loved one take their own life) as well as feelings of guilt and responsibility for being unable to prevent the suicide; (2) feelings of shame, stigma, social isolation, and family relational disturbance; (3) perceived rejection or abandonment by the deceased; and (4) horror/trauma symptoms in response to the suicide event itself. Each of these issues may be important in assisting a survivor of suicide through their grief process, so we will discuss each of these themes in turn.

Why? Guilt. Responsibility

When grieving most deaths, the bereaved need not ask why. The cause of death is clear—their loved one had a disease, their body was failing in old age, or even there was a horrible accident. But in the case of suicide, survivors may wonder why their loved one made this choice and potentially feel guilty or responsible for not predicting or preventing their loved one from ending their life. These internal thoughts may be accompanied by external attributions resulting in suicide loss that is "complicated by the societal perception that the act of suicide is a failure by the victim and the family to deal with some emotional issue and ultimately society affixes blame for the loss on the survivors" (Cvinar 2005, 14). Relatedly, after forty years as a suicide loss grief therapist, Jordan (2020) believes that the two most challenging aspects in suicide loss are the "perceived intentionality" of the death—the survivor's belief that the loved one chose to die by suicide with clear volition of action, and "perceived responsibility" for the suicide—that survivors usually first ascribe to themselves and perhaps later assign to others including family members or professionals, despite the fact that none are to blame.

Shame. Stigma. Social Isolation. Family Disruption

Well-meaning people in general often handle death and expressions of sympathy poorly. Perhaps we have offered or received sympathetic statements that intend to comfort but miss the mark, such as "it's not your fault" or "now you won't have to take care of them all the time." Statements like these are likely offered with kindness but tend to pick at the wounds of shame felt by survivors. Better condolences might include "I am thinking about you," or "I am here to support you." These types of statements help to lessen the very real social isolation encountered by suicide loss survivors by offering solidarity and social support. Support is deeply needed, because suicide loss survivors describe failings in their support systems including that anticipated supports do not appear or communicate, friends may withdraw from the relationship, and others offer unhelpful advice that results in increased pain (Dyregrov 2004, 31–2).

Although it might seem instinctive that the friends and family of a person who completed suicide would be natural supports to one another, this is not always the case. Following any death, families frequently fail to support one another for fear that the other family members do not want to talk about the deceased, the death, or their own grief, potentially for fear of disrupting the others' good days or not wanting to be burdensome. Specifically related to suicide, this interpersonal isolation and disruption can be intensified if family and friends feel anger and frustration at one another for not preventing the death, even though this is not a rational or adaptive thought process.

In addition to feeling alone in their own close relationships, people bereaved by suicide experience more stigma and shame than people who lost loved ones due to all other sudden natural and other unnatural deaths. These feelings of stigma affect family and friends of the deceased similarly and regardless of their perceptions of social support (Pitman et al. 2016, 27). Speaking specifically to the role of perceived stigma leading to social isolation, both family and friends tend to conceal the cause of a death due to suicide (Sveen and Walby 2008, 24), suggesting that survivors are uncomfortable and afraid of others' reactions to the true nature of their loss. People bereaved by suicide also commonly report negative changes in their relationships after their loss. In general, they feel that their relationships become strained, distant, and awkward, and that many of these negative changes occur in their previously closest relationships, emphasizing notable social withdrawal among family members and fear of additional losses in close friendships (Azorina et al. 2019, 4).

Rejection. Abandonment

In the previous section we discussed feelings of isolation and perhaps abandonment among the living, but these feelings can also apply to your relationship with the deceased. When people have an opportunity to prepare for their own natural death, they will often communicate their feelings of love and affection to their family and friends with comments such as "I will miss you so much when I am gone," or "I wanted to be there to see you grow up." These utterances reflect the dying person's own sense of loss and anticipatory grief. These statements also tell the soon-to-be bereaved that the dying person values them and wants their relationship to continue if that were possible. Unfortunately, in the specific case of suicide, those left behind may feel wronged by the deceased whom they may perceive intentionally chose to leave them or may feel that the deceased did not love them enough to stay with them. An important part of grieving a suicide is to find a way to continue the relationship with the deceased after their death, and despite their final action. Therapy may be useful to help the bereaved let go of feeling slighted or abandoned and assist the bereaved to restore access to a full lifetime's worth of stories and memories.

Horror. Trauma

Finally, as noted in the discussion of PTSD symptoms, suicide is often violent. Friends or family may witness the act, find the body, or vividly image the unnatural death event in their heads. This additional aspect of dealing with a death marked by intense feelings of fear, terror, and horror leads to its own unique set of post-traumatic responses that are not encountered if a loved one passes gently at home, hospice, or in the hospital. Kristensen and colleagues (2012, 77) explain, "any sudden loss makes it difficult for relatives to grasp the reality that a close family member has died. Suddenness also hinders bereaved relatives from bidding a final farewell and carrying out any last services for the loved one. Further, violent deaths may strike in horrifying ways, with relatives as helpless witnesses." We deeply appreciate the traumatic nature of losing a loved one to suicide, and we strongly encourage suicide loss survivors to seek professional assistance for managing post-traumatic stress symptoms including overwhelming intrusive memories, nightmares, and fear/anxiety.

Conclusion

This chapter has discussed many salient suicide loss-related diagnostic and treatment considerations. We hope that those bereaved by suicide will seek and receive the help they may need in coping with this loss. Because everyone's grief is an individualized process, family, friends, and professionals are encouraged to repeatedly, proactively, and regularly offer support, even when the bereaved has not responded in receptive ways to previous offers because they might respond differently in the future (Pitman et al. 2018, abstract). We emphasize that seeking and receiving assistance needs to be a continual and bidirectional process because many suicide loss survivors are deterred from seeking help due to feelings of shame (Pitman et al. 2016, 27). Overt demonstrations of social support lessen feelings of isolation and discomfort. Whether originating from the bereaved or those around them, once "survivors feel secure enough to share personal information with others (reflecting a sense of belongingness), emotional aspects of the psychological trauma are likely to be revealed, leading, in turn, to feelings of intimacy and togetherness" (Levi-Belz and Aisenberg 2021, 1033).

John R. Jordan (2020), a suicide loss grief therapy expert, indicates that therapeutic interventions with survivors need to devote special attention to developing a secure and nurturing therapeutic alliance with their clients;

provide comprehensive educational information about suicide, trauma, and grief; assist the bereaved in revisiting and restoring their bond with the deceased; and support survivors as they work to reconstrue a world that has often been dramatically altered by the suicide of a loved one. Individual therapy may be complemented by suicide loss survivor support groups, psychoeducational offerings, and family systems interventions (Jordan 2001, 98–9). The potential value of family systems interventions is true in all types of bereavement but is particularly important for suicide survivors. Because of the risk of additional suicides, and the damage done to family communication and processing, "the facilitation of adaptive family emotional functioning throughout the mourning process is crucial" for suicide loss survivors (Jordan 2001, 99).

We end by emphasizing that with support and time, suicide loss survivors can expect improvements in their symptoms, distress, and dysfunction in daily life. Evidence indicates that symptoms of depression, anxiety, and stress decrease over time (Kõlves et al. 2019, 92). Feelings of rejection, stigmatization, and searching for meaning also decline in the two years following a suicide loss (Kõlves et al. 2019, 93). Unfortunately, little improvement was noted in feelings of shame, responsibility, guilt, and loss of social support (Kõlves et al. 2019, 97). Therefore, we reassert that when a suicide loss survivor "feels supported by others, senses that they belong to family and community, and can communicate pain without feeling like a burden, their healing process accelerates" (Levi-Belz and Birnbaum 2022, 10–11). We hope that the intentional awareness of symptom severity and categorization, and enhanced sensitivity to suicide loss-specific issues and interventions such as those described herein, will help improve psychological distress and suicide loss-associated factors more completely.

Note

1 If you are, or anyone you know is experiencing suicidal thoughts or feelings now, please seek support by calling the Suicide and Crisis Prevention Lifeline by dialing 988.

Bibliography

Abrutyn, Seth, and Anna S. Mueller. 2014. "Are Suicidal Behaviors Contagious in Adolescence? Using Longitudinal Data to Examine Suicide Suggestion." *American Sociological Review* 79 (2): 211–27. https://doi.org/10.1177/0003122413519445.

Addis, Michael E. 2008. "Gender and Depression in Men." *Clinical Psychology Science and Practice* 15 (3): 153–68. https://doi.org/10.1111/j.1468-2850.2008.00125.x.

American Psychiatric Association. 2013. *Diagnostic and Statistical Manual of Mental Disorders*. https://doi.org/10.1176/appi.books.9780890425596.

American Psychiatric Association. 2022. *Diagnostic and Statistical Manual of Mental Disorders*. https://doi.org/10.1176/appi.books.9780890425787.

Azorina, Valeriya, Nicola Morant, Hedvig Nesse, et al. 2019. "The Perceived Impact of Suicide Bereavement on Specific Interpersonal Relationships: A Qualitative Study of Survey Data." *International Journal of Environmental Research and Public Health* 16 (10): 1801. https://doi.org/10.3390/ijerph16101801.

Brent, D. A. 2005. "Family Genetic Studies, Suicide, and Suicidal Behavior." *Child and Adolescent Psychiatry: University of Pittsburgh Part C: Seminars in Medical Genetics* 15: 13–24.

Caselli, Ivano, Marta Ielmini, Alessandro Bellini, Daniele Zizolfi, and Camilla Callegari. 2023. "Efficacy of Short-term Psychodynamic Psychotherapy (STPP) in Depressive Disorders: A Systematic Review and Meta-analysis." *Journal of Affective Disorders* 325: 169–76.

Cavanagh, J. T. O., A. J. Carson, M. Sharpe, and S. M. Lawrie. 2003. "Psychological Autopsy Studies of Suicide: A Systematic Review." *Psychological Medicine* 33 (3): 395–405. https://doi.org/10.1017/s0033291702006943.

Cvinar, Jacqueline G. 2005. "Do Suicide Survivors Suffer Social Stigma: A Review of the Literature." *Perspectives in Psychiatric Care* 41 (1): 14–21. https://doi.org/10.1111/j.0031-5990.2005.00004.x.

Djelantik, A. A. A. M. J., Geert E. Smid, Anna Mroz, Rolf J. Kleber, and Paul A. Boelen. 2020. "The Prevalence of Prolonged Grief Disorder in Bereaved Individuals Following Unnatural Losses: Systematic Review and Meta-analysis." *Journal of Affective Disorders* 265: 146–56.

Dyregrov, Kari. 2004. "Micro-Sociological Analysis of Social Support Following Traumatic Bereavement: Unhelpful and Avoidant Responses From the Community." *OMEGA Journal of Death and Dying* 48 (1): 23–44. https://doi.org/10.2190/t3nm-vfbk-68r0-uj60.

Feigelman, William, Julie Cerel, John L. McIntosh, David Brent, and Nina Gutin. 2018. "Suicide Exposures and Bereavement Among American Adults: Evidence From the 2016 General Social Survey." *Journal of Affective Disorders* 227 (October): 1–6. https://doi.org/10.1016/j.jad.2017.09.056.

Grafiadeli, Raphaela, Heide Glaesmer, Laura Hofmann, et al. 2021. "Suicide Risk After Suicide Bereavement: The Role of Loss-related Characteristics, Mental Health, and Hopelessness." *Journal of Psychiatric Research* 144 (October): 184–9. https://doi.org/10.1016/j.jpsychires.2021.09.056.

Hofmann, Stefan G., Anu Asnaani, Imke J. J. Vonk, Alice T. Sawyer, and Angela Fang. 2012. "The Efficacy of Cognitive Behavioral Therapy: A Review of Meta-analyses."

Cognitive Therapy and Research 36 (5): 427–40. https://doi.org/10.1007/s10608-012-9476-1.

Horowitz, Mardi J., Bryna Siegel, Are Holen, George A. Bonanno, Constance Milbrath, and Charles H. Stinson. 2003. "Diagnostic Criteria for Complicated Grief Disorder." *FOCUS: The Journal of Lifelong Learning in Psychiatry* 1 (3): 290–8. https://doi.org/10.1176/foc.1.3.290.

Jordan, John R. 2001. "Is Suicide Bereavement Different? A Reassessment of the Literature." *Suicide and Life-Threatening Behavior* 31 (1): 91–102. https://doi.org/10.1521/suli.31.1.91.21310.

Jordan, John R. 2008. "Bereavement After Suicide." *Psychiatric Annals* 38 (10). https://doi.org/10.3928/00485713-20081001-05.

Jordan, John R. 2020. "Lessons Learned: Forty Years of Clinical Work with Suicide Loss Survivors." *Frontiers in Psychology* 11 (April). https://doi.org/10.3389/fpsyg.2020.00766.

Kelly, John F., Keith Humphreys, and Marica Ferri. 2020. "Alcoholics Anonymous and Other 12-step Programs for Alcohol Use Disorder." *Cochrane Library* (March). https://doi.org/10.1002/14651858.cd012880.pub2.

Killikelly, Clare, Louisa Lorenz, Susanna Bauer, et al. 2019. "Prolonged Grief Disorder: Its Co-occurrence with Adjustment Disorder and Posttraumatic Stress Disorder in a Bereaved Israeli General-Population Sample." *Journal of Affective Disorders* 249 (February): 307–14. https://doi.org/10.1016/j.jad.2019.02.014.

Kõlves, Kairi, Qing Zhao, Victoria Ross, et al. 2019. "Suicide and Sudden Death Bereavement in Australia: A Longitudinal Study of Family Members Over 2 Years After Death." *Australian & New Zealand Journal of Psychiatry* 54 (1): 89–98. https://doi.org/10.1177/0004867419882490.

Kristensen, Pål, Lars Weisæth, and Trond Heir. 2012. "Bereavement and Mental Health After Sudden and Violent Losses: A Review." *Psychiatry* 75 (1): 76–97. https://doi.org/10.1521/psyc.2012.75.1.76.

Levi-Belz, Yossi, and Daniela Aisenberg. 2021. "Interpersonal Predictors of Suicide Ideation and Complicated-grief Trajectories Among Suicide Bereaved Individuals: A Four-year Longitudinal Study." *Journal of Affective Disorders* 282 (January): 1030–5. https://doi.org/10.1016/j.jad.2021.01.006.

Levi-Belz, Yossi, and Shai Birnbaum. 2022. "Depression and Suicide Ideation Among Suicide Loss Survivors: A Six-Year Longitudinal Study." *International Journal of Environmental Research and Public Health* 19 (24): 16561. https://doi.org/10.3390/ijerph192416561.

Lundorff, Marie, Helle Holmgren, Robert Zachariae, et al. 2017. "Prevalence of Prolonged Grief Disorder in Adult Bereavement: A Systematic Review and Meta-analysis." *Journal of Affective Disorders* 212: 138–49.

McGrath, John J., Ali Al-Hamzawi, Jordi Alonso, Yasmin Altwaijri, et al. 2023. "Age of Onset and Cumulative Risk of Mental Disorders: A Cross-national Analysis of

Population Surveys From 29 Countries." *The Lancet Psychiatry* 10 (9): 668–1. https://doi.org/10.1016/s2215-0366(23)00193-1.

McLean, Carmen P., Hannah C. Levy, Madeleine L. Miller, and David F. Tolin. 2022. "Exposure Therapy for PTSD: A Meta-analysis." *Clinical Psychology Review* 91 (December): 102115. https://doi.org/10.1016/j.cpr.2021.102115.

Mitchell, Ann M., Yookyung Kim, Holly G. Prigerson, and MaryKay Mortimer-Stephens. 2004. "Complicated Grief in Survivors of Suicide." *Crisis* 25 (1): 12–18. https://doi.org/10.1027/0227-5910.25.1.12.

Mitchell, Ann M., Teresa J. Sakraida, Yookyung Kim, Leann Bullian, and Laurel Chiappetta. 2008. "Depression, Anxiety and Quality of Life in Suicide Survivors: A Comparison of Close and Distant Relationships." *Archives of Psychiatric Nursing* 23 (1): 2–10. https://doi.org/10.1016/j.apnu.2008.02.007.

Pitman, Alexandra, David Osborn, Michael King, and Annette Erlangsen. 2014. "Effects of Suicide Bereavement on Mental Health and Suicide Risk." *The Lancet Psychiatry* 1 (1): 86–94. https://doi.org/10.1016/s2215-0366(14)70224-x.

Pitman, Alexandra, David Osborn, Khadija Rantell, and Michael King. 2016. "The Stigma Perceived by People Bereaved by Suicide and Other Sudden Deaths: A Cross-sectional UK Study of 3432 Bereaved Adults." *Journal of Psychosomatic Research* 87: 22–9.

Pitman, Alexandra, Tanisha De Souza, Adelia Khrisna Putri, Fiona Stevenson, Michael King, David Osborn, and Nicola Morant. 2018. "Support Needs and Experiences of People Bereaved by Suicide: Qualitative Findings From a Cross-Sectional British Study of Bereaved Young Adults." *International Journal of Environmental Research and Public Health* 15 (4): 666. https://doi.org/10.3390/ijerph15040666.

Prendergast, Michael, Deborah Podus, John Finney, Lisa Greenwell, and John Roll. 2006. "Contingency Management for Treatment of Substance Use Disorders: A Meta-Analysis." *Addiction* 101 (11): 1546–60. https://doi.org/10.1111/j.1360-0443.2006.01581.x.

Sanford, Rebecca, Julie Cerel, Vanessa McGann, and Myfanwy Maple. 2016. "Suicide Loss Survivors' Experiences with Therapy: Implications for Clinical Practice." *Community Mental Health Journal* 52 (5): 551–8. https://doi.org/10.1007/s10597-016-0006-6.

Sveen, Carl-Aksel, and Fredrik A. Walby. 2008. "Suicide Survivors' Mental Health and Grief Reactions: A Systematic Review of Controlled Studies." *Suicide and Life-Threatening Behavior* 38 (1): 13–29. https://doi.org/10.1521/suli.2008.38.1.13.

Szuhany, Kristin L., Matteo Malgaroli, Carly D. Miron, and Naomi M. Simon. 2021. "Prolonged Grief Disorder: Course, Diagnosis, Assessment, and Treatment." *Focus: The Journal of Lifelong Learning in Psychiatry* 19 (2): 161–72. https://doi.org/10.1176/appi.focus.20200052.

Wagner, Birgit, Laura Hofmann, and Raphaela Grafiadeli. 2021. "The Relationship Between Guilt, Depression, Prolonged Grief, and Posttraumatic Stress Symptoms

After Suicide Bereavement." *Journal of Clinical Psychology* 77 (11): 2545–58. https://doi.org/10.1002/jclp.23192.

Wallace, Denise, Nicholas R. Cooper, Alejandra Sel, and Riccardo Russo. 2023. "The Social Readjustment Rating Scale: Updated and Modernised." *PLoS ONE* 18 (12): e0295943. https://doi.org/10.1371/journal.pone.0295943.

World Health Organization. 2018. *International Statistical Classification of Diseases and Related Health Problems*. 11th ed. World Health Organization.

Young, Ilanit Tal, Alana Iglewicz, Danielle Glorioso, et al. 2012. "Suicide Bereavement and Complicated Grief." *Dialogues in Clinical Neuroscience* 14 (2): 177–86. https://doi.org/10.31887/dcns.2012.14.2/iyoung.

3

A Caring God

Perspectives from the Older Testament for Suicide Loss Survivors

Gordon Brubacher

When our son David chose his own death in September 2022, my wife Rhonda and I found ourselves surrounded by caring communities. One was Rhonda's extended family (we live in her home area), another was made up of my colleagues in the Theology Department at Creighton University, and a third, members of First Mennonite Church, our faith home in Lincoln, Nebraska. Our daughter Sara, in Kitchener, Ontario, where she was staying at the time, and where David lived and died, experienced the same caring community at Stirling Avenue Mennonite Church. All these wonderful communities were just what surrounding people should be at such a time. All, whether consciously or not, reflected a caring God. Inspired by that experience, this chapter offers reflections on voluntary death from the Older Testament (OT) for suicide loss survivors.[1] It first critiques and rejects harmful (mis)use of the OT in traditional Christian stigmas and prohibitions, contesting the darkness of that teaching. It then presents, as a life-giving alternative, the OT theme of a caring God.

Suicides in the Old Testament

Contrary to widely held opinion, suicide itself is not censured morally anywhere in the OT. Here are the commonly listed episodes (biblical quotes are NRSVue unless otherwise indicated).

Abimelech Son of Gideon/Jerubbaal (Judg. 9:52-57)

Abimelech came to the tower and fought against it and came near to the entrance of the tower to burn it with fire. But a certain woman threw an upper millstone on Abimelech's head and crushed his skull. Immediately he called to the young man who carried his armor and said to him, "Draw your sword and kill me, so people will not say about me, 'A woman killed him.'" So, the young man thrust him through, and he died. When the Israelites saw that Abimelech was dead, they all went home. Thus, God repaid Abimelech for the crime he committed against his father in killing his seventy brothers; and God also made all the wickedness of the people of Shechem fall back on their heads, and on them came the curse of Jotham son of Jerubbaal.

Samson the Judge (Judg. 16:28-31)

Then Samson called to the LORD and said, "Lord GOD, remember me and strengthen me only this once, O God, so that with this one act of revenge I may pay back the Philistines for my two eyes." And Samson grasped the two middle pillars on which the house rested, and he leaned his weight against them, his right hand on the one and his left hand on the other. Then Samson said, "Let me die with the Philistines." He strained with all his might, and the house fell on the lords and all the people who were in it. So those he killed at his death were more than those he had killed during his life. Then his kindred and all his family came down and took him and brought him up and buried him between Zorah and Eshtaol in the tomb of his father Manoah. He had judged Israel twenty years.

King Saul and His Armor-bearer (1 Sam. 31:3-5)

The battle pressed hard on Saul, and the archers found him, and he was badly wounded by them. Then Saul said to his armor-bearer, "Draw your sword and thrust me through with it, so that these uncircumcised may not come and thrust me through and make sport of me." But his armor-bearer was unwilling, for he was terrified. So Saul took his own sword and fell on it. When his armor-bearer saw that Saul was dead, he also fell on his sword and died with him.

Ahithophel the Royal Counselor (2 Sam. 17:23)

When Ahithophel saw that his counsel was not followed, he saddled his donkey and went off home to his own city. He set his house in order and hanged himself; he died and was buried in the tomb of his father.

Zimri the Conspirator Assassin (1 Kgs. 16:18-19)

> When Zimri saw that the city was taken, he went into the citadel of the king's house; he burned down the king's house over himself with fire and died—because of the sins that he committed, doing evil in the sight of the Lord, walking in the way of Jeroboam, and for the sin that he committed, causing Israel to sin.

Jonah the Prophet (Jonah 11:12)

> He said to them, "Pick me up and throw me into the sea; then the sea will quiet down for you, for I know it is because of me that this great storm has come upon you."

The reader will note with interest that moral or ethical judgment on the act is missing entirely. Modern studies uniformly find that *suicide itself is not censured morally in the passages quoted above, nor anywhere else in the OT.*[2]

It is true that cultural framework plays an important role in both presentation and interpretation, as shown by variations between the accounts of King Saul's death, or by the morally ambiguous actions of Samson who is nonetheless listed among the heroes of faith in Hebrews 11:32 (Cho 2022, 13, 26–7). However, the element of cultural framework does not change the basic fact that no moral judgments on suicide are found in these narratives.[3]

(Mis)Use of the Older Testament

Various theologians from Lactantius onward have misunderstood or misused the OT in particular in their own teaching on suicide.[4] What follows is a survey of that misuse, which produced the traditional prohibitions and the harmful stigmas that followed (Mason 2021; Potter 2021). This survey can hopefully play a role in contesting the darkness of that teaching.

Lactantius (*c.* 240–320)

Lactantius in *The Divine Institutes* criticized Greek and Roman views on suicide, and in the process anticipated Augustine of Hippo (354–430) in some respects. He wrote:

> *[N]othing can be more wicked than [killing oneself]*. For if a homicide is guilty because he is a destroyer of man, *he who puts himself to death is under the same guilt*, because he puts to death a man. . . . Yea, *that crime may be considered to be greater, the punishment of which belongs to God alone* . . . the death of an innocent person cannot be unavenged . . . we have a great Judge who alone always has the power of taking vengeance in His hands (Lactantius, Book III; emphasis added).

This argument draws on certain OT passages:

- "You shall not murder" (Exod. 20:13);
- "For your own lifeblood I will surely require a reckoning: from every animal I will require it and from human beings, each one for the blood of another, I will require a reckoning for human life" (Gen 9:5); and
- "Vengeance is mine" (Deut 32:35; so most English translations; NRSVue reads "for the day of vengeance").

However: *none of these biblical texts has any overt connection to taking one's own life*. We note in particular Lactantius' early allusion to the Fifth Commandment, "You shall not murder" (Exod 20:13).[5] Augustine soon made it the centerpiece of his own use of the OT to prohibit suicide. Also of interest, as Allyson Mower has observed, is the fact that "Lactantius is the first writer in the Christian tradition to argue, as he does in this work, that *killing oneself is worse than killing another person*, a view that gains considerable currency in later Christian thought" (Mower 2015a; emphasis added). In addition to the passage quoted above, Lactantius refers to this briefly in his *Epitome of the Divine Institutes* (4. 2), a summary of the *Institutes* which he penned later in life (Knight 2023).

Augustine of Hippo (354–430)

Augustine, widely viewed as one of the most important early church theologians, was certainly the most influential on the ethics of suicide (Droge and Tabor 1991, 185–6; Ortiz 2019). While there is no reason to doubt his good intentions, his programmatic treatment has caused much harm and suffering to innocent people, so we need to know what he said and understand what he meant.[6]

In his opposition to the Donatist branch of Christianity,[7] which allegedly encouraged suicide as escape from persecution or simply as a shortcut to heaven, Augustine employed detailed biblical and philosophical arguments for his prohibition of suicide (Adamiak and Dohnalik 2023, 3824). His primary arguments are found in *City of God* 1.17-27, using the OT especially in 1.20-21. The most relevant parts, using two of the Ten Commandments, are worth quoting here (1.20; emphasis added):

> *[T]he law, rightly interpreted, even prohibits suicide, where it says, "Thou shalt not kill."* This is proved especially by the omission of the words "thy neighbor," which are inserted when false witness is forbidden: "Thou shalt not bear false witness against thy neighbor." . . . For the love of our neighbor is regulated by the love of ourselves, as it is written, "Thou shalt love thy neighbor as thyself."
>
> How much greater reason have we to understand that a man may not kill himself, since in the commandment, "Thou shalt not kill," there is no limitation added nor any exception made in favor of anyone, and least of all in favor of him on whom the command is laid!
>
> If, when we say, Thou shalt not kill, we do not understand this of the plants, since they have no sensation, nor of the irrational animals that fly, swim, walk, or creep, since they are dissociated from us by their want of reason, and are therefore by the just appointment of the Creator subjected to us to kill or keep alive for our own uses; if so, then it remains that *we understand that commandment simply of man. The commandment is, "Thou shall not kill man;" therefore neither another nor yourself, for he who kills himself still kills nothing else than man*[emphasis added].

In his own mind, Augustine was clear. The Fifth Commandment prohibits the murder of a human being, and this prohibition includes suicide on grounds that it is the murder of a human being. He supported this interpretation of the Fifth Commandment by contrasting it with the Eighth on bearing false witness because that one has a limiting phrase for application (one's neighbor) whereas the Fifth does not. However, one should clearly note that *the Fifth Commandment does not say anything about suicide*; to find it there, *we need to invent this idea* and insert it into this commandment ourselves.

To the above, one can add further judgments by Augustine from 1.17–27: "he who kills himself is a homicide" (1.17); a woman taking her own life after being violated "commits certain homicide" (1.18); and "suicide is a detestable and damnable wickedness" (1.25). He also ridiculed those who take their lives to escape shame or unbearable suffering (a running theme in 1.17–27) as "of a feeble rather than a strong spirit, and dictated not by honourable feeling forestalling shame, but by weakness shrinking from hardships" (1.23). The extent to which Augustine employed harsh, judgmental, uncompromising language can be surprising (cf. Droge and Tabor 1991, 183 n. 61, 185). He asserted that "Sound judgment is to be preferred even to examples" (1.22), which in context functionally meant that correct dogma or ideology were more important than the actual suffering of real people in their experienced reality on the ground. (This writer disagrees.)

By contrast, Augustine holds up the example of "the saintly Job, who endured dreadful evils in his body rather than deliver himself from all torment by self-inflicted death" (1.26; see Job 3:11, 17–19; 6:8–13; 7:9–10, 21). But whether Augustine actually understands the Book of Job in this matter is certainly open to question.[8]

This hard-line prohibition against taking any human life created some problems of consistency for Augustine, as he himself recognized. Hence he followed with a section titled: "Of the Cases in Which We May Put Men to Death Without Incurring the Guilt of Murder" (1.21). It opens: "However, there are some exceptions made by the divine authority to its own law, that men may not be put to death," and he described these exceptions in two categories. The first includes cases that are justified "by a just law that applies generally," namely, warfare and capital punishment. The second category includes cases that are sanctioned "by a special intimation from God Himself," and here two types are presented. One is by direct divine command, such as Abraham's willingness to sacrifice his son at God's explicit command (Gen. 22:2–3). Another entails a great deal of ambiguity because it asserts a secret divine command or permission which one can only adduce hypothetically. He posits as two such cases: Jephthah, who sacrificed his daughter in order to keep a reckless vow (Judg. 11:29–40); and Samson (an example repeated in 1.26), whose final action looks like suicide to the reader.

By way of assessment, one can only say that *Augustine was mistaken in his interpretation and application of the OT on virtually all counts.* The Fifth Commandment, which prohibits the murder of a human, does not include suicide. The Eighth Commandment about bearing false witness against one's neighbor is irrelevant because it is on an entirely different topic. Invoking a hypothetical secret voice of God to support actions which appear to contradict his main doctrine is an "argument" completely empty of content in that anyone could claim this about anything. Furthermore, it borders on taking the name of God in vain.

The views and attitudes of Augustine quickly acquired a life of their own and became the primary Western Christian doctrine throughout the medieval period and beyond. They were soon adopted as part of both canon and civil law by various church councils and governments (Droge and Tabor 1991, 5–6; Adamiak and Dohnalik 2023, 3825–6). They were notably upheld along the way by Aquinas in particular, so we turn to Aquinas in our survey now.

Thomas Aquinas (*c.* 1225–74)

Thomas Aquinas made Augustine's argument from the Fifth Commandment the central pillar of his own proscription against suicide (Mower 2015b). His primary arguments are found in the *Summa Theologiae*, in the section which he titled "Whether One is Allowed to Kill Himself" (2a 2ae, quest. 64, art. 50). Citing Augustine from Book 1 of *The City of God*, Aquinas wrote: "We understand the commandment 'Thou shalt not kill' to pertain to man. Kill no other man, nor yourself; for he who kills himself kills another man." Aquinas added in the same section: "To God alone belongs the power over death and life, according to Deuteronomy 32: 'I kill and I make to live.'" Quoting and applying Deuteronomy 32:39 was a new development in Christian use of the OT for prohibiting suicide, and this calls for assessment:

> See now that I, even I, am he;
>   there is no god besides me.
> I kill, and I make alive;
>   I wound, and I heal;
> *and no one can deliver from my hand* [emphasis added].

We see that the last line in that verse, "no one can deliver from [God's] hand," *actually appears to contradict Aquinas.* If no one can deliver from God's hand, then no one can kill oneself against God's will. *The line is taken out of context and misused.*

Dante Alighieri (1265–1321) and William Blake (1757–1827)

Here one would be remiss to omit the role of Dante in reinforcing the dogmatic prohibitions described above (cf. Antus 2020, 395). For this we call upon one poet, A. Alvarez, to describe the work of another:

> Certainly, Dante never questioned the orthodox judgment of the crime. Instead, he sustained it by devoting one of the grimmest cantos of the *Inferno* to the suicides. In the Seventh Circle, below the burning heretics and the murderers stewing in their river of hot blood, is a dark, pathless wood where the souls

> of suicides grow for eternity in the shape of warped, poisonous thorns. The Harpies, with their great wings and feathered bellies, human faces and clawed feet, nest in these stunted trees and pick at their leaves. The whole wood is full of the sound of lament(Alvarez 1972, 144).

A celebrated work of art by William Blake, titled "The Wood of the Self-Murderers: The Harpies and the Suicides," furthered Dante's influence, and has rightly made its way into the psychiatric literature on the subject (Harris 2003). Dante's influence is also described in a splendid novel by Matthew Pearl, titled *The Dante Club*, which portrays a group of scholars at Harvard in the 1860s translating, studying, and teaching Dante (Pearl 2003).

Observations on (Mis)Use of the Older Testament

All these forms of misusing the OT might remind us of an apt observation by John Gardner: "The society which scorns excellence in plumbing as a humble activity and tolerates shoddiness in *theology* because it is an exalted activity will have neither good plumbing nor good *theology*: neither its pipes nor its theories will hold water" (Gardner 1961, 86; I changed the original from "philosophy" to "theology").

What kind of God is seen in the OT interpretation described above? Lactantius portrays a judging and avenging God, "a great Judge who alone always has the power of taking vengeance in His hands" (*Divine Institutes*, Book 3). Augustine presents a stern God who demands "purity" (*City of God*, 1.17–19), who is authoritarian and commanding (1.20–21), and who seems to glower at those who might commit the terrible, unforgivable action of ending their own lives. This portrayal of God is aptly described and understandably rejected by A. Alvarez as "God's savage, cheeseparing judgment" in his brilliant and oft-cited book, *The Savage God: A Study of Suicide* (Alvarez 1972, 149). People of faith who are affected by suicide often suffer from the stigma that was created by this portrait of God, because it is still widely accepted, in varying degrees, in some Christian circles to this day.[9] A differing perspective from the OT is needed, and available.

The Caring God

What, if anything, might the OT contain which would bear on the subject of suicide and the people affected by it? One thing could be the important stream of thought which describes a caring God. After all, "It is not enough to say that one believes in God. What is important finally is the *kind* of God in whom one believes" (Fretheim 1984, 1). While the OT does not specifically say that God cares about people who are affected by suicide, we can identify the ways in which God *does* care about humanity and see that this care would extend especially to people who are so affected. Some of the metaphors for God in the OT[10] would surely imply that care.

"In many and various ways" (Heb 1:1), the OT portrays a loving, caring, protecting, committed God throughout. This is a God to whom people affected by suicide can relate. Because misuse of the OT has done so much harm by misrepresenting the nature of God, this section on the caring God in the OT is the longest of the chapter.

The caring God is presented above all as *highly relational*. Fretheim observes that "biblical metaphors for God, with few if any exceptions, have relatedness at their very core. . . . [They reveal] a God who had entered deeply into the life of the world and was present and active in the common life of individuals and communities" (2007, 610). As a result, "God is thus portrayed not as a king dealing with an issue at some distance, nor even as one who sends a subordinate . . . God enters fully into [a] hurtful situation and makes it his own" (Fretheim 1984, 128). Numerous passages and themes in the OT breathe a deep belief in a relational God who cares, in many and various ways. These include the following.

A Blessing God

A caring God is presented in the OT within the framework of the major biblical theme and message of God's will for basic well-being for everyone. This is expressed, for example, in the theme of blessing, which refers to the things which constitute basic well-being, such as having enough food, water, clothing, shelter, family, and community—the basics for life on this good earth together under God (cf. Scharbert 1977, 294). The theme of blessing for all is launched already in the creation story, which says "God blessed [the humans]" (Gen. 1:28). The Sabbath Commandment is described as a day which the Lord has blessed (Exod. 20:11), which means it is intended for well-being, not just some rule because God says so. In fact, it is specifically described as humanitarian, prescribing human rights and worker protection in a time and place in which most people were worked far too hard by those who controlled them. It protects everyone, even those with no citizenship rights, and specifically lists some types of vulnerable people at the time.

The theme of blessing travels a long way. It even goes so far as to envision an era in which three enemy nations—Egypt, Assyria, Israel—will, can, or should be partners in worship and in bringing basic well-being to their known world (Isa. 19:23–25). People would have said "Never!" because those three were bitter enemies at the time. It is more than a big tent; it is a planet-sized pavilion with shelter for all. It pictures a whole new world, like a new creation, willed by a blessing God. And from blessing it is only a short step to a loving, committed God.

A Loving God

A loving, committed God is portrayed, affirmed, and celebrated throughout the OT, often for people in distress. This God is frequently described using two Hebrew words in particular, namely, *ʾahav* "love" and *hesed* "steadfast love," so we should look first at the basic meanings of those words. The Hebrew word *ʾahav* and its derivatives means much the same as the English word "love," plus more. It commonly denotes a sense of commitment, shown through actions, for the well-being of another, no matter what the cost. It applies to the social, national, and international spheres, not only to individual relationships. In the OT, love is an action word (cf. Sakenfeld 2008; Wallis 1977, 105–6).

The important and frequent Hebrew word *hesed*, commonly translated "steadfast love," contains a whole range of meanings, including mercy, kindness, loving-kindness, grace, and loyalty (Birch 1991, 152). It is striking to note that this word is used very frequently of God (Gosling 1996, 277–80). Katherine Doob Sakenfeld, perhaps the most respected scholar on love in the OT, shows how major aspects of *hesed* include the fact that it is "requested of or done for another with whom one is already in relationship," and in basic form it consists of specific actions (Sakenfeld 1992, 378). Elsewhere, she writes that God's steadfast love is foundational, that it is "intimately associated with help in any time of individual or communal distress, and in its abounding mercy it is the fountain from which flows divine mercy and forgiveness" (Sakenfeld 2008, 718; cf. Zobel 1986, 48, 54).

Various themes emerge from a study of how these words are used. It is no surprise that they occur mainly in the Psalms, which respond in faith to the gifts and reversals of life, in joy or in sorrow, as individuals or as the united community of faith. In the process, they convey unshakable belief in a loving God, a belief which can serve people who are affected by suicide to this day.

It *permeates*. The steadfast love of God permeates the world from beginning to end, and it is in fact built into creation itself (Pss. 33:5; 35:5). Psalm 136:5-9 celebrates the creation process with the recurring refrain: "for his steadfast love endures forever." Indeed, it is said to be global, such that all nations and peoples can praise the Lord for his steadfast love (Ps. 117:1-2; cf. Zobel 1986, 62–3).

It *endures*. The steadfast love of God is no less than "*everlasting*." Mere mortals have a brief existence, "But [in contrast] the steadfast love of the Lord is *from everlasting to everlasting*" (Ps. 103:15–17; cf. Jer. 31:3), and "his steadfast love endures forever" (Ps. 118:1–4, 29; cf. 136:23; see Zobel 1986, 55–6, 57).

Moreover, it is *consistent*—one can *count on it*. These psalms affirm and celebrate God's steadfast love as characterized by *faithfulness*. "For the Lord is good; his steadfast love endures *forever* and his faithfulness *to all generations*" (Ps. 100:5; cf. Ps. 89:1, 2, 5, 8, 14; Jer. 31:3). Again, in contrast to mortals, it is known for reliability; it is not capricious (Zobel 1986, 62). Psalm 23 ends with a striking scenario: the psalmist and his former enemies are now family together in the household of God (verse 6; my translation):

> Surely well-being and your *hesed* will tail-gate me
> all the days of my life,
> and I shall dwell under the protection of the Lord
> my whole life long.

In fact, God *owns* goodness. Various psalms affirm aspects of God's goodness to the extent that they give God ownership of these traits. They speak not merely *about* them but use the language of God's ownership: "*your* steadfast love," "*your* mercy," "*your* goodness," and "*your* faithfulness" (Pss. 25:6, 7; 31:7; 36:7; 89:1, 2; cf. Lam. 3:23). God is fundamentally characterized by these traits and known to be so.

Great *expectations* follow. People in distress can appeal to God's steadfast love or goodness, *expecting that God will act accordingly*: "Help me, O Lord my God! Save me *according to* your steadfast love" (Ps. 109:26). This approach indicates belief in a standard to which God measures up or is expected to measure up. Numerous instances are found in the Psalms (e.g., Pss. 25:7; 35:24; 51:1; 69:16; 119:76, 156; cf. Zobel 1986, 56).

It follows also that *hope* is linked to God's steadfast love, describing a *hope-giving* God: "Let your steadfast love, O Lord, be upon us, even as we *hope* in you" (Ps. 33:22; cf. 9:18; 33:22; 42:11; 43:5; 130:5, 7; 131:3). For suicide loss survivors, hope is a special four-letter word, adding great power to the *hesed* of the loving God.

A Mothering God

A parenting, mothering God is yet another portrait found in the OT. For example, as Fretheim correctly observes: "God is not simply father; God is a certain *kind* of father. God is *a loving father, always* (Hos. 11:1). And God is not simply mother; God is a certain *kind* of mother. God is *a mother who will not forget her children, ever* (Isa. 49:15)" (Fretheim 1984, 12; emphasis added). For example, a tender vignette in Hosea portrays the Lord as a parent caring for Israel as a toddler at its origins in the Exodus from Egypt, yet Israel tended to go wrong from the very beginning (Hos. 11:1-4; cf. Brubacher 2025, 1080). This could well be an image of God as mother, "a healing, nourishing motherly presence," part of the larger picture of "a compassionate mother who will never forget her child (Isa. 49:14–17); and a comforting presence as a mother can be comforting (Isa. 66:13)" (Van Wijk-Bos 2007, 587).

The *mothering compassion* of God is notably conveyed by the frequent Hebrew verb *riham* "show compassion, mercy, pity," along with the related noun *rihamim* "compassion, love, mercy, pity" and the adjective *rahum* "compassionate." These words appear to be cognate with the noun *rehem*, which means "womb." Hence they denote womb-like feelings, such as the feelings of a pregnant woman for her unborn child, or those of a woman for the baby nursing at her breast (cf. Trible 1978, 34; Fretheim 2007, 609). Even more striking is the fact that the numerous uses of these words commonly describe God having compassion (Simian-Yofre 2004, 440–1, 451–2; de Roo 2009, 419), and they convey the image of a very mothering God indeed. Certainly, this meaning would fit well in Isa. 49:15:

> Can a woman forget her nursing child
>   or show no compassion [*riham*] for the child of her womb?
> Even these might forget,
>   yet I will not forget you.

As Fretheim observes, "The image of a child in its mother's womb or at its mother's breast is capable of conveying a sense of closeness with God that is unique" (2007, 609). Many other places convey this sense of mothering compassion as well, a God who cares indeed (e.g., Jer. 31:20; Hos. 14:3; Isa. 49:13; 54:10; Pss. 57:1; 119:156; 145:8–9). They portray yet another mode of the God who cares for all, and not least for those in distress.

A Forgiving God

Forgiveness can be a powerful word of grace to counter the persistent legacy of the Augustinian distortion that suicide is a terrible sin (cf. Wolfelt 2009, 42–3). Hence the OT portrait of a forgiving God is relevant even though sin is not at issue here—the OT does not teach that suicide is a sin. Still, for readers who may have been taught this error, the forgiving God should be highlighted in order to be true to the biblical witness, and this may help to alleviate guilt and its harmful effects. In addition, if God is forgiving, suicide loss survivors can also be forgiving to loved ones who took their own lives. A series of interrelated passages about a forgiving God comes to mind, and we begin with Psalm 86:15:

> But you, O Lord, are a God merciful and gracious,
> *slow to anger* and abounding in *hesed* and faithfulness.

Here the "*slow*" divine anger is contrasted with abounding *hesed* and is enveloped in words of grace. That it is *slow* indicates a thoughtful God who is not impulsive but thinks things through, even in regard to anger—a decidedly nonhuman trait. As Helmer Ringgren has observed, the steadfast love and faithfulness of God "are infinitely more powerful than the inevitable consequences of sinning" (1977, 13). Indeed, anger is not a trait of God at all: "if there were no sin, there would be no wrath" (Fretheim 2007, 612).

Very similar passages in the series—almost verbatim—are found in Numbers 14:18; Psalms 103:8; 145:8; Joel 2:13; and Jonah 4:2. All contrast the slow divine anger with divine abounding *hesed* and enclose it in words of grace—merciful, gracious, abounding in *hesed* and faithfulness (cf. Zobel 1986, 57, 62). Just as one might be hard pressed to give a "balanced" view of rape (there is none), these passages do not present a "balanced" view of mercy and judgment in God. If anything, God is irrationally merciful by human standards (cf. Exod. 33:19; 34:6; Isa. 55:6-9; Hos. 14.4; Birch 1985, 52–3; Sakenfeld 2008, 717).

The caring God is *incomparably forgiving*. In a ballad celebrating the power of the Lord at the Reed Sea crossing, one line posits the incomparability of God: "Who is like you, O Lord, among the gods?" (Exod. 15:11). It then describes God with no peer as a warrior, which is all very well in the context and situation. However, the biblical tradition proceeds to transform this incomparability into something very different indeed, especially in Micah 7:18-20. Verse 18 reads:

> Who is a God like you, pardoning iniquity
> and passing over the transgression

of the remnant of his possession?
He does not retain his anger forever
because he delights in showing *hesed*.

The prophet Micah stuns his audience by proclaiming that their God is the greatest in something entirely different, namely, *forgiveness*. It is true that the prophet also recognizes divine anger as an appropriate initial response to wrong actions, but his very point is the transitory nature of that emotion. Instead, his emphasis is on the divine forgiveness and the surprising counter-emotion which goes with it: the Lord "*delights* in showing steadfast love." It is not the dutiful, grudging sort—it pleases him, makes him happy to show it, perhaps to show it off.

We find a similar idea in Jeremiah, where the prophet invites his audience to brag about a triad of traits in which their God delights: "I act with *steadfast love, justice, and righteousness* in the earth, *for in these things I delight*, says the Lord" (Jer. 9:24). The divine social media pages are no doubt strewn with "likes" for these character traits, even though this might offend a frowning theologian. For suicide loss survivors, a God who delights in showing *hesed,* and in whom forgiveness transcends punishment, is a God for all seasons, and for now.

A Faithful God

A traditional hymn titled "Great Is Thy Faithfulness" (Chisholm 1923) captures the spirit and vocabulary of much that we have seen above. It reads (emphasis added):

Great is *Thy faithfulness*, O God my Father;
There is no shadow of turning with Thee;
Thou *changest not, Thy compassions, they fail not*;
As Thou hast been Thou *forever* wilt be.

[Refrain:]
Great is *Thy faithfulness*!
Great is *Thy faithfulness*!
Morning by morning new *mercies* I see:
All I have needed Thy hand hath provided—
Great is *Thy faithfulness*, Lord, *unto me*!

Summer and winter and springtime and harvest,
Sun, moon, and stars in their courses above

Join with *all nature in manifold witness*
To *Thy great faithfulness*, *mercy*, and *love.*

Pardon for sin and a peace that endureth,
Thine own dear presence to cheer and to guide,
Strength for today and *bright hope* for tomorrow—
Blessings all mine, with ten thousand beside!

Great indeed, is it not? In this hymn we have the opportunity of making God's faithfulness great again, even though it has been all along. It is true that the portraits of a loving, faithful God in this hymn are mainly in terms of a patron/client relationship. This is, however, a positive point; this God is not only willing but able to do something about human distress. Moreover, the divine patron is not impersonal or distant in this relationship: "God sees the suffering from the inside; God does not look at it from the outside, as through a window" (Fretheim 1984, 128). A God like this (not like Augustine's) can surely be good news for suicide loss survivors.

Summary and Conclusion

This chapter offers perspectives on voluntary death from the OT for suicide loss survivors. It summarizes the commonly listed episodes of suicide in the OT and agrees with the great majority of modern scholarship that, contrary to widely held opinion, suicide in and of itself is not censured morally anywhere in the OT. It then surveys, critiques, and rejects the harmful use of the OT in what became traditional Christian teaching on suicide. Lactantius, Augustine, Aquinas, Dante, and Blake all (mis)used the OT in particular to diverge from the biblical witness in their own teaching and portrayals of the subject, misreading in particular the famous Fifth Commandment, "You shall not murder" (Exod. 20:13), often in harsh, judgmental language which portrays a harsh, judgmental God. It is fair to say that they were mistaken in their interpretation and application of the OT on virtually all counts.

The heart of this chapter presents instead the major OT theme of a caring God, a life-giving alternative to the traditional prohibitions and harmful stigmas, contesting the darkness of that teaching. It portrays a highly *relational* God, a *loving, blessing* God *committed to human well-being*, characterized by a steadfast love which endures. This God is *consistent*, known for reliability, characterized by *faithfulness*, a *hope-giving* God, a parenting, mothering, *compassionate* God. This God is *incomparably forgiving*, "a God merciful and gracious, slow to anger and abounding in steadfast love and faithfulness" (Ps. 86:15), a God who even *delights* in showing steadfast love. The caring God brings a gospel message of the divine will for basic well-being for everyone, often and especially for people in distress. For suicide loss survivors, this is a God for all seasons, and for now.[11]

Notes

1 "Suicide" is a relatively modern term, first gaining usage in the late 1760s (Daube 1972, 428), and it can be defined as "the voluntary killing of oneself" (Cho 2022, 1). "Voluntary death" and "choosing death" would also seem useful terms because they lack some of the negative baggage commonly associated with "suicide" (Droge and Tabor 1991, 4; cf. Wolfelt 2009, 15–16, 23). In what follows, the three terms are used with much the same meaning, unless a specific term is needed. On the other hand, "suicide loss survivors" is a useful term for people who were close to someone who died by suicide. For the complex, difficult experience of suicide loss survivors, see, for example (Bryan 2022, 49–50).

2 For example, Paul Cho concludes in a detailed and brilliant study that "no one who voluntarily kills himself in the Hebrew Bible is censured for the act" (Cho 2022, 2–3; cf. Koch 2005; Droge and Tabor 1991, 57; Goldstein 1989, 51–5). Much the same applies to suicide and related matters in the NT. Droge and Tabor summarize their detailed study: "Despite the claim of Augustine and later theologians, the New Testament expresses no condemnation of voluntary death" (Droge and Tabor 1992, 125).

3 Elsewhere in the OT, suicide ideation, risk of death, or willingness to die can even be interpreted as positive. Examples include Judah, Moses, Elijah, Queen Esther, Job, and the Suffering Servant in Isaiah (surveyed in Cho 2022; cf. Levinson 2022; Koch 2005; Droge and Tabor 1991). These, however, are not the subject of this chapter.

4 Josephus (*c.* 37–100 CE) partly foreshadowed some Christian theologians when he argued in a speech to his fellow rebels against Rome that suicide rather than surrender would be "an act of impiety towards God who created us. . . . For it is from Him that we have received our being, and it is to Him that we should leave the decision to take it away; . . . and God, their father, visits upon their posterity the outrageous acts of the parents" (Josephus, *Jewish War*, Bk III). These details allude to several OT passages (Gen. 1:27; Deut. 32:39; Exod. 20:5), but none have any actual connection to suicide.

5 Adamiak and Dohnalik find that Lactantius "was probably the first to explicitly link suicide with the commandment 'Thou shalt not kill'" (2023, 3823). On the numbering of the Ten Commandments, see Potter (2021, 3).

6 The general shortcomings of Augustine's arguments for the prohibition of suicide are well documented (e.g., Droge and Tabor 1992, chap. 7). This chapter will focus on his (mis)use of the OT in particular.

7 On the vocabulary and meaning of orthodoxy and heresy, see Droge and Tabor (1991, 137), and the literature cited there.

8 Contrast, for example, the detailed study of Job's unfolding attitude to voluntary death by Paul inCho (2022, 29–59).

9 Dominance by the Augustinian dogmatic perspective notwithstanding, it should be noted that a certain amount of pushback gradually developed, expressing a somewhat more charitable view toward suicides. However, these isolated voices of dissent did little to change the situation until the modern era (Droge and Tabor 1991, 7–8; Adamiak and Dohnalik 2023, 3826–7), and in any case they rarely, if ever, used the OT. The Augustinian view continued to be adopted and active in varying degrees in many Christian circles (Potter 2021, 3–4; Ortiz 2019).

10 Virtually all language about God is ultimately metaphorical because that is the best we humans can do—we compare God to something we know. A metaphor for God asks the reader to believe that God is like a known entity (such as a father) *in some significant respect*. It does not, however, mean to indicate that God is like the known entity in *all* respects. In general, *the significant element of similarity* can be deduced either from immediate context, or from the larger context, or from the widely known nature of the entity, or from the manner in which the metaphor is commonly employed elsewhere in the OT or in the literature of the wider world of the Bible, or by some relevant combination of the above. Good discussions of the nature and use of metaphors for God in the OT are found in Van Wijk-Bos 2007; Fretheim 1984, 5–12; Weems 1995, 23–5; Trible 1978.

11 Unless otherwise stated, all translations of the Bible are from the New Revised Standard Version, updated edition, National Council of Churches Friendship Press. New Revised Standard Version Bible, copyright 1989, Division of Christian Education of the National Council of the Churches of Christ in the United States of America. Used by permission. All rights reserved.

Bibliography

Adamiak, Stanisław, and Jan Dohnalik. 2023. "The Prohibition of Suicide and Its Theological Rationale in Catholic Moral and Canonical Tradition: Origins and

Development." *Journal of Religion and Health* 62: 3820–33. https://pmc.ncbi.nlm.nih.gov/articles/PMC10682050/.

Alvarez, A. 1972. *The Savage God: A Study of Suicide.* Random House.

Antus, Elizabeth L. 2020. "'The Silence of the Dead': Remembering Suicide Victims and Reimagining the Communion of Saints." *Theological Studies* 81 (2): 394–413.

Augustine of Hippo. 2000. *The City of God.* Translated by Marcus Dods, with an introduction by Thomas Merton. Modern Library paperback ed. Random House.

Birch, Bruce C. 1985. *What Does the Lord Require? The Old Testament Call to Social Witness.* Westminster/John Knox.

Birch, Bruce C. 1991. *Let Justice Roll Down: The Old Testament, Ethics, and Christian Life.* Westminster/John Knox.

Brubacher, Gordon. 2025. "Introduction and Biblical Context Notes for Hosea." In *Anabaptist Community Bible*, edited by John D. Roth, 1069–84. MennoMedia.

Bryan, Craig J. 2022. *Rethinking Suicide: Why Prevention Fails, and How We Can Do Better.* Oxford.

Chisholm, Thomas O. 1923. "Great Is Thy Faithfulness." https://library.timelesstruths.org/music/Great_Is_Thy_Faithfulness/. Performed by Donnie McClurkin & CeCe Winans, https://www.youtube.com/watch?v=BNiKt_5WH-8.

Cho, Paul K. K. 2022. *Willingness to Die and the Gift of Life: Suicide and Martyrdom in the Hebrew Bible.* Eerdmans.

Daube, David. 1972. "The Linguistics of Suicide." *Philosophy & Public Affairs* 1 (4): 387–437. https://www.jstor.org/stable/2265099.

de Roo, Jacqueline C. R. 2009. "*Rahum, Rihamim.*" In *The Concise Dictionary of Classical Hebrew*, edited by David J. A. Clines, 419. Sheffield Phoenix.

Droge, Arthur J., and James D. Tabor. 1992. *A Noble Death: Suicide and Martyrdom Among Christians and Jews in Antiquity.* HarperCollins.

Fretheim, Terence E. 1984. *The Suffering of God: An Old Testament Perspective.* Overtures to Biblical Theology. Fortress.

Fretheim, Terence E. 2007. "God, OT View of." In *The New Interpreter's Dictionary of the Bible*, edited by Katherine Doob Sakenfeld, vol. 2, 603–18. Abingdon.

Gardner, John W. 1961. *Excellence: Can We Be Equal and Excellent Too?* Harper.

Goldstein, Sydney. 1989. *Suicide in Rabbinic Literature.* KTAV Publishing House.

Gosling, Frank. 1996. "*ḥeseḏ.*" In *The Dictionary of Classical Hebrew*, edited by David J. A. Clines, vol. 3, 277–80. Sheffield Phoenix.

Harris, James C. 2003. "The Wood of the Self-Murderers: The Harpies and the Suicides." *Archives of General Psychiatry*, April. https://doi.org/10.1001/archpsyc.60.3.229. PubMed. https://www.researchgate.net/publication/10868045_The_Wood_of_the_Self-Murderers_The_Harpies_and_the_Suicides.

Josephus, Flavius. 1927. "The Defeat at Jotapata." In *The Jewish War*, translated by Henry St. John Thackeray, vol. 2 (I–III), Book III. London: William Heinemann;

Harvard University Press. Edited by Allyson Mower. 2015. https://ethicsofsuicide.lib.utah.edu/category/author/josephus/.

Knight, Kevin, ed. 2023. *Epitome of the Divine Institutes*. Translated by William Fletcher. From *Ante-Nicene Fathers*, vol. 7. Edited by Alexander Roberts, James Donaldson, and A. Cleveland Coxe. Christian Literature Publishing Co., 1886. Revised and edited for New Advent by Kevin Knight. http://www.newadvent.org/fathers/0702.htm.

Koch, H. J. 2005. "Suicides and Suicide Ideation in the Bible: An Empirical Survey." *Acta Psychiatrica Scandinavica* 112: 167–72.

Lactantius. 1886. *The Divine Institutes*, Book III, Chapters 18–19. Translated by William Fletcher. In *The Ante-Nicene Fathers*, vol. 7. Online at Christian Classic Ethereal Library. https://ethicsofsuicide.lib.utah.edu/category/author/lactantius/.

Levinson, Hanne Løland. 2022. "Death Wishes in the Hebrew Bible." *The Ancient Near East Today* 10 (12). https://anetoday.org/levinson-death-hebrew-bible/.

Mason, Karen. 2021. "Suicide Stigma in Christian Faith Communities: A Qualitative Study." *Religions* 12 (7). https://www.mdpi.com/2077-1444/12/7/540.

Mower, Allyson. 2015a. "Introduction to 'Lactantius, *The Divine Institutes*, Book III, Chapters 18–19.'" In *The Ethics of Suicide Digital Archive*, edited by Margaret Pabst Battin. https://ethicsofsuicide.lib.utah.edu/category/author/lactantius/.

Mower, Allyson. 2015b. "Introduction to 'Thomas Aquinas, *Summa Theologiae*: Whether One is Allowed to Kill Oneself.'" In *The Ethics of Suicide Digital Archive*, edited by Margaret Pabst Battin. https://ethicsofsuicide.lib.utah.edu/selections/thomas-aquinas/.

New Revised Standard Version of the Bible, Updated ed. 2021. National Council of Churches of Christ in the United States of America.

Ortiz, Jared. 2019. "Saint Augustine Contra Suicide." *The Catholic World Report*, September 29. https://www.catholicworldreport.com/2019/09/29/saint-augustine-contra-suicide/.

Pearl, Matthew. 2003. *The Dante Club*. Random House.

Potter, John. 2021. "Is Suicide the Unforgivable Sin? Understanding Suicide, Stigma, and Salvation through Two Christian Perspectives." *Religions* 12 (11). https://doi.org/10.3390/rel12110987.

Ringgren, Helmer. 1977. "*ʾāhb*." In *Theological Dictionary of the Old Testament*, edited by G. Johannes Botterweck and Helmer Ringgren, rev. ed., vol. 1, 1–19. Translated by John T. Willis. Eerdmans.

Sakenfeld, Katherine Doob. 1992. "Love (OT)." In *The Anchor Bible Dictionary*, edited by David Noel Freedman, vol. 4, 375–81. Doubleday.

Sakenfeld, Katherine Doob. 2008. "Love in the OT." In *The New Interpreter's Dictionary of the Bible*, edited by Katherine Doob Sakenfeld, vol. 3, 713–18. Abingdon.

Scharbert, Josef. 1977. "*brk*." In *Theological Dictionary of the Old Testament*, edited by G. Johannes Botterweck and Helmer Ringgren, rev. ed., vol. 1, 279–308. Translated by John T. Willis. Eerdmans.

Simian-Yofre, H. 2004. "*rḥm*." In *Theological Dictionary of the Old Testament*, edited by G. Johannes Botterweck, Helmer Ringgren, and Heinz-Josef Fabry, vol. 13, 437–52. Translated by David E. Green. Eerdmans.

Trible, Phyllis. 1978. *God and the Rhetoric of Sexuality*. Overtures to Biblical Theology. Fortress.

Van Wijk-Bos, Johanna W. H. 2007. "God, Metaphors for." In *The New Interpreter's Dictionary of the Bible*, edited by Katherine Doob Sakenfeld, vol. 2, 586–8. Abingdon.

Wallis, Gerhard. 1977. "*'āhābh*." In *Theological Dictionary of the Old Testament*, edited by G. Johannes Botterweck and Helmer Ringgren, rev. ed., vol. 1, 101–18. Translated by John T. Willis. Eerdmans.

Weems, Renita J. 1995. *Battered Love: Marriage, Sex, and Violence in the Hebrew Prophets*. Overtures to Biblical Theology. Fortress.

Wolfelt, Alan D. 2009. *Understanding Your Grief: Ten Essential Touchstones for Finding Hope and Healing Your Heart*. Companion Press.

Zobel, H. J. 1986. "*ḥeseḏ*." In *Theological Dictionary of the Old Testament*, edited by G. Johannes Botterweck and Helmer Ringgren, rev. ed., vol. 5, 44–64. Translated by David E. Green. Eerdmans.

4

Toward a More Certain Hope

Expanding Theological Awareness for Consoling Suicide Loss Survivors

Nicolae Roddy

The taboo surrounding suicide often makes it difficult for people to know just what to say to someone grieving the loss of a loved one to suicide. Motivated by genuine sympathy or mere social convention, their words are surely intended to bring comfort to the bereaved. Some people say very little, instead offering a comforting presence akin to the Jewish practice of "sitting shiva," in which close friends quietly accompany mourners through the first days of numbing grief regardless of the cause of death (Diamant 1999). There are also well-meaning friends who, in the discomfort of the moment, express their condolences in rather insensitive and theologically misinformed ways, with the unintended result of heaping additional weight upon a suicide loss survivor's unspeakable grief, helplessness, guilt, or shame. Such social ineptitude is not always unintended. As recently as December 2018, a Roman Catholic priest presiding over the funeral of a teen suicide in the Detroit Archdiocese completely ignored prearranged parental wishes for how they wanted their son to be remembered and instead made sure that the hundreds of mourners in attendance understood the young man's act to be a grievous sin that could preclude him from entering heaven.[1]

Informed by critical insights from historical theology, this article offers a platform of support to suicide loss survivors with theological concerns about the afterlife, with special emphasis on the love of God at the heart of the perennially controversial topic of universal salvation (or *apocatastasis*).[2] Presuming no special revelation about the nature of life after death, let alone the mind of the Supreme Being, it presents the historical and doctrinal complexity of the topic in a way that offers a platform of hope for survivors whose loved ones experienced such utter hopelessness at a crucial moment in time that ending their lives seemed to be the only way out. It also encourages prudence for theologically self-assured persons who inadvertently and without malice add emotional insult to injury.

Smorgasbord of Theological Opinions about the Afterlife

At a memorial gathering in the days following my father's suicide, I overheard a guest assure a cousin of ours that my father's soul had "gone to be with God." The kind consoler was immediately interrupted by another guest, who made it clear that the soul of a suicide does not go directly to heaven but must first endure the fires of Purgatory.[3] No doubt other afterlife perspectives, spoken or unspoken, were present at the time. Perhaps the person hovering over the dessert table harbored the medieval conviction that a person who takes their own life (Lat. *felo-de-se*) consigns their immortal soul to the unquenchable fires of hell for all eternity, or an agnostic shrugging off speculation in stoical indifference over a cup of coffee, or a self-avowed atheist snatching a cookie and steering away from perceived superstitious blather. These afterlife beliefs, along with possible others—Hindu, Buddhist, Jewish, Muslim, variously Indigenous, and so on—populate our world of ideas speculating over the objectively unknowable reality of life after death.

People who invest steadfast faith in a particular religious tradition usually regard the views of others as misinformed and inferior to their own, failing to acknowledge variations that exist in their own tradition. For example, one might suppose that belief in a final judgment and its bifurcated afterlife (eschatology) would be uniformly shared among Christians, but closer examination reveals a plurality of afterlife sub-traditions. Only in pre-modern times would it have been possible to argue for an overall monolithic view of Christian cosmology, namely, the one promulgated and reinforced by the Roman Catholic Church, which into the Renaissance managed to hold sway even over budding sciences like astronomy. With the revival of classical humanism, Dante's ordered universe began to crumble from challenges to Church authority. It was further assailed by Enlightenment ideas such as Deism, critiqued by thinkers like Feuerbach and Nietzsche, and eventually culminated in the so-called New Atheist movement of our own day (Hitchens 2007; Dawkins 2006; Harris 2004). If one is to retain faith in God—not as mere belief, but as an investment of trust—one must be willing to open a window to Infinitude and experience the liberating fullness that melts away our finite expectations and presuppositions about it. What remains is God's goodness and hope for all of creation, including us rebellious self-willed sinners.

In the chasm that exists between traditional Church dogma on the one hand, and the bold New Atheism movement on the other, theological and philosophical possibilities flourish. The horrors of the twentieth century spawned new discourse regarding the nature of evil in the world (theodicy). Some Jewish intellectuals, like the late Elie Wiesel, Holocaust survivor and author of *Night* (Wiesel 1960), have held God accountable for abrogating the principle of divine justice by failing to intervene in the Nazi extermination of six million innocent Jews and other groups and individuals the regime considered undesirable. Calling to mind Abraham's bold intercession for any righteous people who might be living in the doomed cities of Sodom and Gomorrah (Gen. 18:22-33), this theodicy argues that God is able (but for some reason unwilling) to prevent widespread human suffering and slaughter—boldly holding God complicit in crimes against humanity (Allen 2021, 273–319). By contrast, the theodicy of process, a movement that also arose in response to the Holocaust, offers arguments to the effect that God is ostensibly willing to intervene in human suffering, but for whatever reason (usually based on arguments affirming freedom of choice) God is somehow prevented from acting (Cobb and Griffin 1976). Standing at opposite ends of the spectrum, these examples span a broad diversity of theological ideas about the nature of God, love, and justice, good and evil, the nature of the cosmos, and the mystery of life after death.

The Essential Role of Doubt for Genuine Faith

I remember watching an episode of *Real Time with Bill Maher* shortly after Mother Teresa of Calcutta's personal diary was discovered and made public. According to her biographers, her private writings were not intended to be made public, but in them we discover that this extraordinary Croatian nun, canonized by Pope Francis in 2016, confesses to having experienced prolonged stretches of doubt resulting in serious crises of faith over the course of her life (Kolodiejchuk 2007). At that time, Maher, a popular comedian, political commentator, acerbic satirist, and relentless maligner of religion, doubled down on his usual disparagement of religious devotion by asserting that Mother Teresa's loss of faith supported his assertion, echoing Freud, that religion is a kind of neurological disorder.[4] After all, he seems to reason, if the saintly Mother Teresa has doubts, then the whole faith perspective must be delusional.

Before the release of her diary, I confess to having written off Mother Teresa's tireless love and devotion for the diseased and destitute denizens of Calcutta's streets and alleyways as driven by some sort of dissociative disorder or martyr complex. But unlike Maher, once the Mother of Calcutta's private confessions became public, I came to acknowledge her as an authentic saint—an enduring icon of love for God and neighbor to inspire the world. To my mind, her unassailable sacrificial service punctuated by occasional bouts of gnawing existential doubt witnesses to the genuineness of her faith as a subjective and deeply personal state in communion with infinite and ineffable ultimate Reality—God, if you will. Through the conscious act of maintaining an authentic and open frequency with this ultimate Reality, faith—which involves an abiding investment of trust—takes on a life of its own.[5]

By contrast, the blind faith that zealous religious devotees sometimes claim to have often manifests something more akin to blindness than authentic faith. It is an attitude unconsciously rooted in insecurity and fear of the possibilities that lie beyond the artificial walls subconsciously constructed to shield oneself from the terror of an ineffable cosmos. The furthest observable object in the universe is incomprehensibly distant and new cosmological discoveries replace older theories about the universe every few years. How is one to fathom the incomprehensible distance from here to the furthest observable object in the universe some 13.8 billion light-years away, let alone all the yet unknown and unreachable aspects of cosmic reality?[6] Unfortunately for many, it is much simpler to self-deceptively surrender to the loving arms of the blond European Jesus in the portrait on the wall than face the searing countenance of the One upon whose face no one can look upon and survive (Exod. 33:20).

In sum, whether people categorize themselves as religious, "not religious but spiritual," or wholly materialist, living out one's commitment to a chosen worldview requires a modicum of existential doubt for it to be authentic (Tillich 1975, 116–17). Doubt must never be considered antithetical to faith (whether in something or nothing) but an essential part of it, like yeast that leavens a loaf of bread. A reality-based faith resonates at the core of one's being as something unassailably real and true while necessarily maintaining a modicum of authenticating doubt in the face of the cruelest and most unimaginably vile evils the universe has to offer, including the terror of the incomprehensibly vast Unknown. Assurance of this kind of faith, to the greatest extent possible, can only come from maintaining full and honest agreement between the head and the heart, ever open to new and expanded possibilities, including the possibility that the God of our understanding—like the God of longsuffering, albeit self-righteous Job (32:1)—does not exist in the way we imagine. At any rate, the fathomless mystery of Ultimacy should keep us guarded in our certainty and prudent in our speech, especially regarding suicide.

Western Christian Attitudes toward Suicide

It may be surprising to discover the extent to which traditional religious doctrine obscures scriptural and historical evidence to the contrary. Sacred authority requires unassailable monolithic doctrines that delimit clear boundaries between orthodoxy and perceived heterodoxy or heresy.[7] Because religious institutions abhor uncertainty, the body of challenging, contradictory data turns out to be more varied and ambiguous than ecclesiastical leadership would have the faithful believe. Religious orthodoxy asserts itself to be a kind of lifeboat in the tumultuous sea of theological possibilities; however, it floats along a current of unprivileged ideas that were rejected at some point along the way but remain no less "orthodox" in the sense that Scripture and the Church Fathers would appear to support them.

The topic of suicide provides an especially apt example of the uneasy tension between doctrine and popular conviction, one that can produce confusion and inner turmoil for grieving survivors. Experiencing the self-harm and sudden death of a loved one is painful enough without added pressure from religious authority and dogma. From prehistoric times, suicide has continued to disrupt the social dynamics of families and communities, affecting economic well-being and the risk of offending perceived superhuman powers and protectors. In classical antiquity, suicide could also be lauded as a noble and courageous act (Tondo 2014). This idea appealed to some Christian writers during the age of imperial persecutions as martyrs and confessors boldly offered themselves up for the faith. Writing at the turn of the third century, Tertullian reflects such an attitude in his praise of martyrdom, helping to lay the groundwork for Christianity's celebration of the cult of martyred saints (Brown 1982).[8]

Once the age of great persecutions had passed, the idea of Christian martyrdom as a noble death gave way to the conviction that offering up one's life was a sin against God, tantamount to murder as prohibited by the commandment "You shall not kill" (Exod. 20:13). This idea can be traced back to Clement of Alexandria and Lactantius, but it was Augustine of Hippo (354–430) who systematically developed it in opposition to the Donatist practice of "pious suicide" (Shaw 2011, 740; Adamiak and Dohnalik 2023). In his classic work *The City of God*, Augustine goes further than any Christian thinker before him in condemning the act of suicide for any reason.[9] Slightly more than two decades following his death, the Council of Arles (452) provided ecclesiastical support for Augustine's wholesale condemnation of suicide.

In the centuries that followed, the Church began stepping up efforts to discourage and prevent suicide by requiring strict penitential remedies for anyone who had made the attempt and excluding the souls of suicides from burial in church cemeteries. The *Decretum Gratiani*, a twelfth-century compendium of canon law, preserves a fragmented text of Leo the Great's fourth-century commentary on Judas Iscariot, whose desperate act, he writes, was a sin against God. Asserting that repentance and confession are necessary for reconciliation, he further affirms its role in preventing suicide (Adamiak and Dohnalik 2023). In addition, the *Decretum* reinforces a decree from the Council of Braga (561), adopted by later synods, that funeral rites for victims of willful suicide be denied, albeit tempered with some consideration for those who ended their lives out of apparent madness. In 693, a synod in Toledo prescribed posthumous excommunication for those who took their lives, and in 1096, the Third Council of Nimes ruled that the bodies of suicides cannot be laid to rest in consecrated soil (Adamiak and Dohnalik 2023).

These ecclesiastical pronouncements filtered through local parish homilies among peasant folk gave rise to the appearance of bizarre rituals across Europe, such as dragging the corpse of a suicide through the streets of the village, burying it at some rural crossroad instead of in a cemetery, or driving a stake through its heart (Ekeberg and Retterstøl 2021), likely aimed at placating disquieted spirits.[10] The general cultural ignorance and fear among the medieval populace, reinforced by the intolerant sociocultural dominance of institutionalized Christendom,[11] further isolated the suicide from the community of the faithful and the blessed repose of its dead. This pervasive tradition raises questions about the efficacy of the pre-modern Church's well-intentioned attempt to prevent suicide while leveraging the dispensation of grace to those who fell victim to it.

Distancing victims of suicide from the loving embrace of the faithful only serves to strengthen the power of the taboo, which despite recent positive developments lingers to this day.

In the early nineteenth century, the fledgling science of psychiatry was established, which held that most suicide victims were mentally ill. But it was not until the late twentieth century that the Church began to rethink the failing guardrails of its moral legalism to adopt a more compassionate understanding of the mental health aspects of suicide. Only as recently as 1983 was the practice of denying funerals and church burials to suicides canonically rescinded. Finally, in 1997, the *Catechism of the Catholic Church* (CCC) was emended to acknowledge suicidal ideation on a mental health spectrum: "Grave psychological disturbances, anguish, or grave fear of hardship, suffering, or torture can diminish the responsibility of the one committing suicide" (§2282b). Moreover, "We should not despair of the eternal salvation of persons who have taken their own lives. By ways known to him alone, God can provide the opportunity for salutary repentance. The Church prays for persons who have taken their own lives" (§2283).

While these developments contribute to a greater understanding of the plight of the suicidal person to create a more compassionate position for those who despair of a loved one's eternal salvation, the Christian tradition generally has not gone far enough in exploring the resources of Scripture and the writings of the Church Fathers to arrive at a higher hope, namely, faith in the unfailing and supreme love of God, or as St. Paul writes, "the power to comprehend, with all the saints, what is the breadth and length and height and depth and to know the love of Christ that surpasses knowledge, so that you may be filled with all the fullness of God" (Eph. 3:18-19). The crux of the problem remains in the need for striking a balance between compassionate understanding for people who feel compelled to end their lives and the fear that undermining traditional guardrails (such as instilling fear of eternal torment) will make an act of suicide more likely to occur.

A Platform for Hope

The pre-Socratic poet and philosopher Xenophanes suggested that if horses could draw, their gods would be horses, referring to the universal human proclivity of imbuing gods with human form and qualities. Similarly, nineteenth-century German philosopher Ludwig Feuerbach (1804–72) suggested that gods (and therefore God) are products of human projections of their own collective conceptions, ideals, and values (Feuerbach 2008). The suggestion that human beings project self-generated delusions upon reality was developed further in the writings of Feuerbach's near contemporary, Friedrich Nietzsche (1844–1900), most notably in *The Antichrist* (Nietzsche 1993). Moreover, theologians today who assert that the creator God of Genesis 1 transcends human projections of physicality and gender ignore the influence of Hellenistic thought in our understanding of the Hebrew text, whose writers freely ascribed human anatomical features to the God of Scripture (Markschies 2019). The varied projections of human characteristics and propensities upon one's Higher Power go unchallenged as long as their claims remain within the boundary of the community's range of acceptance. For example, a believer who harbors a strong conviction that God's eternal love and forgiveness indomitably transcend all other modes of being may sit comfortably alongside a fellow worshiper who fully agrees that God is love but imagines the Deity equally to be a stern Judge who would condemn a person to the eternal fires of hell for errors of judgment made during an infinitesimally brief earthly lifespan.

But what might it mean to say, "God is love" (1 Jn 4:8, 16)? Does it not mean something more than simply saying God loves? Even so, it would mean that God loves human beings supremely and without deficiency in a way that far exceeds anything humanly possible. Saying God *is* love grounds that love in the very essence of the Divine, boundless and eternal. In fact, it may be tempting to capitalize the word "love" here because the Christian affirmation that "God is love" roots that love in the divine essence (Gr. *ousia*; Lat. *substantia*), manifested through the Three Persons (*hypostases*) of the Holy Trinity, and extending God's divine energies (*energeiai*) to all of creation. Created in the *imago Dei*, humans may aspire to some level of selfless love, but ego prevents human love from attaining anything near the pure and boundless love of God, for mortality has its limitations.

The upshot of all this is that whatever personal qualities a person might assign to the Ultimate Being, we nevertheless "see through a glass darkly" (1 Cor. 13:12). If we are willing to accept the proposition that God is love, then we must acknowledge that God's love must infinitely exceed any human ability to fully comprehend it—more elusive than trying to wrap our minds around the distance to the furthest reaches of the cosmos. Trying to fathom the ineffable reality of the Ultimate—God, if you will—in a way that remains truly open toward the Infinite helps us to realize the naïve and feeble ways we impose our limited projections upon it—projections that derive from flawed perspectives based on our own finite experiences and expectations. This is not to say that God cannot be known through revelation, reason, or, like the enlightened Deists, solely from observing the natural world—only that the *essence* of God cannot be fully comprehended. For St. Paul, revelation was sufficient to convince him of the absolute inviolability of God's love, a love that does not fail: "For I am convinced that neither death, nor life, nor angels, nor rulers, nor things present, nor things to come, nor powers, nor height, nor depth, nor anything else in all creation will be able to separate us from the love of God in Christ Jesus our Lord" (Rom. 8:38-39, NRSV).

Even with certain faith in God's absolute and infinite love, one must still consider the matter of God's justice, which in its extreme accommodates the idea that eternal torment in the fires of hell is somehow fitting punishment for the misguided choices made by misinformed mortals in the relative eyeblink of finite time. While such a doctrine has been promulgated for centuries, leaving some to find it beyond questioning, it is also the case that Christian tradition harbors its own prevailing and countervailing theological position (*theologoumena*) that God's supreme and unfailing love supersedes all manner of human failing, including outright defiance. One could argue that a person who dies and comes face-to-face with the living God could theoretically still defy and reject divine reality and that for God to offer salvation to such a person would be a violation of that person's free will. But how could a truly free and rational human being reject ultimate truth appearing before their very eyes? Doing so would present a contradiction, for rejecting what is presented as ultimately true would raise questions over whether the denier is truly free and whole. This does not mean that God forces belief at the expense of the human will, for being consigned to oblivion remains an option. What defies rational thought is the exclusivist position that God would punish those theoretically free and rational people who, beholding the reality of eternal life, would choose to refuse it.

Universal Salvation and Scripture

Anyone looking to Scripture for a definitive answer to the question of universal salvation, especially those wishing to argue against it, will be frustrated by ambiguity. Internet discussions on the topic lead one down into a veritable rabbit-hole of debate and dissension. The categories of universalism and exclusivism (and their variations) enjoy ample scriptural evidence from their entrenched proponents. For example, those who hold a juridical view of a punishing God who metes out eternal punishment for temporal sins may derive support from the gospels, most notably Mt. 25:31-46, which states that those who choose not to feed and care for the welfare of others will "go away into eternal punishment" (v. 46). The implications of a literal application of this verse would likely make today's fiscal conservatives nervous; however, it should be obvious that the purpose of the statement is not to reify eternal torment but to reinforce the demand to feed and care for the poor (Rhee 2012). The localized social world of first-century Judea is often reflected in the gospels' use of metaphors. The Valley of Hinnom (or Gehenna), popularly thought to have been a place of burning refuse located just south of Jerusalem, is a site where according to prophetic tradition children were sacrificed to the god Moloch (Jos. 15:8; 2 Kgs. 23:10; Jer. 2:23, 7:31-32, 9:6, 13–14), thus providing a metaphorical warning to those who would not heed the words of Jesus (Mt. 5:22-30).

These and other proof-texts should be interpreted with a modicum of historical critical understanding that takes into account the polemical nature of the gospels, where interaction between Jewish leaders and those who accepted Jesus of Nazareth as the Christ (Messiah) provoked mutual animosity. The polemic between the Jesus communities and other Jewish sects and parties is especially evident in John's gospel, where those who believe that Jesus is the Christ are "saved" in the present, and those who do not believe are already condemned (cf. Jn 3:16-18).

By contrast, several NT passages offer a less damning fate for nonbelievers, including just these few:

- "And when I am lifted up from the earth, I will draw [Gr. ἐλκύο, literally, 'to drag'] all humankind unto myself" (Jn 12:32);
- ". . . Jesus, who must remain in heaven until the time of universal restoration (ἀποκατάστασις πάντων) that God announced long ago through his holy prophets" (Acts 3:21);
- "For I am convinced that neither death, nor life, nor angels, nor rulers, nor things present, nor things to come, nor powers, nor height, nor depth, nor anything else in all creation will be able to separate us from the love of God in Christ Jesus our Lord" (Rom. 8:38-39);
- "For in him [Christ] all the fullness of God was pleased to dwell, and through him God was pleased to reconcile all things to himself, whether on

earth or in heaven, by making peace through the blood of his Cross" (Col. 1:19-20).

In support of these texts, Aidan Kimel, an Orthodox priest who has written prolifically on the topic of universal salvation, witnesses to the unfailing, all-encompassing love of God through the parables of the Good Shepherd (Jn 10:1-21), the woman searching for a lost coin (Lk. 15:8-10), and the Prodigal Son (Lk. 15:11-32). Accepting the proposition that God is love and that this love never fails, demands the assertion that God's love "accomplishes what it promises and never returns to him empty" (Kimel 2024). To assert that human beings in their fallen and limited condition should somehow be able to subvert the eternal scope of God's love and render it a failure seems unreasonable and unlikely. Kimel asks his readers to imagine the parables' alternative outcomes:

> The good shepherd goes out to search for the one lost sheep, but eventually returns to his flock, his head bowed in resignation and disappointment. The woman turns her house upside down to find her treasured lost coin, but never finds it. The father waits for the return of his son, but the son never returns, and the father dies from his grief. Does this sound like the gospel we are called to preach? Does this sound like the victory of Pascha? Christ is risen, we triumphantly sing (but under our breaths we whisper, but many are damned) . . . Love never abandons the beloved, nor is it impotent before our sin and free will. (Kimel 2024)

As persuasive as scriptural references and their interpretations may seem to some, mere proof-texting is of little help in bolstering arguments for or against the role of divine justice in light of God's supreme love and mercy.

Universalism and Its Persistence in the Christian Theological Tradition

The theological term for universalism is *apokatastasis*. Despite variations on the view, it survives from the second century and remains widely accepted today (Congdon 2023). The controversial Christian thinker Origen of Alexandria (*c.* 185–253) was able to imagine God's supreme love and mercy transcending all cosmic imperfections to bring about the restoration of creation to its original state (*apokatastasis*).[12] So, too, the fourth-century Cappadocian Father Gregory of Nyssa, along with several others (see Ramelli 2014). Although some of Origen's ideas have been rejected by various synods, most notably regarding the preexistence of souls, his particular views on *apokatastasis* were not. No authoritative witnesses are found to have stood in direct opposition to the idea, including any of the Seven Ecumenical Councils (Kimel 2020).

The dogged tenacity of universalist convictions persists, as attested in a recent study that contrasts the concept of universalism in Gregory of Nyssa with that of the twentieth-century Jesuit theologian Karl Rahner (Ludlow 2000). Spanning sixteen centuries and bridging the thought of two brilliant theologians, an Origenist and a Thomist respectively, the study demonstrates just how pervasive universalism continues to be. While universalism has never been fully accepted as doctrine, neither has it ever been expressly condemned. Those who would make it otherwise challenge the notion that God's love is supreme and unfailing. They would seem to support the view that a life of misinformed choices based on false negative influences during a relative eyeblink of finite existence should somehow endure eternal torturous consequences.

One of the main exclusivist objections to a universalist position is the idea that somehow Christ's suffering and death on the Cross would have been for naught, rendering Christian evangelism unnecessary (McClymond 2020). However, if one affirms the doctrine of the Incarnation through which, according to St. Maximus the Confessor, heaven and earth and all things therein are reconciled (Thunberg 1999), this need not be the case. Contrary to the exclusivist position, universalism does not negate or minimize the salvific significance of the birth, life, death, and resurrection of Jesus Christ at all, but extends its efficacy to all human beings, as supported by many of the NT passages presented above.

Those who would assert that God is constrained by some divine compulsion to permit or even to will eternal damnation would have to reject the notion that God is love, or that God's supreme and unfailing love can somehow fail through some sort of deficiency. God's justice is mitigated by love, not vice-versa. As Orthodox theologian David Bentley Hart lays out most succinctly, "To say that, on the one hand, God is infinitely good, perfectly just, and inexhaustibly loving, and that, on the other hand, he has created a world under such terms as oblige him either to impose, or to permit the imposition of, eternal misery on finite rational beings, is simply to embrace a complete contradiction" (Hart 2019, 202–3).

Another objection is based on a defense of so-called free will, that somehow a human being has the right to reject God's love and mercy for whatever reason, or that such rejection is even possible. Theoretically, such a choice to reject may well be possible. However, the question arises over whether free will is ever truly free—that it can exist in a sort of vacuum shielded from any external influence. Garcin, a character in Jean-Paul Sartre's famous play *No Exit*, hopelessly opines, "Hell is other people"; however, Garcin's problem lies not with other people, but within Garcin himself. If hell is other people, then heaven must be found in always having someone else to blame. The point is this: whether one really imagines that when confronted by the ultimate reality of God's love over and against all other conditions, one would or could still refuse it. Theoretically, perhaps; but in reality?

Conclusion

Christian believers who speak with certainty about the afterlife may be admired for their faith but should exercise restraint when it comes to sharing their personal convictions with others in a way that does not encourage hope. Nothing is more intensely personal than one's own experience of the Sacred, which carries the power to affect others for good or ill. Anything that goes beyond commending the soul of the suicide victim to a life of blessed repose in the embrace of God's supreme and unfailing love—a God who is said to be Love itself—diminishes God. It also violates the command to love one another by taking advantage of a grieving survivor's vulnerability no matter how well-intentioned the motivation. There is simply no reason to inflict further distress. St. Paul writes: "Beloved, let us love one another, because love is from God; everyone who loves is born of God and knows God [. . .] No one has ever seen God; if we love one another, God abides in us, and his love is perfected in us" (1 Jn 4: 7-12).

Because speculation about salvation (soteriology) and the afterlife takes place in the present, its arguments remain suspended somewhere between affirmations of God's unsurpassed and unfailing love on the one hand, and the reasonable certainty of God's justice (or judgment) on the other. Scripture's take on what it might mean for human beings to be created in the image of God (Gen. 1:26-27) may be helpful; however, the writer does not fully explain what it means. It takes the whole of Scripture—the Prophets and the Psalms—to unpack it. There we find that the most often used analogies for God in the Older Testament are King (*melek*) and Shepherd (*ro'eh*), whose steadfast love and mercy (*chesed*) are manifested through attributes of justice (*mishpat*) and righteousness (*zedakah*). For the Apostle Paul, Christ represents the true image of God (Col. 1:15), which does not alter but reinforces the responsibility of shepherding those in our charge, exercising unconditional love beyond the people we already know and care about, and toward those we may not know or even like. Love is an action and as such must be actualized through the twinned attributes of justice and righteousness. For humans, these attributes must be held vigilantly in self-monitored balance; for righteousness without justice devolves easily into self-righteousness, while justice without righteousness lacks mercy. This illustration of what it might mean to be created in the image of God, based on a data-driven approach to Scripture, establishes the fact that divine love and mercy, not judgment, rise above all.

Given the ubiquity of scriptural, canonical, and extra-canonical data regarding universal salvation, arguments for or against are ultimately rooted in a tyranny of the Ego, demanding that God see things as we see them and turning matters of faith, hope, and love into bitter pills of absolute certainty to be foisted upon others. In the end, where one comes down on the matter of universal salvation is often based on the projection of one's individual mentality, examined or unexamined, either way ineffective in convincing people to abandon what they already tenaciously hold to be true. It is unthinkable that the profound depths of despair leading to suicide—the complete and utter absence of hope that relief from such a torturous imprisonment could ever come—would be overlooked by a loving God, nor subject to some deterministic afterlife structure that would demand a fiery purgation, let alone eternal torture as ostensibly imagined by juridically minded Christians.

For these reasons, it would seem incumbent on those seeking to console bereaved suicide loss survivors to adopt an attitude of humility by keeping one's personal convictions about afterlife scenarios unspoken. For the theist, it should be enough to affirm that souls of hopeless departed ones are with God and leave it at that; for setting divine judgment in opposition to divine love creates a false equivalency construct. God's unfailing love and mercy (Heb. *chesed*; Gr. *eleos*) overcome the world, especially as humans imagine them. "For judgment will be without mercy to anyone who has shown no mercy; mercy triumphs over judgment" (Jas. 2:13; see also Hadith Qudsi 1, *Forty Hadith Qudsi*, "My mercy prevails over my wrath").[13]

Notes

1 *The Christian Post*. https://www.christianpost.com/news/outrage-after-priest-suggests-at-funeral-that-teen-who-committed-suicide-might-not-go-to-heaven.html (2018). The priest has since undergone professional retraining and has apologized publicly for his insensitive remarks.

2 Universal salvation is the belief that all human souls will eventually be "saved" by God's infinite love and mercy, with various theological opinions over the ways salvation plays out. See Congdon (2023).

3 Purgatory (Lat: *purgatorium*) is a dogma of the Roman Catholic church, which posits a transitory, after-death state for human souls in need of purification for admittance into heaven. "All who die in God's grace and friendship, but still imperfectly purified, are indeed assured of their eternal salvation; but after death they undergo purification, so as to achieve the holiness necessary to enter the joy of heaven" *Catechism of the Catholic Church* (§1030).

4 The website of the *Catholic League for Religious and Civil Rights*, an organization founded by Fr. Virgil Blum, SJ, in 1973 to counter anti-Catholic discrimination, notes that Maher's comment (which I recall witnessing firsthand) aired February 8, 2008, on the HBO series, "Real Time with Bill Maher." According to the *Freedom from Religion Foundation* web site, Maher's comment on religion as a neurological disorder aired on "The Tonight Show" in 2004 (https://ffrf.org/publications/day/bill-maher/).

5 Although, one must continue to question the legitimacy of any putative connection with the supernatural by critiquing it against the wider population of faith and morally right action, lest one "hear voices" leading them toward the psychopathy of a Charles Manson or David Koresh.

6 According to the NASA website, "Current observations suggest that the Universe is about 13.8 billion years old. We know that light takes time to travel, so that if we observe an object that is 13 billion light-years away, then that light has been traveling toward us for 13 billion years. Essentially, we are seeing that object as it appeared 13 billion years ago" (https://imagine.gsfc.nasa.gov/features/cosmic/farthest_info.html).

7 Simply put, heterodoxy refers to some deviation from the norms of orthodox faith or practice, while heresy indicates a complete departure from fundamental orthodox beliefs.

8 Tertullian extols the merits of Christian martyrdom in his early work "To the Martyrs" (*Ad Martyras*). For English translations see C. Dodgson, *Library of the Fathers* (Oxford, 1842), 150–7, or S. Thelwall, *Ante-Nicene Fathers* 3 (1885): 693–6, both of which are accessible online.

9 Augustine (1956).

10 I can personally attest to the veracity of Romanian belief that the souls of suicides can sometimes wander about as troubled spirits (*strigoi*) in the vicinity of their villages, and to the practice of driving a stake into the chest to prevent them from doing so.

11 Christendom, which is not synonymous with Christianity, refers to western society of the Middle Ages, during which time the Roman Catholic Church dominated virtually every aspect of European society and culture.

12 Although Origin is considered a saint in the Coptic church, his belief in the preexistence and transmigration of souls generated sufficient opposition to prevent him from being fully embraced by most other eastern churches. Many of his writings have not survived; still, his influence on early Christian thinkers cannot be overstated.

13 Unless otherwise stated, all translations of the Bible are from the New Revised Standard Version, updated edition, National Council of Churches Friendship Press. New Revised Standard Version Bible, copyright 1989, Division of Christian Education of the National Council of the Churches of Christ in the United States of America. Used by permission. All rights reserved.

Bibliography

Adamiak, Stanislaw, and Jan Dohnalik. 2023. "The Prohibition of Suicide and Its Theological Rationale in Catholic Moral and Canonical Tradition: Origins and Development." *Journal of Religion and Health* 62 (6): 3820–33. https://doi.org/10.1007/s10943-023-01900-w.

Allen, Wayne. 2021. *Thinking About Good and Evil: Jewish Views from Antiquity to Modernity*. Jewish Publication Society.

Augustine. 1956. *The City of God*, 1.17–27, translated by Marcus Dods. In *NPNF*, edited by Philip Schaff, vol. 2. Grand Rapids: Eerdmans.

Bell, Rob. 2011. *Love Wins: A Book About Heaven, Hell, and the Fate of Every Person Who Ever Lived*. HarperOne.

Brown, Peter. 1982. *The Cult of the Saints*. University of Chicago Press.

Catechism of the Catholic Church (CCC). 1997. Libreria Editrice Vaticana. https://www.vatican.va/archive/ENG0015/_INDEX.HTM.

Cobb, John B., and Ray Griffin. 1976. *Process Theodicy: An Introductory Exposition*. The Westminster Press.

Congdon, David W. 2023. *Varieties of Christian Universalism: Exploring Four Views*. Baker Academic.

Dawkins, Richard. 2006. *The God Delusion*. Mariner Books.

Diamant, Anita. 1999. *Saying Kaddish: How to Comfort the Dying, Bury the Dead, and Mourn as a Jew*. Schocken.

Ekeberg, Øivind, and Nils Retterstøl. 2021. "Christianity and Suicide." In *Oxford Textbook of Suicidology and Suicide Prevention*, 2nd ed., edited by Danuta Wasserman. Oxford University Press. https://doi.org/10.1093/med/9780198834441.003.0009.

Feuerbach, Ludwig. 2008. *The Essence of Christianity*. Originally published in 1841. Dover Publications.

Harris, Sam. 2004. *The End of Faith: Religion, Terror, and the Future of Reason*. W. W. Norton.

Hart, David Bentley. 2019. *That All Shall be Saved: Heaven, Hell, and Universal Salvation*. Yale University Press.

Hitchens, Christopher. 2007. *God Is Not Great: The Case Against Religion*. Atlantic.

Kimel, Aidan. 2020. "Did the Fifth Ecumenical Council Condemn Universal Salvation?" *Eclectic Orthodoxy*. https://afkimel.wordpress.com/2020/05/31/did-the-fifth-ecumenical-council-condemn-universal-salvation/.

Kimel, Aiden. 2024. "Two Briefly Stated Arguments in Favor of Universal Salvation." *Eclectic Orthodoxy*. https://afkimel.wordpress.com/2024/05/11/two-briefly-stated-arguments-in-favor-of-universal-salvation/.

Kolodiejchuk, Brian. 2007. *Mother Teresa: Come Be My Light: The Private Writings of the Saint of Calcutta*. Doubleday.

Koslow, Stephen H., Pedro Ruiz, and Charles B. Nemeroff. 2014. *A Concise Guide to Understanding Suicide*. Cambridge University Press.

Ludlow, Morwenna. 2000. *Universal Salvation: Eschatology in the Thought of Gregory of Nyssa and Karl Rahner*. Oxford University Press.

Markschies, Christoph. 2019. *God's Body: Jewish, Christian, and Pagan Images of God*. Translated by Alexander Johannes Edmonds. Baylor University Press.

McClymond, Michael J. 2020. *The Devil's Redemption: A New History and Interpretation of Christian Universalism*. Baker Academic.

Nietzsche, Friedrich. 1993. *The Antichrist*. Originally published in 1895. Translated by H. L. Mencken. Routledge.

Ramelli, Ilaria. 2014. *The Christian Doctrine of Apokatastasis: A Critical Assessment from the New Testament to Eriugena*. Supplements to Vigiliae Christianae 120. Brill.

Rhee, Helen. 2012. *Loving the Poor, Saving the Rich: Wealth, Poverty, and Early Christian Formation*. Baker Academic.

SCOBA (Standing Conference of the Canonical Orthodox Bishops in the Americas). 2007. "Pastoral Letter on Suicide." https://www.goarch.org/whats-new/-/asset_publisher/rlvS19snJYAk/content/scoba-pastoral-letter-on-suicide.

Shaw, Brent D. 2011. *Sacred Violence: African Christians and Sectarian Hatred in the Age of Augustine*. Cambridge University Press.

Thunberg, Lars. 1999. *Microcosm and Mediator: The Theological Anthropology of Maximus the Confessor*. Open Court Publishing.

Tillich, Paul. 1975. *Systematic Theology*. 2 vols. University of Chicago Press.

Tondo, Leonardo. 2014. "Brief History of Suicide in Western Cultures." In *A Concise Guide to Understanding Suicide*, edited by Stephen H. Koslow, Pedro Ruiz, and Charles B. Nemeroff, 3–12. Cambridge University Press.

Wasserman, Danuta. 2021. *Oxford Textbook of Suicidology and Suicide Prevention*. 2nd ed. Oxford University Press. https://doi.org/10.1093/med/9780198834441.003.0009.

Wiesel, Elie. 1960. *Night*. Translated by Stella Rodway. Hill & Wang.

5

LGBTQ+ Youth and Suicide

Catholic Reflections

Todd A. Salzman and Michael G. Lawler

In 1998, three filmmakers founded the Trevor Project with the mission to end suicide among lesbian, gay, bisexual, transgender, and queer youth (LGBTQ+). The project grew out of their award-winning short film, *Trevor*, a gay, thirteen-year-old boy who, rejected by his friends because of his homosexual orientation, ended up attempting suicide. The filmmakers understood that some viewers of their film would be in the same situation as Trevor, and they sought a support help-line telephone number to be aired with the film. Finding none, they decided to establish their own, and the Trevor Project was born to promote, via education and advocacy, acceptance of LGBTQ+ persons and suicide prevention among that group (Champions of Change, n.d.).

A critical part of the Trevor Project's endeavor is research on LGBTQ+ youth, and, on May 1, 2023, it released its *National Survey on the Mental Health of LGBTQ Young People* (The Trevor Project 2023a). The survey documents the serious negative mental health impacts of anti-LGBTQ+ policies, language, and victimization. It shows that, in LGBTQ+ youth between the ages of thirteen and twenty-four who had suffered victimization as a result of their sexual orientation or gender identity, 73 percent had suffered from anxiety and 58 percent from depression. Many had seriously *considered* suicide in the past year and an alarming number had attempted suicide. LGBTQ+ young adults report suicide ideation and attempt suicide more than five times the rate of their non-LGBTQ+ peers (Almeida et al. 2009; Hatzenbuehler, Hilt, and Nolen-Hoeksema 2010). The rates of suicide ideation and attempted suicide were highest among transgender youth: 50 percent of transgender males had seriously considered suicide and 22 percent had attempted it; the rates for transgender females were 48 percent and 12 percent respectively. The corresponding rates for cisgender females were 37 percent and 10 percent, and for cisgender males 28 percent and a surprising 0 percent. Suicidal rates, the study reported, have worryingly trended upward in the past three years. Young people who had been harmed, either physically or psychologically, in the past year due to their sexual orientation or gender identity reported triple the rate of those who were not. Transgender, nonbinary youth of color reported higher rates than their peers (The Trevor Project 2020). A critically important datum for those who deal with LGBTQ+ youth is that *young people from affirming homes, schools, or religious communities reported lower rates of attempting suicide*. This is a datum for everyone who wants to work as a Trevor Project caring person to hear and take to heart (The Trevor Project 2020).

Though not a study of specifically LGBTQ+ youth, a study from UCLA Health reported that suicide was the second leading cause of death among American 15- to 24-year-old. Nearly 20 percent of high school students had seriously thought about suicide and 9 percent has attempted it. The apparent good news is that those rates are lower than any other adult group (Cohen 2023). Professor of Psychiatry, Dr. Carl Fleisher, of UCLA Health, notes that today's teenagers and young adults have rising rates of suicide compared to teenagers and young adults 10–15 years ago. The causes of this higher rate are due to where they stand developmentally and, especially, where they stand in their young lives in the eyes of their peers (Cohen 2023). The Catholic Church's message of the infinite dignity of all human beings (Dicastery for the Doctrine of the Faith [hereafter DDF] 2024), but very negative language about LGBTQ+ persons, that their sexual orientation or gender identity is "objectively disordered," and that any same-sex sexual act is "intrinsically disordered" (Congregation for the Doctrine of the Faith [hereafter CDF] 1975, n. VIII) for instance, plays strongly into the rising rates, especially for young Catholics, many of whom have left the church because of that and similar condemnatory language. A PRRI survey in 2016 showed that 39 percent of American youth raised in the Catholic Church were more likely than those raised in another religion to cite negative treatment of LGBTQ+ persons as their primary reason for leaving the church (Jones et al. 2016). In a 2023 study, that number had risen to 47 percent (PRRI Staff 2024). Given these alarming and frightening statistics, in this collection on suicide, we focus on suicide among LGBTQ+ persons.

In this chapter, we first describe the stigma, discrimination, and violence, including suicide, that confront LGBTQ+ people. Second, we demonstrate the correlation between Catholic doctrinal language that promotes and fosters these realities. Third, we explain and critically analyze that doctrinal language to demonstrate its lack of theological and moral credibility. We conclude that Catholic language and doctrinal teaching regarding LGBTQ+ people must be reformed to reduce the stigma, discrimination, and violence the language and teaching promote and to create a loving, welcoming, Christian community of "radical inclusion" for LGBTQ+ people (McElroy 2023).

Stigma, Discrimination, and Violence

The Vice President of Research for the Trevor Project, Dr. Ronita Nath, points out that "as the existence of LGBTQ+ young people continues to be put up for debate, it's critical to consistently underscore that these challenges are not inherent to LGBTQ identity, but rather stem from stigma, discrimination, and violence" (The Trevor Project 2023b). Unfortunately, much of the stigma, discrimination, and violence is motivated by religious language that directly promotes discrimination and indirectly promotes homophobia and violence against LGBTQ+ young people. The most egregious violent attack in the United States on members of the LGBTQ+ community occurred on June 12, 2016, in Orlando Florida at the Pulse gay nightclub where a single gunman brutally murdered forty-nine people. This senseless and violent act was a clear manifestation of extreme homophobia directed against LGBTQ+ persons. This homophobia is based, not on any understanding of the dignity of such persons as human beings or of their relationships to family, friends, and social communities, but solely on ignorance, hate, and a distorted view of who LGBTQ+ persons are. Many spoke out against this violent act, including many Catholic bishops. Although those bishops decried the senseless violence and violation of human dignity, only Bishop Robert Lynch honestly and courageously makes a clear connection between that violence and religion: "sadly it is religion, including our own, which targets, mostly verbally, and also often breeds contempt for gays, lesbians and transgender people. Attacks today on LGBTQI+ men and women often plant the seed of contempt, then hatred, which can ultimately lead to violence" toward other and, we add, self (National Catholic Reporter Staff 2016). His statement draws a correlational, if not a causal, link between Catholic language and doctrinal teaching about LGBTQ+ persons and the homophobic attitudes and violence that language and teaching on occasion promotes (Janssen and Scheepers 2019). It also highlights the tension in Catholic teaching that, on the one hand, declares the infinite dignity of all human beings (DDF 2024) and condemns discrimination (Catechism 1994) and, on the other hand, promotes not unjust discrimination against LGBTQ+ people (Catechism 1994), declares homosexual orientation objectively disordered, and condemns same-sex sexual acts (CDF 1975, n. VIII). Although the Pulse attack is the most extreme case of physical violence directed against LGBTQ+ persons, it is not an isolated event and Catholic and religious doctrinal language have led to other forms of physical and spiritual sexual violence, pain, and trauma, including suicide ideation and suicide among LGBTQ+ persons (Gibbs 2015).

One of the most poignant and tragic examples of Catholic induced trauma is the suicide of Alana Chen, a young lesbian woman struggling with her sexual identity and Catholic teaching against same-sex relationships. She sought "religious counseling" from a priest at St. Thomas Aquinas Catholic Church in Denver, which Alana described as conversion therapy. Carissa, her sister, sees a causal relationship between Alana's suicide and the Church's role in counseling and the doctrinal teaching underlying it. "I think the church played a huge role in the years of trauma and treatment that she went through and ultimately her suicide, and they're just going to have to live with that. We all will now" (Julig 2020).

The Correlation between Religious Language, Trauma, Depression, and Self-Harm

Numerous sociological studies demonstrate substantially higher rates of mental illness, depression, and self-harm for LGBTQ+ youth and adolescents (see Gibbs 2015). An important question for our chapter is how religion in general, and religious doctrinal teaching in particular, either contribute to these higher rates or give comfort, support, and hope to LGBTQ youth and young adults. The Trevor Project conducted an overview of the research on this very question. It concluded that religiosity can protect against suicide attempts and ideation by providing a supportive and welcoming community that embraces people and their sexual identities, influences beliefs concerning suicide, and provides hope (Trevor Project 2020; Lawrence, Oquendo, and Stanley 2016). However, where religious institutions are not supportive of LGBTQ+ identities, as are many religious institutions in the United States, including Catholicism, religiosity does not have a protective effect against suicidality and often induces "soul violence," that is, theological and/or spiritual violence against LGBTQ+ people (Sanders 2020, 4–5). One study of young adults between eighteen and twenty-four concluded that parents' negative religious beliefs about homosexuality were associated with double the risk of attempted suicide in the past year (Trevor Project 2020; Gibbs 2015).

In his research on the relationship between religiosity and suicidality, Gibbs explains the risk and protective factor model researchers use to understand mental health outcomes. Risk factors contribute to negative mental and behavioral health outcomes such as suicide or suicide ideation; protective factors protect against such outcomes. In addition to common strains of risk and protective factors, minority stress theory posits that minority groups, such as LGBTQ+ people, experience unique stress factors that stem from sexual and gender identity, such as homophobia, discrimination, bullying, and negative communal and religious attitudes toward them, and that these "chronic stressors are associated with negative mental outcomes" (Gibbs 2015). Several studies have identified these minority group stressors with suicidal behavior among LGBTQ+ young adults. In general, religiosity can be a protective factor against negative mental outcomes and promote positive mental health. However, "a strong correlation . . . exists between [the] level of religiosity and negative attitudes toward homosexuality" (Gibbs 2015). As a result, many LGBTQ+ people who grow up in a religious community experience discrimination, exclusion, and homophobia within that community and these risk factors extend to religiously influenced family situations as well. Parental and religious support of, and openness toward, sexual identity is a protective factor; parental and religious rejection and judgment of, and closedness toward, sexual identity is a risk factor (Gibbs 2015; Sanders 2020).

As discussed above, Catholic doctrine contains both protective and risk factors in its doctrinal teaching regarding LGBTQ+ people. On the one hand, it teaches that all human beings are created in the image and likeness of God with infinite dignity (DDF 2024) and that homosexuals "must be accepted with respect, compassion, and sensitivity" (Catechism 1994, n. 2358). On the other hand, it teaches very negative views of LGBTQ+ people, which it attempts to justify biblically and theologically. These teachings often shape the self-perception and understanding of LGBTQ+ individuals and cause what sociologist Arthur Frank refers to as "narrative ambush" (2010), religious biblical and doctrinal stories that communicate a negative narrative about a person's very worth and identity that "set life on edge, make life seem unlivable, and often lead to suicide" (Sanders 2020, 1). Those teachings are that homosexual orientation is "objectively disordered" (CDF 1975); that gay and lesbian sexual acts are "intrinsically disordered and can in no case be approved of," and the same judgment applies to same-sex marriage in which same-sex acts are practiced (CDF 1975); and not "unjust discrimination" against LGBTQ+ people is morally acceptable (Catechism 1994) and required to protect human dignity and the common good, and even promotes such discrimination legislatively (United States Conference of Catholic Bishops [hereafter USCCB] 2019; see Salzman and Lawler 2025). In light of the substantial number of people leaving the Church because of its teaching on LGBTQ+ issues, it is clear that people in the pews are internalizing the judgmental and condemnatory narrative ambush and risk factor language and doctrinal teaching over and above the accepting and loving protective factor language and doctrinal teaching. Anecdotally, we have heard several risk factor homilies in our Catholic religious community, opposing the legalization of same-sex civil marriage that was ruled on by the Supreme Court of the United States in 2015 and morally condemning homosexual sexual acts and, more recently, condemning gender affirming care and even denying the reality and existence of transgender people (USCCCB 2023).

Catholic Doctrinal Teaching Regarding LGBTQ+ People: A Critical Analysis

The Catholic Church codifies doctrinal language against LGBTQ+ people and their sexual acts that promotes many of the religiously based mental health risk factors of stigma and discrimination that can lead to personal and other violence noted by the Trevor Project and numerous sociological studies. We investigate several of those teachings and their justification including the nature of the human person (CDF 1975), "the constant teaching of the Magisterium . . . the moral sense of the Christian people" (CDF 1975, VIII), and not "unjust discrimination" against LGBTQ people, and find all of them wanting as accurate interpretations of the ethics of sexuality in general, and LGBTQ+ people in specific, in the twenty-first century. Critically analyzing those teachings and their justification and reforming those teachings can alleviate Catholic based mental health risk factors.

Human Nature, Gender Identity, and Sexual Orientation

The nature of the human person or human nature is grounded in a theological anthropology. To understand Catholic doctrinal teaching on LGBTQ+ ethical issues, one must first define Catholic sexual anthropology. That anthropology is a strict sex binary that posits an intrinsic link between sex and gender. Sex is determined biologically by a person's genitalia at birth; gender is determined culturally as the expression of this biological sex. According to Pope Francis, "biological sex and the socio-cultural role of sex (gender) can be distinguished but not separated" (2016, n. 56; USCCCB 2023, n. 6). This statement reflects Catholic sexual anthropology, a strict ontological binary where one's biological sex determines one's gender. Male is masculine and female is feminine. Any sexual anthropology that does not conform to this definition Pope Francis labels pejoratively as "gender ideology," which promotes "a personal identity and emotional intimacy radically separated from the biological difference between male and female" (2016, n. 56; USCCCB 2023, n. 6).

This binary, however, once rigid and unquestionable, is now seriously challenged in favor of a broad sexual continuum that embraces male, female, and intersex. "At conception the genital regions of all human fetuses appear identical and then, around seven weeks, most but not all begin to develop clearly along male and female lines" (Preves 2003, 25). In fact, over seventy combinations of sex chromosomes have been detected (Gudorf 1994), which account for this biological continuum. Gender determines whether a person is culturally acknowledged as masculine or feminine and is a cultural construction in dialogue with sex (see Butler 2006). Whereas Pope Francis' perception of the relation between sex and gender is intrinsic and essential, scientifically and experientially there is a clear distinction between sex and gender where there is no intrinsic link. This lack of intrinsic link is evident in transgender people and intersex people with ambiguous genitalia.

Transgender refers to persons who experience gender dysphoria and feel a disjunction or disconnect between their developed biological sex and their culturally assigned gender. A World Population Review reported the number of transgender persons worldwide at 2 percent (n.d.), but Pew Research reported in 2022 that 5 percent of young adults in the United States between the ages of eighteen and twenty-nine claimed they were transgender or sexually nonbinary (Brown 2022). These numbers are significant, and they are numbers of real people, whose existence deserves to be acknowledged. One of the greatest mental health risk factors for transgender people is to deny their very existence. Unfortunately, the denial of transgender people is a logical, though logically incoherent, conclusion in Catholic sexual anthropology.

Catholic theological anthropology does recognize the reality of homosexual orientation. However, it considers this orientation a distortion of human nature and labels it an "objective disorder." The CDF's *Persona humana* draws a distinction between homosexuals whose condition is transitory and "homosexuals who are definitively such" (1975, VIII). We interpret "definitively such" to mean those who by *human nature* are LGBTQ+. In every human being, the church teaches that there is an abstract reality named *human nature*. That human nature is an interpreted reality and always in need of ongoing interpretation as circumstances change and dialectical interpretations of how it is to be understood and of what is and what is not included in human nature arise. Nature and natural law have always had a prominent place in Catholic theological ethics, and all sexual activity that deviates from God's "wisely ordered laws of nature" (Paul VI 1968, n. 11) and is not open to the transmission of life is taught to be ethically wrong. The fundamental principles which dictate this ethical judgment are said to be contained "in the divine law . . . *accessible to our minds*" (Paul VI 1968, n. 3; emphasis added). This phrase, "accessible to our minds," however, raises serious questions about its interpretation. Already in the thirteenth century, Thomas Aquinas taught that natural law is "'nothing other than the light of understanding placed in us by God" (Catechism 1994, n. 426). He argues that, although the precepts of the natural law are universal and immutable, their application varies according to the circumstances of peoples' real lives. Our approach to the meaning of human nature follows the direction mapped out by Aquinas: women and men know their human nature by being attentive to, by understanding, and by making judgments and decisions based on the reality of their shared human lives.

Young Catholics, including young LGBTQ Catholics, get their understanding of nature from the teaching of their church. That teaching that gay and lesbian human nature is disordered is condemnatory and discriminatory and leads to acts of discrimination, sometimes serious acts of discrimination like physical assault and even murder of gays and lesbians. One nineteen-year-old gay Catholic student told us that after one such assault he thought that, if this was what his life was going to be like, he would be better off dead and considered suicide. Thanks, however, to the love and care of his parents, he did not become part of the suicide statistics given above.

Historical women and men have no access to pure, uninterpreted nature. Nature reveals to our attention, understanding, judgment, and decision only its naked fact; we know from our experience that we have a human and not a vegetable nature. Everything beyond that knowledge, including what human nature demands of us in terms of ethical action, is the result of interpretation by attentive, intelligent, rational, and responsible persons. We experience nature only as socially interpreted. The uninterpreted experience of human nature, as indeed of every other reality in our lives, is restricted to its mere facticity and is void of meaning, a quality that does not inhere in nature but is assigned to it by rational human beings in interpretive acts. "The potter, and not the pot," Alfred North Whitehead correctly judges, "is responsible for the shape of the pot" (Whitehead 1959, 8). It is inevitable that different groups of equally reasonable, historically, and culturally conditioned human beings will have different interpretations of nature and the ethical obligations deriving from it, and that any given interpretation may be right or wrong. Because every interpretation of nature is a culturally constructed reality, what nature is interpreted to really be must always to be subjected to scrutiny, even if the interpretation is advanced by the Catholic magisterium. That includes its teaching on the ethics of gay and lesbian reality.

We recognize sexual orientation as an essential, definitive dimension of human nature. Unlike church teaching that claims homosexual orientation is "objectively disordered" (*Catechism* 1994, n. 2358),[1] we argue that sexual orientation or identity, heterosexual, homosexual, bisexual, intersexual, or transgender is naturally and objectively ordered. Currently, there is no scientific consensus on the origins of sexual orientation or sexual identity. Catholic teaching recognizes this lack of scientific consensus, acknowledging that the psychological genesis of homosexuality "remains largely unexplained" (*Catechism* 1994, n. 2357). Despite this acknowledgment, ignoring the available scientific data on the reality of sexual orientation and basing itself largely on doubtful scripture and tradition, Catholic teaching continues to claim that a homosexual orientation is objectively disordered. Relying on the data now supplied by human experience and science, many Catholic ethicists challenge this claim. The nineteen-year-old student mentioned above told us that he never heard of that challenge in his years in Catholic schools.

Neuroscientific and genetic studies have evolved dramatically in their ability to identify areas in the brain that shape a person's sexual orientation. Based on scientific research, Jacques Balthazart asserts that "sexual orientation is probably under the control of embryonic endocrine/genetic phenomena in which there is little room for individual choice" (2012, x). This hypothesis has been substantiated by scientists employing different methodologies. Simon LeVay's extensive research on the origins of homosexual orientation begins with sexual orientation in humans and supports these specific observations in humans with animal studies (2010). Balthazart's research comes from the other direction, beginning with sexual orientation in animals and then seeing how these studies apply to humans. Nonetheless, both scholars reach the same conclusion: "homosexuality in humans is to a very large extent, if not exclusively, determined by biological factors acting prenatally or soon after birth and that the social or educational environment plays at best a subsidiary role in this determinism" (Balthazart 2012, xi). Based on such studies, theologian James Allison challenges the claim that a homosexual orientation is objectively disordered. "There is no longer any reputable scientific evidence of any sort," he correctly argues, "psychological, biological, genetic, medical, neurological—to back up the claim" (2009, 9).

These studies provide scientific, biological explanations of the genesis of homosexuality and challenge the assertion that homosexual orientation is objectively disordered. David Matzko McCarthy presents a theological explanation for why the church's claim that homosexual orientation is objectively disordered is both inconsistent and inaccurate. Church teaching defines heterosexual orientation as normative, the "natural" explanation of the nuptial metaphor, and defines homosexual orientation as objectively disordered. Homosexual orientation is objectively disordered in the *desire* for a person of the same-sex (USCCB 1997) and because it creates a "strong tendency" toward same-sex *acts* that are intrinsically evil (CDF 2003, 3). This emphasis on desire and act highlights the inconsistency of Catholic teaching on the term "orientation" when it comes to heterosexual or homosexual orientation. Whereas heterosexual orientation focuses on the complementarity of two embodied persons, biologically, affectively, socially, and spiritually (CCE 1983), homosexual orientation focuses on their desire and acts.

Matzko McCarthy provides a theological definition of homosexual orientation which, aside from the absence of heterosexual complementarity, is consistent with Catholic teaching's understanding of heterosexual orientation. "Gay men and lesbians are persons who encounter the other (and thus discover themselves) in relation to persons of the same sex. This same-sex orientation is a given of their coming to be, that is, *the nuptial meaning of human life emerges* for a gay man in relation to other men and for a woman when face to face with other women" (McCarthy 2002, 212–13; emphasis added). In a steadfast, just, and loving union, then, same-sex couples give their bodies to one another and are "theologically communicative"; that is, they are witnesses to the community of God's "constancy and steadfast fidelity" (McCarthy 2002, 213). In their witness, they have "iconic significance" in their sexuality through embodied interpersonal union, just as heterosexual couples, both fertile and infertile, have iconic significance in their sexuality in their embodied interpersonal unions. Heterosexual orientation complementarity is not a determining factor. Rather, two embodied persons, heterosexual or homosexual, in permanent interpersonal union, who reflect God's constant love and steadfast fidelity, are the determining factor. In the case of fertile heterosexual couples, embodied interpersonal union is potentially procreative; in the case of infertile heterosexual and same-sex couples, embodied interpersonal union is not potentially procreative. Embodiment and the nuptial metaphor, however, are essential to all three interpersonal unions.

What can be categorized as "natural" in interpersonal unions and sexual activity, therefore, will vary depending on whether the person's sexual orientation is homosexual, heterosexual, or bisexual. Same-sex acts are natural for people with a same-sex orientation. Heterosexual acts are natural for people with a heterosexual orientation. Same-sex and/or heterosexual acts are natural for people with a bisexual orientation. They are natural because they are expressions of the true and definitive sexual orientation of the person, created in the image and likeness of God. We are not to be understood as arguing here that same-sex acts are ethical because they are natural for those with a same-sex orientation; that would be to treat natural facts as ethical justification and to commit the naturalistic fallacy. To be ethical any sexual act, whether same-sex, heterosexual, or bisexual, must be not only natural, in accord with a person's definitive sexual orientation, but also just and loving (Farley 2006; Salzman and Lawler 2008). The Second Vatican Council, which codified the method for reading and interpreting scripture, has ethical implications for judging the immorality of same-sex acts.

The Bible and Catholic Teaching on Same-Sex Acts

Persona humana notes that the condemnation of homosexual acts is an established teaching in sexual ethics and considers scripture a primary justification for this teaching. At the end of this document the CDF asserts that Catholic doctrine "must be handed on in a way capable of properly enlightening the consciences of those confronted with *new situations* and it must be enriched with a discernment of all the elements that can truthfully and usefully be brought forward about the meaning and value of human sexuality" (CDF 1975, n. XIII; emphasis added). This assertion pays homage to the teaching of the Council about the approach to reading the scriptures and other ancient texts, and we fully endorse it. What we do not endorse is the CDF's ignoring of Council teaching, as we will show, in its own text.

Christianity is one of the religions of the Book and Christians rightly appeal to their Bible, believed to be the very word of God, to substantiate their theological and ethical claims. As far back as 1943, Pope Pius XII introduced into official Catholic biblical tradition the teaching that the "foremost and greatest endeavor" of every interpreter of the sacred scriptures "should be to discern and define clearly the sense of the biblical words that is called literal" (Pius XII 1943, n. 23). He went on to explain that the literal sense "is not to be determined by the rules of grammar or philology alone; the interpreter must go back wholly in spirit to those remote centuries of the East and with the aid of history, archaeology, ethnology, and other sciences, accurately determine what modes of writing the authors of that ancient period would be likely to use and did use" (Pius XII 1943, n. 35). Pius officially initiated the historically conscious approach to reading the Bible and Vatican II canonized it.

The reader of the Bible, Vatican II taught, "must investigate what meaning the sacred writer intended to express and actually expressed in particular circumstances by using contemporary literary forms *in accordance with the situation of his own time and culture*" (Second Vatican Council 1965a, n. 12). In 1994 the Pontifical Biblical Commission explained what this means in practice. Religious texts, it teaches, "are bound in reciprocal relationship to the societies in which they originate. . . . Consequently, the scientific study of the Bible requires as exact a knowledge as possible of the social conditions distinctive of the various milieus in which the traditions recorded in the Bible took shape" (Pontifical Biblical Commission 1994, D1). Of great interest here is the CDF's confession that "difficulties arise from the historical condition that affects the expression of revelation. . . . It sometimes happens that some dogmatic truth is first expressed incompletely (but not falsely) and, at a later date when considered in a broader context of faith or human knowledge, is expressed more fully and perfectly" (CDF 1973, n. V). The CDF clearly knows and is defensive about the historicity of the biblical texts. Why, then, we ask, does it ignore that historicity in its document on certain sexual questions, specifically on the ethics of same-sex acts?

Persona humana teaches that in sacred scripture same-sex acts "are condemned as a serious depravity and even presented as the sad consequence of rejecting God," citing only Romans 1:24-27 in support of this teaching. This leads it to the judgment that "homosexual acts are intrinsically disordered and can in no case be approved of" (CDF 1975, n. VIII), a judgment that, fifty-five years later, continues to be the cornerstone of the Catholic Church's approach to every discussion about the ethics of same-sex acts. A later document from the CDF, *Homosexualitatis problema*, is more expansive. It teaches that there is "a clear consistency within the sacred scriptures for judging the ethical issue of homosexual behavior. The church's doctrine regarding this issue is thus based not only on isolated phrases taken out of context . . . but rather on the solid foundation of a constant biblical testimony" (1986, n. 50). It then lists the texts on which this solid foundation is built: Gen. 19:1-11; Lev. 18:22; 20:13; Rom. 1:26-7; 1 Cor. 6:9; 1 Tim. 1:10 (CDF 1986). We have offered elsewhere a full exegesis of all these texts, seeking out "that meaning that the sacred writer, in a determined situation and given the time and circumstances of his time and culture, intended to express and did express through the medium of a contemporary literary form" (Salzman and Lawler 2008, 215), and we will not rehearse that extensive exegesis here. We will, rather, only outline its basic facts, to offer a possible antidote to the misunderstanding that gives rise to too many LGBTQ suicides.

The first fact is linguistic and ontological: there is no word in ancient Hebrew for *homosexual* because every man and woman was believed to be *heterosexual*. Homosexual was unheard of in the time and culture of the Old Testament.[2] If there is condemnation of male same-sex acts in the scriptures, and there is in the texts cited by the CDF, it is condemnation of the same-sex acts of *perverted heterosexuals*. The same-sex acts condemned in Genesis 19 are acts of *heterosexual* anal rape (Olyan 1994) threatened by perverted heterosexual men. Such acts cannot be ethically equated today to the just and loving same-sex acts of men and women with a definitive homosexual orientation. Though the act of violent heterosexual rape committed by perverted heterosexual men is condemned in Genesis 19, however, it is but a secondary meaning of the text. What is primarily condemned is the violation of the Jewish law of hospitality by perverted heterosexual men. This is made clear in the text when Lot, who is culturally free to offer his two virgin daughters to the men of Sodom for sex, begs them "to do nothing to these men for *they have come under the shelter of my roof*" (Gen. 19:8; emphasis added), that is, under the shelter of my hospitality. This interpretation is reinforced by the Old Testament itself, where Sodom is regularly mentioned but not once is its crime said to be same-sex acts. The Book of Wisdom explicitly charges the men of Sodom with inhospitality (Wis. 19:14) and so does Jesus in the context of the inhospitality accorded his disciples (Lk. 10:10-12; Matt. 10:14-15). Good Jew that he was, he also makes hospitality a cause of salvation and inhospitality a cause of damnation in the great final judgment scene (Matt. 25:34-46). Genesis 19, when read in the "*time and circumstances of* [the writer's] *time and culture*" is not about homosexuals and their same-sex acts. It is about the sexual acts of perverted heterosexuals violating the crucial Jewish law of hospitality. There is a vast difference between hospitality and homosexuality.

The second fact concerns the Leviticus text cited by the CDF: "you shall not lie with a male as with a woman" (Lev. 18:22). Again, as with Genesis 19, the text prohibits two *heterosexual* males lying with one another, not two same-sex males. The transposition that the CDF and the church make from that time and circumstance of presumed universal heterosexuality to a modern time and circumstance of distinction between heterosexuality and definitive homosexuality is entirely illegitimate by its own rules of interpretation. It is culturally important to understand that it is two males who are forbidden to lie with one another, and that two women lying with one another do not fall under Leviticus' proscription. In English the "*you*" in "you shall not lie" can apply to either women or men but in Hebrew the *you* that is used is used only of males. That it is only male same-sex acts that are proscribed introduces another Jewish consideration that applies to the text, that of male honor and the actions appropriate to it.

The third fact is the cultural issue of honor, carried exclusively by males, particularly by the patriarch who headed an extended family and for all intents and purposes owned the females in it, whether they were wives, daughters, or slaves. Patriarch Lot, therefore, could culturally offer his two virgin daughters for sex to the men of Sodom (Gen. 19:8). For a man to behave like a woman, however, to lie with and be passively penetrated by another man, offended not only his male honor but also that of his whole extended family. It was an abomination, not directly because he engaged in same-sex acts but because those same-sex acts, so contrary to the established heterosexual culture of the times, injured the honor of his whole extended family and threatened the whole patriarchal and hierarchical social and sexual context of his culture. "Passive partners demean male honor" (Malina 2001, 156). There is a further cultural consideration that explains the judgment in Leviticus 20:13 that men lying together shall be put to death, this time a monumental biological error. The ancient Hebrew, Greek, and Roman understanding of what happens in sexual intercourse is that a man passed on seed that contained the whole of life, later called by Paracelsus in the sixteenth century a *homunculus* or little man. The female simply provided the "field" or "ground" in which the seed could develop into a full-fledged human person (see duBois 1988). To spill the seed where the *homunculus* could not develop, in a male body, for instance, was held as tantamount to murder, and murder was always punishable by death (Malina 2001). Such a biologically flawed argument can no longer be taken seriously.

Christians consider the Old Testament fulfilled and superseded by the New Testament, and so we now consider what the New Testament says about homosexuality and homosexuals. We first emphasize that nothing has changed in the Jewish culture of the New Testament; every woman and man is still assumed to be heterosexual. Though same-sex acts are well-known, the condition of definitive homosexuality remains unknown. The first text the CDF presents as contributing to "a solid foundation" for the church's condemnation of homosexual acts is Paul's letter to the Romans 1:26-27. The literal context of Paul's remarks is standard Jewish accusations against gentile idolatry. The existence of God, he asserts, ought to be plain to gentiles but they do not acknowledge God. Rather, "they exchanged the glory of the immortal God for images resembling a mortal human being." What is radically wrong with gentiles is not that they engage in same-sex acts but that they engage in idolatry. Because they are idolaters, "God gave them up to dishonorable passions." Driven by their idolatry, Roman women *exchanged* their natural heterosexual acts for same-sex acts and Roman men *gave up* their natural heterosexual acts for same-sex and *dishonorable* acts (Rom. 1:26). Notice here that it is only men whom Paul declares dishonorable; Jewish women in his time and culture have nothing to do with honor, except to do nothing that would harm it. Men are the guardians of honor and one of the ways they seriously harm honor is to give up their natural heterosexual acts for same-sex acts with another man, in short to *reduce* themselves to the status of a woman (D'Angelo 2001). Paul's conclusion belies the CDF's claim of a solid foundation in the text for Catholic teaching on homosexuality. "Since they did not see fit to acknowledge God, God gave them up to a base mind and to improper conduct." The improper conduct he lists is extensive: "envy, murder, strife, deceit, malignity, gossips, slanderers, haters of God, insolent, haughty, boastful, inventors of evil, disobedient to parents, foolish, faithless, heartless, ruthless" (Rom. 1:28-31). Significantly missing is any mention of same-sex activity.

In 1 Cor. 6:9, Paul lists among those who will not inherit the kingdom of God *malakoi* and *arsenokoitai*. *Malakos* is the Greek word for soft, *arsenokoitos* is a very uncommon Greek word, whose translation to English is widely contested. There is some evidence that *malakos* and its cognate *malakia* (softness) were used of female sexual behavior, though they were not restricted to that meaning (Scroggs 1984). Bearing in mind our discussion of Leviticus 18:22 and the primacy of male honor there involved, it is not difficult to grasp that Paul was speaking of male dishonor when heterosexual men behave sexually like women, when men who were expected to be thoroughly masculine are reduced in the social and sexual hierarchy of the time and culture to the status of soft women. Such behavior, as we have already seen, was judged to be an abomination in itself without any additional judgment on same-sex activity. There is, however, no unanimity of translation. The King James Bible translated *malakos* along the lines of *effeminacy*, the 1946 Revised Standard Version translated it incorrectly as *adulterers*, and the 1977 New Revised Standard Version, based on documents discovered since the 1946 edition, returned to the King James' interpretation and translates *malakoi* and *arsenokoitai* together as *sexual perverts*, men and women perverting their presumed heterosexual natures and acting sexually as women and men respectively. Given everything we have argued about the times and cultures of both Old and New Testaments, this latter translation seems to us to be based on "as exact a knowledge as possible of the social conditions distinctive of the various milieus in which the traditions recorded in the Bible took shape" (Pontifical Biblical Commission 1994, D1) demanded by Vatican II and the Pontifical Biblical Commission.

What can we conclude from the foregoing analysis of the Bible on same-sex activity? First, we can conclude that the same-sex acts of both women and men with a definitive same-sex orientation are not a biblical concern. There is no mention of them in Israel's earliest ethical codes, there is nothing about it in the "words" that God spoke in the Decalogue (Exod. 20: 1-17), there is nothing about it in Jesus' gospel teaching, there is not even a word for it in Hebrew or Greek. There is no word for it, as we pointed out, because it was not a recognized reality in the culture at the time. There is condemnation of same-sex activity in the Bible, but it is condemnation of the same-sex activity of perverted *heterosexual* men, not of the just and loving same-sex activity of definitively homosexual men or women. Second, we can conclude that biblical scholar Bruce Malina's conclusion about Paul's text to the Romans actually applies to the entire Bible. "If we return to the twenty-first century after this excursion into the first century [or earlier], we can see that Paul's perspectives, if taken consistently, simply do not make sense" (Malina 2001, 168). They make as much sense as the perspectives Paul might have had on Microsoft, Mercedes Benz, and the Bank of Ireland. Paul does not live in our time and culture in which Microsoft is a recognized economic behemoth, Mercedes is a recognized luxury automobile, the Bank of Ireland is a trusted financial institution, and homosexual orientation is a recognized natural condition, nor do we live in his time and culture of bad procreational biology. Lisa Sowle Cahill puts the issue succinctly: "Realizing the impossibility of transposing rules from biblical times to our own, interpreters look for larger themes, values, or ideals which can inform moral reflection without determining specific practices in advance" (Cahill 1992, 5–6).

Third, we can conclude that the larger biblical theme with respect to homosexuality and same-sex behavior is that both Old and New Testament saw the evil of same-sex acts embedded in the perversion of the presumed universal heterosexual order. What they say about the same-sex activity of heterosexual men cannot be transposed without careful ethical discernment to the same-sex acts of men and women of natural same-sex orientation with persons of the same sex. Their same-sex acts may be or not be unethical, but any judgment of their ethics will have to be substantiated by proof other than the Bible's condemnation of the same-sex activity of *heterosexual* men. Richard Sparks' judgment is our final judgment: "On scriptural evidence alone we are left short of a clear and clean condemnation of what might be called committed or covenantal homosexual acts" (Sparks 1996, 81). Fourth, we can safely conclude that current Catholic teaching is simply misguided and wrong, based as it is, at least in part, on a wrongly interpreted and, therefore, unsound scriptural exegesis.

Moral Sense of the Catholic People and Same-Sex Acts

Persona humana asserts that those who excuse homosexual relations between certain people "do so in opposition to the constant teaching of the Magisterium and to the moral sense of the Christian people" (CDF 1975, n. VIII). We have shown that the constant teaching of the Magisterium, claimed to be rooted in the sacred scriptures, has not paid attention to the biblical texts in the way that Vatican II demands. We will now show that the teaching is neither received nor supported in the contemporary moral sense of the Christian people, since contemporary scientific data indicate that the teaching of the church is presently not so supported. A 62-year-old lesbian told us several years ago that "I have suffered all my life from the teaching of the Catholic Church about my sexual orientation, and it is only recently that I have discovered that the vast majority of practicing Catholics reject that teaching." We will now show how correct she was about that rejection.

The Second Vatican Council revalidates a forgotten doctrine of Catholic theology, that of *sensus fidei*, the sense of faith, which connotes the connatural and intuitive knowledge that faith has of God and the things of God. *Sensus fidelium*, sense of the faithful, is a connatural and intuitive knowledge of God and the things of God, a charism of discernment, possessed by the whole church. It is a charism which sometimes recognizes a teaching of the church as a truth of God and, therefore, to be received and believed, and sometimes recognizes a teaching of the church as not a truth, or not the whole truth, of God and, therefore, to be received and believed, at best, developmentally (see Lawler 2005). In the first instance, it is an important element in the validation of church doctrine and, in the second instance, an important element in the development of church doctrine, as was abundantly demonstrated in the cases of the false doctrines of usury, slavery, and religious freedom.

Sensus fidelium has biblical root in Paul's exhortation to the Philippians to "have this common mind among yourselves, which is yours in Christ Jesus" (2:5). It has patristic root in Vincent of Lerins' fifth-century rule of faith: "what is believed everywhere, always, and by all" (Vincent of Lerins 1846, 640). It has Scholastic root in Aquinas, who taught that the faithful understand a teaching *per modum connaturalitatis*, that is, they incline connaturally and intuitively in faith and adhere to what they believe to be the true meaning of the word of God (Aquinas 1225). It was offered as proof of Catholic doctrine against the Reformers by Robert Cardinal Bellarmine: "what all the faithful hold as a matter of faith is necessarily true and of faith" (cited in Dulles 1986, 240). It was sharply focused for moderns by John Henry Cardinal Newman, who taught that it was "a sort of instinct, or *phronema,* deep in the bosom of the Mystical Body of Christ . . . which leads to all true doctrine" (Newman 1961, 73). It was validated as contemporary Catholic doctrine by the Second Vatican Council, which taught that the doctrine of the Catholic Church is preserved in *all* the faithful, laity and hierarchy together. "The body of the faithful *as a whole*, anointed as they are by the Holy One (1 John 2:20, 27), cannot err in matters of belief. Thanks to a supernatural sense of the faith [*sensus fidei*] which characterizes the people *as a whole*, it manifests this unerring quality when, 'from the bishops to the last of the faithful' it manifests its universal agreement in matters of faith and morals" (Second Vatican Council 1964, n. 12; emphasis added). This teaching makes sense, of course, only in a church believed to be and lived as a communion instituted by Christ, constituted by the Spirit of Christ, and "composed of all those who receive him in faith and in love" (Second Vatican Council 1965b, n. 32), an historical communion "of life, love, and truth" (Second Vatican Council 1964, n. 9). There is hierarchy in such a worldwide communion as the Catholic Church, but it is not a hierarchy in which all authority is located only in the leaders of the church.

We now proceed to consider the survey data related to homosexuality and same-sex acts, but before doing so we issue a warning. We are in full agreement with Pope John Paul II when he insists that, while "the church values sociological and statistical research, such research *alone* is not to be considered in itself an expression of the *sensus fidei*" (John Paul 1981, n. 5; emphasis added). On the one hand, sociological, statistical data is not of itself an expression of theological *sensus fidei*. On the other hand, it does provide data for church dialogue on the contemporary faith of the church, both the actual faith of believing Catholics and what it is they actually believe. Distinguished sociologist David Martin reminds us that "doctrines do not land like meteorites from outer space but grow organically where they have a fertile niche or cranny" (1997, 69). Sociological research scientifically examines those niches and crannies and the Catholic doctrines that take root in them. So now to that research and what it teaches us about *sensus fidei* on definitive homosexuality and same-sex acts today.

In December 2013 and January 2014, the Spanish media company Univision, in response to Pope Francis' request for Church consultations for the Synods on Marriage and Family, conducted a global survey on Catholic ethical beliefs. Only one of its questions is of interest to the topic of this chapter: "Do you support or oppose marriage between two persons of the same sex?" Thirty percent of Catholic respondents from eleven nations with the largest Catholic populations reported that they supported such marriages, 66 percent of respondents reported that they opposed such marriages, and 4 percent gave no response (Univision Communications 2014). These numbers are slightly skewed by the overwhelming responses from the two African countries included, Congo and Uganda, where those responding were opposed to same-sex marriages 98 percent and 99 percent respectively, an understandable response in two patriarchal cultures. In the Univision poll, 54 percent of Americans supported marriage between same-sex couples. A subsequent Gallup poll reported 56 percent of Americans supported same-sex marriage in 2014 rising to 63 percent support in 2019 (McCarthy 2019), and a similar Pew Research study reported 56 percent support in 2014 rising to 61 percent in 2019 (Pew Forum 2019). Of particular interest to this chapter is that in 2019, Pew reported that American Catholic support for same-sex marriage was at 61 percent, not different from the national figure. A Pew Global Snapshot of Same-Sex marriage in 2019 reported same-sex marriage legally widespread in Western Europe, in the Americas from Canada to Argentina, in Australia, and in New Zealand, but legal in Africa only in South Africa and in Asia only in Taiwan. Eleven European countries had legal civil unions/partnerships, including the Czech Republic where support for same-sex marriage was at a high 65 percent (Masci and Desilver 2019). Linda Woodhead reports two important facts from the United Kingdom: 52 percent of Catholics support same-sex marriage and 0 percent say they look to religious figures for ethical guidance, preferring instead their own understanding, judgment, and decision (Woodhead 2013). None of this data is encouraging news for the Catholic Church, especially as Woodhead points out that Catholics claim not that the teachings are too *hard* but that they are simply *wrong*. It is too bad that our lesbian friend did not learn these statistics earlier in her life; it would have saved her from much emotional and religious trauma and suffering.

The sociological data on the morality of same-sex sexual acts and marriage indicate, at the very least, that *sensus fidelium* raises questions about the moral credibility of Catholic teachings on these issues. At the most, it indicates that these teachings must be revised. Another teaching that must be revised, which is in direct contradiction to its own social teaching, is Catholic teaching on the just discrimination against LGBTQ+ people.

Discrimination as a Risk Factor: Not "Unjust Discrimination"

Discrimination is one of the risk factors that minority groups are especially vulnerable to and contribute to mental illness, suicide ideation, and suicide. There is both a risk factor and protective factor in Catholic teaching on discrimination and LGBTQ+ people. The risk factor is that "every sign of *unjust* discrimination in [homosexuals'] regard should be avoided" (Catechism 1994, n. 2358), implying that there is just discrimination against homosexuals in specific, and LGBTQ+ people in general. The CDF asserts that discrimination is just and moral in the case of homosexual coaches, teachers, military personnel, and applicants to foster or adopt children (1992). The suggestion that there can be "just discrimination" against LGBTQ+ people simply because they are LGBTQ+ is a contradiction in terms, for discrimination against them on this basis alone is always unjust.

The protective factor is in Catholic social teaching, which teaches discrimination is never morally justified. "The equality of men [and women] rests essentially on their dignity as persons and the rights that flow from it: 'Every form of social or cultural discrimination in fundamental personal rights on the grounds of sex, race, color, social conditions, language, or religion must be curbed and eradicated as incompatible with God's design'" (Catechism 1994, n. 1935). The *Catechism* does not include sexual orientation or gender identity in the list that condemns social or cultural discrimination and the USCCB has vehemently resisted employment non-discrimination legislation in Congress on the basis of sexual orientation and gender identity, even for celibate gay or lesbian people (see USCCB 2019).

Catholic teaching on discrimination is a risk factor for LGBTQ+ people in at least two senses. First, it allows and promotes individual, legal, social, and structural discrimination against LGBTQ+ people. Second, it highlights the inconsistency in Catholic doctrinal teaching that has a double standard depending on whether that person is heterosexual or LGBTQ+. LGBTQ+ are singled out as not deserving moral and legal protection based solely on their sexual orientation or gender identity. The risk factor trumps the protective factor for LGBTQ+ people in Catholic doctrinal teaching and can contribute to mental health issues including anxiety, depression and, in extreme cases, suicidal ideation.

Calls for Reform of Catholic Teaching on LGBTQ+ Issues

Cardinal McElroy of the United States calls for "radical inclusion" in the Church of members of the LGBT community and asserts, correctly, that "It is a demonic mystery of the human soul why so many men and women have a profound and visceral animus [moral dignity] toward members of the LGBT communities." This animus is also evident in the Catholic Church and its doctrinal teaching (McKinless and Davis 2023), which can cause mental health risk factors for LGBTQ+ people. Exclusion from a religious community that teaches God's unconditional love and mercy and yet labels a person's sexual orientation "disordered" and promotes "just discrimination" against that person has an existential impact with salvific implications. It is well documented in the scientific community that discrimination against sexual and gender minorities causes trauma, anxiety, and depression, and violates ontological dignity (Livingston et al. 2020).[3] Even when sexual and gender minorities attempt to conceal their identities to protect themselves against overt discrimination, the concealment itself, staying "in the closet," is associated with greater depression and anxiety. These are compounded by religious perspectives where the isolation and alienation are experienced in a community that is supposed to reflect God's unconditional love, but instead threatens eternal punishment due to a person's sexual actions that flow from her/his particular sexual orientation or gender identity.

Cardinal McElroy calls for "radical inclusion" of LGBTQ+ people in the Church and points out that the *Catechism*'s use of the phrase "objective disorder" to label a homosexual orientation has personal, legal, and ethical implications that indicate LGBTQI people are somehow humanly and ethically disordered (2023). McElroy calls for a doctrinal change to remove this phrase from the *Catechism* and a broader revision of church doctrine on LGBTQ+ sexual ethical issues (McElroy 2023; McKinless and Davis 2023). Such changes would codify and prioritize protective factors in Catholic doctrinal teaching and establish the Catholic Church as a religion that is inclusive and gives hope to LGBTQ+ minority communities where it has too often demonstrated hostility and exclusion to these communities.

European church leaders have gone further in the call to change church doctrine. Cardinal Hollerich of Luxembourg frankly argues that "the sociological-scientific foundation of [Catholic teaching on homosexual people and acts] is no longer correct." It is, he believes, "time for a fundamental revision of the doctrine" on homosexuals and their acts (Catholic News Service 2022a). Bishop Helmut Dieser of Aachen comments that "same-sex feelings and love are not an aberration, but a variant of human sexuality." He maintains that church thinking on human sexuality in general, and homosexuality in particular, is "too simple." "Homosexuality," he argues, is "as science shows—not a glitch, not an illness, not an expression of any kind of deficit" (Catholic News Service 2022b). Similar statements have been made by Cardinal Marx (Catholic News Service 2022c) and the majority of German Bishops (Catholic News Agency 2022). The church must stop speaking of LGBTQ+ people in negative terms that promote mental health risk factors, embrace scientific understandings of human sexuality into its theological anthropology, and formulate doctrines that reflect this understanding. The results of this process will call for a revision of the doctrines themselves.

Conclusion

In this chapter, we have explained and critically analyzed several Catholic doctrinal teachings regarding LGBTQ+ people and the justification for those teachings that promote mental health risk factors and can contribute to suicide ideation or suicide among LGBTQ+ youth and young adults. Its theological anthropology posits a strict ontological sexual binary, the absolute condemnation of homosexual sexual acts and relationships, and the claim of just discrimination against LGBTQ+ people. We have demonstrated that all of these teachings are either anthropologically, ethically, or theologically unjustified and cannot rightly be used, therefore, to justify the doctrinal teaching that contributes to risk factors for the mental health, well-being, and human dignity of LGBTQ+ people.

We opened the chapter with the reality of suicide among LGBTQ+ people and its origin in the social and ecclesial stigma, discrimination, and violence to which they are subjected. It is a simple step to the conclusion and proposal that it is time, indeed well past time, for the Catholic Church to abandon its erroneous doctrinal teachings about LGBTQ+ persons and to replace them with a more positive and supportive teaching. Such a teaching can provide psychological, emotional, spiritual, and relational support to LGBTQ+ people. Such support is essential and demonstrated sociologically to alleviate suicide ideation and suicide among LGBTQ+ youth (Gibbs 2015).

Feminists appeal to Paul's baptismal formula in Gal 3:28 as an argument for human equality and dignity between woman and men (Farley 2006). "There is neither Jew nor Greek, there is neither slave nor free, there is neither male nor female, for you are all one in Christ Jesus." We make bold to add to Paul's list that in Christ there is also neither lesbian, gay, bisexual, transgender, queer, intersex, nor heterosexual, for they are all one in and with him.[4]

Notes

1 It is important to note that, unlike *Persona humana*, which refers to "homosexual orientation" as definitive, the *Catechism* and other magisterial documents refer to "homosexual tendencies" or a homosexual "inclination." The former implies that

homosexual orientation is a given and part of human nature; the latter imply that it is not a given and therefore not part of human nature.

2 The first appearance in English of the word *homosexual* was not until 1892 in the translation of a German work on sexual perversion. Its first appearance in the Bible was in 1946, when, as we shall see, the compilers of the Revised Standard Version (RSV) combined the two Greek words *malakos* and *arsenokoitos* into the one English word, *homosexual.*

3 Livingston et al. (2020).

4 Unless otherwise stated, all translations of the Bible are from the New Revised Standard Version, updated edition, National Council of Churches Friendship Press. New Revised Standard Version Bible, copyright 1989, Division of Christian Education of the National Council of the Churches of Christ in the United States of America. Used by permission. All rights reserved.

Bibliography

Allison, James. 2009. "The Fulcrum of Discovery Or How the 'Gay Thing' Is Good News for the Catholic Church." http://www.jamesalison.co.uk/pdf/eng59.pdf.

Almeida, Joanna, Renee M. Johnson, Heather L. Corliss, Beth E. Molnar, and Deborah Azrael. 2009. "Emotional Distress among LGBT Youth: The Influence of Perceived Discrimination Based on Sexual Orientation." *Journal of Youth and Adolescence* 38 (7): 1001–14. https://www.ncbi.nlm.nih.gov/pmc/articles/PMC3707280/.

Aquinas, Thomas. 1225. *Summa Theologiae*. http://www.documentacatholicaomnia.eu/03d/1225-1274,_Thomas_Aquinas,_Summa_Theologiae_%5B1%5D,_EN.pdf.

Balthazart, Jacques. 2012. *The Biology of Homosexuality*. New York: Oxford.

Brown, Anna. 2022. "About 5% of Young Adults in the U.S. Say Their Gender is Different from Their Sex Assigned at Birth." *Pew Research Center*, June 7. https://www.pewresearch.org/short-reads/2022/06/07/about-5-of-young-adults-in-the-u-s-say-their-gender-is-different-from-their-sex-assigned-at-birth/#:~:text=Some%205.1%25%20of%20adults%20younger,strictly%20one%20or%20the%20other.

Butler, Judith. 2006. *Gender Trouble: Feminism and the Subversion of Identity*. New York: Routledge.

Cahill, Lisa Sowle. 1992. "Is Catholic Ethics Biblical?" *Warren Lecture Series in Catholic Studies*, No. 20. University of Tulsa.

Catechism of the Catholic Church. 1994. Paulist.

Catholic News Agency. 2022. "German Catholic Bishops Welcome Initiative Seeking Change in Church Teaching on Sexuality." *Angelus*, January 25. https://angelusnews.com/news/world/german-catholic-bishops-welcome-initiative-seeking-change-in-church-teaching-on-sexuality/.

Catholic News Service. 2022a. "Cardinal Hollerich Says Church Teaching on Gays 'No Longer Correct.'" *Angelus*, February 2. https://angelusnews.com/news/world/cardinal-hollerich-says-church-teaching-on-gays-no-longer-correct/.

Catholic News Service. 2022b. "German Bishop Calls Current Catholic Teaching on Sexuality 'Too Simple.'" *National Catholic Reporter*, November 10. https://www.ncronline.org/news/german-bishop-calls-current-catholic-teaching-sexuality-too-simple.

Catholic News Service. 2022c. "German Cardinal Calls for Change in Church Teaching on Homosexuality." *National Catholic Reporter*, March 31. https://www.ncronline.org/news/theology/german-cardinal-calls-change-church-teaching-homosexuality.

Champions of Change. n.d. "The Trevor Project." https://obamawhitehouse.archives.gov/champions/suicide-prevention/the-trevor-project.

Cohen, Sandy. 2023. "Suicide Rates Among Young People Continue to Rise, but There Are Ways to Help." *UCLA Health*, February 23. https://www.uclahealth.org/news/article/as-suicide-rates-among-young-people-rise-there-are-ways-to-help.

Congregation for Catholic Education. 1983. *Educational Guidance in Human Love: Outlines for Sex Education*. Rome: Typis Polyglottis Vaticanis.

Congregation for the Doctrine of the Faith. 1973. *Declaration in Defense of the Catholic Doctrine on the Church Against Certain Errors of the Present Day*, June 24. https://www.vatican.va/roman_curia/congregations/cfaith/documents/rc_con_cfaith_doc_19730705_mysterium-ecclesiae_en.html.

Congregation for the Doctrine of the Faith. 1975. *Persona Humana*. https://www.vatican.va/roman_curia/congregations/cfaith/documents/rc_con_cfaith_doc_19751229_persona-humana_en.html.

Congregation for the Doctrine of the Faith. 1986. *Homosexualitatis problema: Letter to the Bishops of the Catholic Church on the Pastoral Care of Homosexual Persons.* https://www.vatican.va/roman_curia/congregations/cfaith/documents/rc_con_cfaith_doc_19861001_homosexual-persons_en.html.

Congregation for the Doctrine of the Faith. 1992. *Some Considerations Concerning the Response to Legislative Proposals on the Non-Discrimination of Homosexual Persons.* http://www.vatican.va/roman_curia/congregations/cfaith/documents/rc_con_cfaith_doc_19920724_homosexual-persons_en.html.

Congregation for the Doctrine of the Faith. 2003. *Considerations Regarding Proposals to Give Legal Recognition to Unions between Homosexual Persons.* http://www.vatican.va/roman_curia/congregations/cfaith/documents/rc_con_cfaith_doc_20030731_homosexual-unions_en.html.

Curtin, Sally G., and Matthew F. Garnett. 2023. "Suicide and Homicide Death Rates Among Young Adults 10–24, United States, 2001–2021." *Centers for Disease Control and Prevention*, June 15, 2023. https://stacks.cdc.gov/view/cdc/128423.

D'Angelo, Mary Rose. 2001. "Perfect Fear Casteth Out Love: Reading, Citing, and Rape." In *Sexual Diversity and Catholicism: Toward the Development of Moral Theology*, edited by Patricia Beattie Jung with Joseph Andrew Coray, 175–97. Michael Glazier.

Dicastery for the Doctrine of the Faith. 2024. *Dignitas Infinita*, April 8. https://press.vatican.va/content/salastampa/en/bollettino/pubblico/2024/04/08/240408c.html.

duBois, Paige. 1988. *Sowing the Body: Psychoanalysis and Ancient Representations of Women*. University of Chicago Press.

Dulles, Avery. 1986. "Sensus Fidelium." *America* 155, no. 12 (November 1): 240–2, 263.

Farley, Margaret A. 2006. *Just Love: A Framework for Christian Sexual Ethics*. Continuum.

Frank, Arthur W. 2010. *Letting Stories Breath: A Socio-Narratology*. University of Chicago Press.

Gibbs, Jeremy J. 2015. "Religious Conflict, Sexual Identity, and Suicidal Behaviors among LGBT Young Adults." *Archives of Suicide Research* 19, no. 4 (October–December): 472–88. https://www.ncbi.nlm.nih.gov/pmc/articles/PMC4706071/.

Gudorf, Christine. E. 1994. *Body, Sex, and Pleasure: Reconstructing Christian Sexual Ethics*. Cleveland: Pilgrim Press.

Hatzenbuehler, Mark L., Lori M. Hilt, and Susan Nolen-Hoeksema. 2010. "Gender, Sexual Orientation, and Vulnerability to Depression." In *Handbook of Gender Research in Psychology*, edited by Joan C. Chrisler and Donald R. McCreary, 133–51. Springer.

Janssen, Dirk-Jan, and Peer Scheepers. 2019. "How Religiosity Shapes Rejection of Homosexuality Across the Globe." *Journal of Homosexuality* 66 (14): 1974–2001. https://www.tandfonline.com/doi/full/10.1080/00918369.2018.1522809#abstract.

John Paul II, Pope. 1981. *Familiaris Consortio*, November 22, 1981. https://www.vatican.va/content/john-paul-ii/en/apost_exhortations/documents/hf_jp-ii_exh_19811122_familiaris-consortio.html.

Jones, Robert P., Daniel Cox, Betsy Cooper, and Rachel Lienesch. 2016. *Exodus: Why Americans are Leaving Religion—and Why They're Unlikely to Come Back*. PRRI. https://www.prri.org/wp-content/uploads/2016/09/PRRI-RNS-Unaffiliated-Report.pdf.

Julig, Carina. 2020. "A Young Woman's Suicide Puts Focus on Church's Counseling for LGBT Catholics." *National Catholic Reporter*, February 17. https://www.ncronline.org/news/young-womans-suicide-puts-focus-churchs-counseling-lgbt-catholics.

Jung, Patricia Beattie, and Joseph Andrew Coray, eds. 2001. *Sexual Diversity and Catholicism: Toward the Development of Moral Theology*. Michael Glazier.

Lawler, Michael G. 2005. *What Is and What Ought to Be: The Dialectic of Experience, Theology, and Church*. Continuum.

Lawrence, Ryan E., Maria A. Oquendo, and Barbara Stanley. 2016. "Religion and Suicide Risk: A Systemic Review." *Archive Suicide Research* 20 (1): 1–21. https://pubmed.ncbi.nlm.nih.gov/26192968/.

Lerins, Vincent of. 1846. "Commonitorium Primum." In *Patrologia Latina*, edited by Jacques-Paul Migne, vol. 50, 637–86. Garnier.

LeVay, Simon. 2010. *Gay, Straight, and the Reason Why*. Oxford University Press.

Livingston, Nicholas, Annesa Flentje, James Brennan, Ethan H. Mereish, Oakleigh Reed, and Bryan N. Cochran. 2020. "Real-Time Associations between Discrimination and Anxious and Depressed Mood Among Sexual and Gender Minorities: The Moderating Effects of Lifetime Victimization and Identity Concealment." *Psychology of Sexual Orientation and Gender Diversity* 7 (2): 132–41. https://www.ncbi.nlm.nih.gov/pmc/articles/PMC8132594/.

Malina, Bruce J. 2001. "The New Testament and Homosexuality." In *Sexual Diversity and Catholicism: Toward the Development of Moral Theology*, edited by Patricia Beattie Jung and Joseph Andrew Coray, 150–74. Michael Glazier.

Martin, David. 1997. *Reflections on Sociology and Theology*. Oxford University Press.

Masci, David, and Drew Desilver. 2019. "A Global Snapshot of Same-Sex Marriage." *Pew Research*, October 29, 2019. https://www.pewresearch.org/fact-tank/2019/10/29/global-snapshot-same-sex-marriage.

McCarthy, David Matzko. 2002. "The Relationship of Bodies: A Nuptial Hermeneutics of Same-Sex Unions." In *Theology and Sexuality: Classic and Contemporary Readings*, edited by Eugene F. Rogers, Jr., 200–16. Blackwell Publishing.

McCarthy, Justin. 2019. "U.S. Support for Gay Marriage Stable, at 63%." *Gallup Poll*, May 22, 2019. https://news.gallup.com/poll/257705/support-gay-marriage-stable.aspx.

McElroy, Robert W. 2023. "Cardinal McElroy on 'Radical Inclusion' for L.G.B.T. People, Women and Others in the Catholic Church." *America*, January 24, 2023. https://www.americamagazine.org/faith/2023/01/24/mcelroy-synodality-inclusion-244587.

McKinless, Ashley, and Zac Davis. 2023. "Cardinal McElroy: Sex and Sin Need a New Framework in the Church." *America*, February 3, 2023. https://www.americamagazine.org/faith/2023/02/03/cardinal-mcelroy-inclusion-sexualty-244650.

National Catholic Reporter Staff. 2016. "Statements by US Bishops on Orlando Shooting." *National Catholic Reporter*, June 22, 2016. https://www.ncronline.org/news/spirituality/statements-us-bishops-orlando-shooting.

Newman, John Henry. 1961. *On Consulting the Faithful on Matters of Doctrine*. Sheed and Ward.

Olyan, Saul M. 1994. "'And with a Male You Shall Not Lie the Lying Down of a Woman': On the Meaning and Significance of Leviticus 18:22 and 20:13." *Journal of the History of Sexuality* 5 (2): 179–206. https://www.jstor.org/stable/i284760.

Paul VI, Pope. 1968. *Humanae vitae*. https://www.vatican.va/content/paul-vi/en/encyclicals/documents/hf_p-vi_enc_25071968_humanae-vitae.html.

Pew Forum. 2019. "Attitudes on Same-Sex Marriage." May 14, 2019. https://www.pewresearch.org/religion/fact-sheet/changing-attitudes-on-gay-marriage/.

Pius XII, Pope. 1943. *Divino Afflante Spiritu*, September 30, 1943. https://www.vatican.va/content/pius-xii/en/encyclicals/documents/hf_p-xii_enc_30091943_divino-afflante-spiritu.html.

Pontifical Biblical Commission. 1994. "The Interpretation of the Bible in the Church." January 6, 1994. https://catholic-resources.org/ChurchDocs/PBC_Interp-FullText.htm.

Preves, Sharon E. 2003. *Intersex and Identity: The Contested Self. New Brunswick*, NJ: Rutgers University Press.

PRRI Staff. 2024. "Religious Change in America." *PRRI*, March 27, 2024. https://www.prri.org/research/religious-change-in-america/.

Salzman, Todd A., and Michael G. Lawler. 2008. *The Sexual Person: Toward a Renewed Catholic Anthropology*. Georgetown University Press.

Salzman, Todd A., and Michael G. Lawler. 2025. *Doctrinal Language: A Source of Pain and Trauma in the Catholic Church*. Paulist Press.

Sanders, Cody J. 2020. *Christianity, LGBTQ Suicide, and the Souls of Queer Folk*. Lexington Books.

Scroggs, Robin. 1984. *The New Testament and Homosexuality*. Augsburg Press.

Second Vatican Council. 1964. *Lumen Gentium*. https://www.vatican.va/archive/hist_councils/ii_vatican_council/documents/vat-ii_const_19641121_lumen-gentium_en.html.

Second Vatican Council. 1965a. *Dei Verbum*. https://www.vatican.va/archive/hist_councils/ii_vatican_council/documents/vat-ii_const_19651118_dei-verbum_en.html.

Second Vatican Council. 1965b. *Gaudium et Spes*. https://www.vatican.va/archive/hist_councils/ii_vatican_council/documents/vat-ii_const_19651207_gaudium-et-spes_en.html.

Sparks, Richard. 1996. *Contemporary Christian Morality*. Crossroad.

Trevor Project. 2020. "The Trevor Project Research Brief: Religiosity and Suicidality among LGBTQ Youth." April 2020. https://www.thetrevorproject.org/wp-content/uploads/2021/08/LGBTQ-Youth-and-Religion-Research-Brief-April-2020.pdf.

Trevor Project. 2023a. "2023 U.S. National Survey on the Mental Health of LGBTQ Young People." https://www.thetrevorproject.org/survey-2023/.

Trevor Project. 2023b. "The Trevor Project's Annual U.S. National Survey of LGBTQ Young People Underscores Negative Mental Health Impacts of Anti-LGBTQ Policies & Victimization." *Trevor Project*, May 1, 2023. https://www.prnewswire.com/news-releases/the-trevor-projects-annual-us-national-survey-of-lgbtq-young-people-underscores-negative-mental-health-impacts-of-anti-lgbtq-policies--victimization-301811364.html.

United States Catholic Conference of Catholic Bishops. 2023. *Doctrinal Note on the Moral Limits to Technological Manipulation of the Human Body*, March 20. https://www.usccb.org/resources/Doctrinal%20Note%202023-03-20.pdf.

United States Conference of Catholic Bishops. 1997. *Always Our Children: A Pastoral Message to Parents of Homosexual Children and Suggestions for Pastoral Ministers*.

Washington, DC: USCCB. https://www.usccb.org/resources/Always%20Our%20Children.pdf.

United States Conference of Catholic Bishops. 2019. "Equality Act Letter to Congress." March 20, 2019. http://www.usccb.org/issues-and-action/marriage-and-family/marriage/promotion-and-defense-of-marriage/upload/Equality-Act-Letter-to-Congress-House-1.pdf.

Univision Communications. 2014. *Global Survey of Roman Catholics: Executive Summary.* https://bendixenandamandi.com/wp-content/uploads/2018/06/UNIVISION-Catholic-Poll-Executive-Summary.decryptedKLR.pdf.

Whitehead, Alfred North. 1959. *Symbolism: Its Meaning and Effect.* Putnam's.

Woodhead, Linda. 2013. "New Poll: Faithful Catholics an Endangered Species." *Religion Dispatches*, December 12, 2013. https://religiondispatches.org/new-poll-faithful-catholics-an-endangered-species/.

World Population Review. n.d. https://worldpopulationreview.com/country-rankings/trans-population-by-country.

6

Racial Trauma and Suicide

Toward Healing through Creative Maladjustment

Christina Jones Davis

The Trauma Revolution

When language falls short, some experiences are most intimately known by a distinctive tenor of suffering and residual impact. What was before, is no longer—only that which remains (Rambo 2010). Trauma is often one such experience. Systematic theologian Serene Jones describes trauma as an annihilating violence to the human brain and body setting them on a loop to replay these moments in which you almost were not (Jones 2019, viii). That which follows is often marked by the incredible dilemma of letting in help from outside that could potentially be salvific, but difficult to receive because what is outside has tried to kill you (Jones 2019, ix).

Experiences of trauma are all but novel, but the act of naming and understanding experiences as "trauma" has increased in recent decades. What began in health care settings as giving attention to treating victims of child abuse and wartime survivors led to the recognition of such issues having long-lasting, lingering symptoms known as post-traumatic stress disorder (PTSD). Over the last thirty years, this understanding of PTSD has expanded to apply to civilian, adult, family, organizational, community, and intergenerational experiences of trauma. All trauma—acute and chronic, individual and collective, severe and less so—is acknowledged to be more persistent and pervasive than ever before.

Pivotal to the widespread awareness of trauma was the trauma-informed care initiatives based on the 1998 study sponsored by the Substance Abuse and Mental Health Services Administration (SAMHSA) (Becker and Gatz 2005, 111–12). Launched in twenty-seven sites, it resulted in a set of guidelines calling for providers to be sensitive to traumatic experiences (Dashorst et al. 2019). Soon after that, Harris and Fallot (2001, 3–22) were among the first to coin the phrase "trauma-informed care," which brought about a paradigm shift that encouraged providers to focus on considerations of past experiences of trauma. The shift was well encapsulated by imploring persons in helping roles not to ask, "What is wrong with you?" but to ask, "What happened to you?" Adopting a trauma-informed approach was further legitimized by SAMHSA (2014, 14–4884), when a comprehensive, global statement about trauma-informed practices was published.

In the same year that SAMHSA's trauma-informed practices were published, I was in my inaugural year as a faculty member at a Seminary where I also served as the clinic director of its onsite counseling center. As a licensed marriage and family therapist having just transitioned from working in a large hospital system in the DC area, I was among the helping professionals who had been privy to several seminars and workshops on adopting trauma-informed care practices. In the years that followed, something happened that I and many others likely did not anticipate. The 2012 purchase of Instagram by Facebook and the 2014 advent of the short-form video hosting platform TikTok sent the social media medium for sharing information soaring. In many ways, social media helped to catapult the spread of information on trauma, and references to trauma became part of wider society's commonly used lexicon (Haslam and McGrath 2020). In fact, by December 2023, TikTok's #TraumaTok space had over five billion views (O'Connor et al. 2024). As I write this chapter now in 2025, trauma in general is a mainstream concern.

As references to trauma become ubiquitous, they grow more generalized. While expanding the use of trauma language signaled a destigmatization of mental illness that removed barriers that might keep persons from seeking help, the problem of "concept creep" was also a factor accounting for nuance in reported experiences across a wide demographic (Haslam et al. 2020). This chapter presents the specific ways race in America affects trauma and identifies ways racial trauma contributes to some of the direst of consequences for Black life, namely, death by suicide. Understanding the trauma of Black persons in America, must begin with the forced African diasporic arrival to this land.

Particularizing Trauma

One need not look simply at contemporary examples to fully comprehend how racism impacts psyches today. One must go several years back to understand a phenomenon called intergenerational transmission. The concept of intergenerational transmission simply means that we inherit biological and environmental behaviors, thoughts, and traits from previous generations. For example, I grew up athletic, in part because my father valued athleticism. As a family, we would play basketball, go jogging through the neighborhood, bike, and engage in other recreational activities on a regular basis. Others may be musically inclined, or bilingual, or even good at gardening, depending on the interests and activities of parents and caregivers. Alternatively, those who struggle to stay in tune were likely not descended from musically inclined forebears.

While the examples I offer may more readily be considered environmentally learned, they may at the same time include biological transmissions that one cannot see. In what ways might I have inherited a genetically influenced capacity for athleticism, or others who are musically inclined inherited an "ear" that aids in their exceptionalism? In the case of intergenerational transmission of trauma, it has been discovered that some learnings get embedded into our very bodies. Epigenetics is the study of how genes are impacted in offspring for generations to come by the experiences of previous generations. For example, descendants of Holocaust survivors display an increased vulnerability to developing psychological disturbances in direct relationship to the negative life experience of the previous generation (Dashorst et al. 2019, 25). Likewise, descendants of Native Americans with shared historical trauma, including boarding schools, massacres, and forced violent removal from their tribal land, experience symptoms of depression, substance dependence, and diabetes (Brown-Rice 2013). And, yes, chattel enslavement of Africans in the United States and sustained collective traumas contribute to making Black people highly vulnerable to developing mental health disorders as well (Mental Health America, n.d.).

It has been just over 400 years since the first shipment of Africans to a British-claimed North American colony. In her book *Post Traumatic Slave Syndrome: America's Legacy of Enduring Injury and Healing*, Joy DeGruy notes that after 265 years of chattel slavery, there were no mass therapeutic or care interventions of any kind. Instead, the traumas of slavery were followed by more trauma under Jim and Jane Crow (DeGruy 2005). It was during Jim and Jane Crow when Black Psychology began to investigate internalized trauma's impact on children in 1947. Kenneth Clark, considered the father of Black Psychology, in collaboration with his wife, Mamie Phipps-Clark, coauthored the famous "doll test" study that investigated identity formation in children and influenced the Brown vs.

Board of Education decision (Clark and Clark 1947). Some sixty-three years later, Anderson Cooper hosted a CNN special showcasing this study having been replicated in 2010. The results of the study were remarkably similar for kids ranging in age from preschool through elementary school (a mean age of five), associating white-skinned dolls with positive characteristics and brown-skinned dolls with negative characteristics (Killen 2012). With intergenerational transmission in mind, these results are not surprising, although they remain deeply telling and troubling in revealing how intergenerational transmission affects us at such a young age.

Concern for youth motivated Beverly Tatum, author of *Why Are All the Black Kids Sitting Together in the Cafeteria*, to try and understand the psychology of racism as displayed in children. She found that racial and ethnic socialization involve the transmission of information regarding race and ethnicity as transferred to children from adults early on (Hughes et al. 2006). She also found that children as young as aged three notice physical differences such as skin color, hair texture, and facial features (Tatum 2003). Perhaps most alarmingly, however, was that attitudes and beliefs toward such differences are simultaneously learned through family, friends, and the media. Furthermore, there is an enormous dissonance that occurs between what is culturally learned, and what some adults consider too taboo to openly discuss with children about race.

We now understand more about how genetics, environmental and social conditions affect the psyche. If the field of psychology was not aware of societal impacts on mental health before September 1, 1967, Dr. Martin Luther King, Jr.—just seven months prior to his assassination—addressed the some of the nation's leading social scientists at a meeting of the American Psychological Association concerning the role of behavioral scientists in the civil rights movement. Even then, his pleas included a need to help a society "poisoned to its soul by racism."

> If the Negro needs social sciences for direction and for self-understanding, the white society is in even more urgent need. White America needs to understand that it is poisoned to its soul by racism and the understanding needs to be carefully documented and consequently more difficult to reject. The present crisis arises because although it is historically imperative that our society take the next step to equality, we find ourselves psychologically and socially imprisoned. All too many white Americans are horrified not with conditions of Negro life but with the product of these conditions-the Negro himself. When the majority of the country could not live with the extremes of brutality they witnessed, political remedies were enacted, and customs were altered. (King 1968)

As a relational-systemic therapist and practical theologian, I echo King's emphasis on social change needed for healing and hope for a day when the majority of the country cannot live with the brutality witnessed in ways that bring about political and cultural change. Nevertheless, witnessing brutality continues.

Black Trauma Broadcasted

According to an article in *The Lancet* medical journal, more than 30,000 people were killed by police between 1980 and 2019 (Lancet 2021). This same article spoke to the mounting evidence showing that deaths at the hands of the police disproportionately impact people of certain races and ethnicities, pointing to systemic racism in policing. Police violence fatalities in the United States disproportionately affect Black, Indigenous, and Hispanic populations (Edwards, Lee, and Esposito 2019, 16793). Recent studies show that over the life span, about one in every 1,000 Black men are killed by the police in the United States, causing them to be two and a half times more likely to be killed by police than white men (Edwards, Lee, and Esposito 2019, 16794). Black women are about one and a half times more likely to be killed by police than are white women (Edwards, Lee, and Esposito 2019, 16794).

While disparities around police violence are not new, a key difference in the late 2010s was the widespread broadcasting of these events for the world to see. What we saw coinciding with proliferation of trauma-informed practices in the 2010s and years that followed were high profile killings of black and brown bodies flooding the media and, subsequently, the consciousness of a nation. Videos of Eric Garner pleading to breathe while being choked by police, videos of Walter Scott being fatally shot in the back while fleeing police, audio of young Trayvon Martin's screams while being pursued and attacked by a vigilante walking home from the corner store, and George Floyd calling for his mother while an officer held a knee to his neck for 9 minutes and 29 seconds. The at-your-fingertip access to video footage on smartphones, and the capacity for videos to be shared, and subsequently "go viral," meant we could all witness these events up-close—repeatedly.

Not only was video footage of the traumatic event ubiquitous, but there was also the aftermath that followed, starting with the debates around what meaning the world was to make of these events and lives lost. There were the protests that followed that, at times, also involved violence or the threat of force on the part of law enforcement. In the end, there were verdicts that all too often did not produce a salve for psychic wounds but rather reinforced the need for the rallying cry "Black Lives Matter" in the face of a world that signaled otherwise.

I was witnessing and experiencing these times in America on multiple levels. Professionally in my work as a clinician I was treating more and more Black clients who were symptomatic and reporting heightened stress, grief, anger, and anxiety in response to what they were witnessing. Simultaneously, my students were asking questions about the capacity for mental health care treatments to effectively treat people of color for whom their struggles were born out of resistance to, or failed ability to cope with, racism and all its implications. They wanted to understand how to effectively diagnose and treat racism.

Personally, I wanted to make meaning of my experience so that I could care for myself. I too was experiencing the impact of all that was happening. The emotionality was extraordinarily high and utterly exhausting. At times I found myself needing to withdraw from social media and the news. Not because I did not care, but because I *did* care and felt helpless and overwhelmed from caring. The persistent grief, the profound anger, the haunting fear for my safety and the safety of loved ones who look like me, the irritability was taking a toll on me. As you may notice, what I just described were several embodied experiences. I became even more curious about them by hearing these experiences echoed by so many others. What we were experiencing reflected features of collective racialized trauma.

Kenneth Hardy, marriage and family therapist and scholar, talks about invisible trauma wounds of internalized devaluation, internalized voicelessness, and rage and how important it is to externalize these ills (Hardy 2023). And yet, many were saturated by these realities. For the sake of my students, clients, and community, I was intent upon identifying ways psychology could help us understand and voice the impact of these events on the mind, body and spirit. I endeavored to research this phenomenon, identify tools, and share as much as I could via talks, trainings, and lectures. Many of these insights I will recount and build upon within this chapter.

Now that I have attempted to outline the socio-historical milieu of Black trauma, I will turn my attention to seeking to clearly define it. As a womanist theologian, I am always concerned with intersections. Just as we know that as we talk about psyches and minds we are also talking about bodies and souls, in the same way, we cannot talk about race without acknowledging that race does not exist outside of the influences of class, gender, sexuality, and other identities. All these experiences are interconnected, and while my emphasis will be on race, these other realities are present and matter.

So what is racialized trauma and how is it defined? To help us understand its origin, let us begin with the *DSM-5*, or the *Diagnostic Statistical Manual* edition 5. The *DSM-5* serves as a guide for mental health professionals to categorize sets of symptoms and give them names. The *DSM-5* lists five criteria necessary for post-traumatic stress disorder. I will accompany each criterion with an example to illustrate how these criteria relate to features of racial trauma.

- Criterion one is exposure to death, threatened death, or actual or threatened serious injury (American Psychiatric Association 2013). This can be by direct exposure, witnessing the trauma, or learning that a relative or close friend was exposed to a trauma (APA 2013). This criterion is illustrated in President Obama's response to the Trayvon Martin murder in 2012, after which he said Michelle and I do not have a son, but if we did he might look a lot like Trayvon. He then went on to share about his experiences of being profiled when shopping in stores as to say I identify closely with Trayvon. In fact, identification with this victim of violence was palpable within larger communities. The proclamation "I am Trayvon Martin" was more than a tagline, it affirmed the notion of Ubuntu theology that states that what happens to one happens to us all because our humanity is bound up together (Battle 2000, 181).
- Criterion two describes the traumatic event as persistently re-experienced (Battle 2000, 173–82). We can trace state sanctioned violence against Black people for centuries, but Black people are still Resmaa 2.5 times more likely to be killed by police than White people today (Smith and Hawkins 2011, 149–62). As has been described, the recent rise of visibility of these events has exponentially increased the awareness of their persistence and access to reexperiences.
- Criterion three is avoidance of trauma-related thoughts or feelings, and trauma-related reminders (Smith and Hawkins 2011). This criterion relates to wanting to turn off T.V. and social media. It may also relate to experiences of a person feeling nervous or afraid if they see a police car behind them. The way one's heart may begin to race. The physiological reaction to the police car is likely not about a cognitive belief that all police are dangerous, as much as it is about trauma-related triggers and reminders.

- Criterion four is negative thoughts or feelings after the trauma, including overly negative thoughts about oneself or the world, exaggerated blame of self or others for causing the trauma, decreased interest in activities, feeling isolated, and difficulty experiencing positive mood (Smith and Hawkins 2011). For many impacted by racial trauma, it may seem as though each time one's mood begins to stabilize a bit, one could turn on the television to discover another violent act and negative thoughts and assumptions about the world come rushing back. Some features within these criteria can look like depression, but as mentioned, trauma-informed care asks the question not what is wrong with a person who is responding this way but "what happened to them."
- Within criterion five, two of the following symptoms are required. Trauma-related reactions that began or worsened after the trauma, such as: irritability or aggression, hypervigilance, heightened startle reaction, difficulty concentrating, difficulty sleeping (Smith and Hawkins 2011). These symptoms were all too familiar within my community. The majority of my Black clients, family, and friends reported feeling irritable after witnessing trauma, having difficulty concentrating, and feeling hypervigilant—there was a shared, collective traumatic experience.

In an attempt to capture how racism and discrimination negatively impacts the physical and mental health of people of color, scholars have coined the term "racial trauma" or "race-based traumatic stress" as a more particularized alternative to PTSD (Comas-Díaz, Hall, and Helen A. Neville 2019, 1). This new language gave a name to contextual experience that the cumulative, pervasive, and deleterious effects of persistent exposure to race-based stress wherein adaptations to this environmental threat develop over time (Polanco-Roman et al. 2021). A study found that adults who were the targets of racism experienced anxiety, depression, decreased life satisfaction, and psychiatric symptoms (Pieterse et al. 2012). Another study found that racial trauma may result from racial harassment, witnessing racial violence, or experiencing institutional racism (Comas-Díaz 2016). Racial trauma may result in experiencing symptoms of depression, anxiety, low self-esteem, feelings of humiliation, poor concentration, or irritability.

Not only did research find that racial discrimination and harassment induced trauma, but the adjustments and coping strategies used to mitigate these effects and maintain safety often undermine the arousal system and regulatory processes to render the individual more vulnerable to future stressors (Polanco-Roman et al. 2021). This supports the framework of Complex PTSD that indicates developmental consequences from cumulative stress and trauma exposure (Cloitre et al. 2009). Mounting research and longitudinal studies of consequences of racial discrimination suggests that increased exposure over time is associated with poorer health outcomes in adulthood and could be a factor to suicide-related risks (Cave et al. 2020). As one can see, racial trauma has many deleterious effects. At times, living with these effects may overextend one's capacity to cope or access to resources. When this happens, options can be few and hope can grow dim, making way for one of the direst of consequences of racism, namely, suicide.

Racial Trauma and Suicidality

Suicidality affects millions in the United States each year (U.S. Substance Abuse and Mental Health Services Administration 2021 and 2022). While a pervasive issue, suicidality often impacts BIPOC communities disproportionately (U.S. Department of Health and Human Services 2025). Among the shifts in language around racial trauma, and social media facilitated trauma-sharing, Black communities have experienced significant increases in deaths by suicide in the last few decades. Namely, deaths by suicide among Black female youth increased 182 percent between 2001 and 2017 and Black male teens saw a 60 percent increase in suicide (Al-Mateen and Rogers 2018). More recently, suicide rates grew by 19.2 percent between 2018 and 2021 and most significantly escalated by 36.6 percent among Black people ages 10–24 (Stone, Mack, and Qualters 2023).

More research is needed to understand just how much upwards trends in suicidality interfaces with the trauma broadcasting surge beginning in the 2010s. What is certain is that these statistics point to the need to closely examine the conditions which influence such increasingly poor outcomes. As we have discussed, intergenerational traumas related to slavery impact the minds and bodies of their descendants today (Kendi 2019). Additionally, contemporary contextual conditions contribute to risk factors for suicidality, including limited access to social supports, pervasive lack of control in life, and feeling trapped (Jewett et al. 2024).

One startling death by suicide that received national attention was that of a beloved Black university administrator, Antoinette Candia-Bailey, who was Vice

President of Student Affairs at Lincoln University. Candia-Bailey was found dead by suicide on January 8, 2024, at age forty-nine. This occurred after having documented her mental health concerns to Lincoln University's first white president, John Moseley. While there are multiple factors that lead to suicide, Candia-Bailey's death spurred conversations around experiences of race-based work stressors of Black employees in academic settings. For example, research has long established that faculty of color receive the lowest scores on student evaluations due to gender and race bias (Smith and Hawkins 2011). This bias, together with the finding that teaching evaluations do not measure teaching effectiveness, continues to impact Black faculty in tenure and promotion portfolios (Uttl, White, and Gonzalez 2017). Faculty of color seeking tenure are already underrepresented, making up fewer that 13 percent of full-time faculty (U.S. Department of Education 2023). How might these contextual factors of Candia-Bailey's professional experiences have contributed to her difficulties? The news of Candia-Bailey's death struck a chord with many Black faculty and administrators around the country, bringing attention to this important question.

Though there is a confluence of factors involved in death by suicide for BIPOC persons, it is worth exploring how racial trauma may contribute. This is especially true when we consider how common race-based stressors and racial trauma are for people of color. Epidemiological studies have shown a direct association between racial discrimination and suicidal ideation and attempts across minoritized adults in the United States (Perez-Rodriguez et al. 2014). Similar connections have been found with Black adolescents (Assari et al. 2017). Additionally, ongoing racial stressors in addition to acute experiences can cause racial trauma with symptoms that persist with longitudinal findings further supporting associations between racial and ethnic discrimination and suicidal ideation and attempts among minoritized racial and ethnic groups of adults (Polanco-Roman et al. 2021).

In one meta-analysis of literature regarding associations of racial discrimination with suicidal ideation (SI) and suicide attempt (SA), forty-three articles that investigated the matter found that racial discrimination has a small but significant effect on both SI and SA (Coimbra et al. 2022). As a theologian and mental health clinician, it is incumbent upon our professions to call upon all the wisdom our fields offer in response to this critical concern. If individuals at the brunt end of systemic racism develop more suicidal thoughts, and have an increased likelihood of attempting suicide, prevention and intervention are key.

Pathways to Healing

In what follows, I explore three pathways to address the issue of racial trauma and suicidality. The first strategy focuses on prevention. Kenneth Hardy, marriage and family therapist and culturally responsive therapy scholar, talks about the invisible wounds of racial trauma as internalized devaluation, internalized voicelessness, and rage (Hardy 2023). When something is nameless, it not only increases doubt and uncertainty but limits agency. By naming experiences of racial trauma, we gift individuals with the choice to speak to their experiences, recognize the impact on them, and externalize them. It is often said that we are only as sick as our secrets, and we now know that the body keeps the score of repressed traumatic events unless we externalize them (Van der Kolk 2014).

When a person shares experiences of racial trauma and is met with acknowledgment, there is healing in the act of sharing as well as the opportunity to explore their options and access agency. This means clinicians, clergy, and those who wish to help must create space for dialog and racial storytelling and participate in validation of experiences of racial trauma. Validation works to combat the force of devaluation and externalize it as not of one's own making.

In addition to verbally externalizing experiences of racial trauma, it is important to do embodied healing work as well. Author and therapist Resmaa Menakem, in his book *My Grandmother's Hands: Racialized Trauma and the Pathway to Mending Our Hearts and Bodies*, implores us to understand that racial trauma is not only cognitive, but also bodily. To heal, it is imperative that we take the stress of racialized trauma seriously. After his death, Martin Luther King Jr.'s autopsy found that while he was just thirty-nine years old, he had the heart of a sixty-year old (Bagwell and Walker 2004). Doctors concluded that the pressure he had experienced in his career had stressed and aged his heart. Here again, the body keeps the score of trauma exposure.

According to Menakem, while cognitive and/or behavioral insights help you heal, they are not the only way healing works. Recent studies and discoveries increasingly point out that we heal through the body, not just through the rational brain. Trauma therapies have become increasing aware of the fight, flight, freeze, or fawn mechanisms in the reptilian brain that take over while being threatened, whether perceived or real. When this happens, the rational brain is off-line. This survival reaction is something that we all have, and we can learn to slow this process down, which is particularly healing when not in real danger.

Healing from this racial trauma does not merely happen in our head. It happens in our body. Internalized racial trauma can be mitigated through body centered practices done as individual practices as well as in community. Menakem offers five key anchors for the body as we attend to our own racial trauma transmissions.

The five anchors for healing racial trauma include one's ability to (1) learn to self soothe, (2) learn to simply notice the sensations instead of reacting to them, (3) learn to accept the discomfort, (4) develop the capacity to stay present, and (5) learn to safely discharge any energy that remains. Safely discharging energy may be through cathartic movements, cleansing breaths, exercise, talking with trusted others, cathartic dancing, drumming, worship, yoga, or journaling. Engaging in these practices along with others outlined in Menakem's book may help metabolize trauma and open pathways to healing.

Finally, a tool that is especially useful in clinical settings is the Individual-in-Contexts Model (ICM) that seeks to address limitations of other psychological and public health approaches to account for systemic forces in suicide screening, assessment and intervention (Hightower and Grant 2024, 149–68). This framework uses critical suicide studies to illuminate the relationship among people, identity, and environments in socially unjust contexts to understand connections between social injustices and suicidality (Hightower and Grant 2024).

Multiple contexts have contributed to historical trauma, eco-racism, global eco-migration crises among Black peoples, racialized public policies, resource-deprived communities, violent interpersonal relationships, and suicide-vulnerable individuals (Kendi 2019). From this perspective, the term "suicide"—and the common narratives about its meanings, causes, and implications—must be critically re-interrogated and reimagined to decrease suffering, improve lives, and prevent suicides that can be prevented (Hightower and Grant 2024). The ICM integrates the factors most likely to impact minoritized groups, like Black communities, and provides a more holistic screening, assessment, and intervention tool. This contextualizing framework, and those like it, are essential to addressing suicidality in minoritized demographics.

Healing as Mal-adaption

In closing, I hope I have helped give a name to experiences of racial trauma, and how they are transmitted and persist in bodies, communities, and reified through systems. I have sought to show how the coming together of trauma awareness through the social media revolution created a proliferation of exposure to Black traumatic events. I have also endeavored to connect the ways racial trauma contributes to suicidal ideation and have identified pathways to healing which include externalization, embodied trauma metabolizing, and the ICM as a framework that accounts for the impact of systemic racism when screening, assessing, and intervening for suicidality in Black communities.

In response to the problem of racial trauma and suicide among BIPOC persons, I have implored, particularly persons of color, to adopt intentional practices of care for self and others and reminded us that we must not stop short of engaging the body as a source of healing. While race is a social construction, it has real lived consequences and is perhaps one of the most powerful myths of all time. But also, because race was socially created, we have the capacity to create something different. Each step we can take with healing our trauma is a way of preventing its transmission and healing our communities for generations to come.

I already shared a portion of Dr. Martin Luther King Jr.'s remarks to the American Psychological Association (APA). Now, his final words to the APA are an appropriate charge with which to conclude:

> Every academic discipline has its technical nomenclature. You who are in the field of psychology have given us a great word. It is the word maladjusted. This word is probably used more than any other word in psychology. It is a good word; certainly, it is good that in dealing with what the word implies you are declaring that destructive maladjustment should be destroyed. You are saying that all must seek the well-adjusted life in order to avoid neurotic and schizophrenic personalities. But on the other hand, I am sure that we will recognize that there are some things in our society, some things in our world, to which we should never be adjusted. There are some things concerning which we must always be maladjusted if we are to be people of good will. We must never adjust ourselves to racial discrimination and racial segregation. We must never adjust ourselves to religious bigotry. We must never adjust ourselves to economic conditions that take necessities from the many to give luxuries to the few. We must never adjust ourselves to the madness of militarism, and the self-defeating effects of physical violence. Thus, it may well be that our world is in dire need of a new organization, The International Association for the Advancement of Creative Maladjustment. Through such creative maladjustment, we may be able to emerge from the bleak and desolate midnight of man's inhumanity to man, into the bright and glittering daybreak of freedom and justice. (King 1968)

May we not lose hope.

Bibliography

Al-Mateen, Cheryl, and Kenneth Rogers. 2018. "Suicide Among African-American and Other African-Origin Youth." In *Suicide Among Diverse Youth: A Case-Based Guidebook*, edited by Andres J. Pumariega and Neha Sharma, 32–49. Springer Nature.

American Psychiatric Association. 2013. *Desk Reference to the Diagnostic Criteria from DSM-5-TR*. American Psychiatric Association Publishing.

Assari, Shervin, Ehsan Moazen-Zadeh, Cleopatra Howard Caldwell, and Marc A. Zimmerman. 2017. "Racial Discrimination During Adolescence Predicts Mental Health Deterioration in Adulthood: Gender Differences among Blacks." *Frontiers in Public Health* 5 (May). https://doi.org/10.3389/fpubh.2017.00104.

Bagwell, Orlando, and W. Noland Walker, dirs. 2004. *American Experience*. "Citizen King." Aired January 19, 2004, on PBS. https://www.pbs.org/wgbh/americanexperience/films/mlk/.

Battle, Michael. 2000. "A Theology of Community: The Ubuntu Theology of Desmond Tutu." *Interpretation: Journal of Bible and Theology* 54 (2): 173–82. https://doi.org/10.1177/002096430005400206.

Becker, Marion A., and Margaret Gatz. 2005. "Introduction to the Impact of Co-occurring Disorders and Violence on Women: Findings from the SAMHSA Women, Co-occurring Disorders and Violence Study." *The Journal of Behavioral Health Services & Research* 32 (2): 111–12. https://doi.org/10.1007/bf02287260.

Brown-Rice, Kathleen. 2013. "Examining the Theory of Historical Trauma Among Native Americans." *The Professional Counselor* 3 (December): 117–30. http://dx.doi.org/10.15241/kbr.3.3.117.

Cave, Leah, Matthew N. Cooper, Stephen R. Zubrick, and Carrington C. J. Shepherd. 2020. "Racial Discrimination and Child and Adolescent Health in Longitudinal Studies: A Systematic Review." *Social Science & Medicine* 250 (February): 112864. https://doi.org/10.1016/j.socscimed.2020.112864.

Clark, Kenneth B., and Mamie P. Clark. 1947. "Racial Identification and Preference Among Negro Children." In *Readings in Social Psychology*, edited by Theodore M. Newcomb and Eugene L. Hartley, 169–78. Holt, Rinehart, and Winston.

Cloitre, Marylene, Bradley C. Stolbach, Judith L. Herman, Bessel Van Der Kolk, Robert Pynoos, Jing Wang, and Eva Petkova. 2009. "A Developmental Approach to Complex PTSD: Childhood and Adult Cumulative Trauma as Predictors of Symptom Complexity." *Journal of Traumatic Stress* 22 (5): 399–408. https://doi.org/10.1002/jts.20444.

Coimbra, Bruno Messina, Chris Maria Hoeboer, Jutka Yik, Andrea Feijo Mello, Marcelo Feijo Mello, and Miranda Olff. 2022. "Meta-analysis of the Effect of Racial

Discrimination on Suicidality." *SSM—Population Health* 20 (November): 101283. https://doi.org/10.1016/j.ssmph.2022.101283.

Comas-Díaz, Lillian. 2016. "Racial Trauma Recovery: A Race-informed Therapeutic Approach to Racial Wounds." In *The Cost of Racism for People of Color: Contextualizing Experiences of Discrimination*, edited by A. N. Alvarez, C. T. H. Liang, and H. A. Neville. American Psychological Association. https://doi.org/10.1037/14852-012.

Comas-Díaz, Lillian, Gordon Nagayama Hall, and Helen A. Neville. 2019. "Racial Trauma: Theory, Research, and Healing: Introduction to the Special Issue." *American Psychologist* 74 (1): 1–5. https://doi.org/10.1037/amp0000442.

Dashorst, Patricia, Trudy M. Mooren, Rolf J. Kleber, Peter J. De Jong, and Rafaele J. C. Huntjens. 2019. "Intergenerational Consequences of the Holocaust on Offspring Mental Health: A Systematic Review of Associated Factors and Mechanisms." *European Journal of Psychotraumatology* 10 (1). https://doi.org/10.1080/20008198.2019.1654065.

DeGruy, Joy. 2005. *Post Traumatic Slave Syndrome: America's Legacy of Enduring Injury and Healing*. Uptone Press.

Edwards, Frank, Hedwig Lee, and Michael Esposito. 2019. "Risk of Being Killed by Police Use of Force in the United States by Age, Race-ethnicity, and Sex." *Proceedings of the National Academy of Sciences USA* 116 (34): 16793–8. https://doi.org/10.1073/pnas.1821204116.

Hardy, Kenneth V. 2023. *Racial Trauma: Clinical Strategies and Techniques for Healing Invisible Wounds*. W. W. Norton & Company.

Harris, Maxine, and Roger D. Fallot. 2001. "Envisioning a Trauma-informed Service System: A Vital Paradigm Shift." *New Directions for Mental Health Services* 89: 3–22. https://doi.org/10.1002/yd.23320018903.

Haslam, Nick, Brodie C. Dakin, Fabian Fabiano, Melanie J. McGrath, Joshua Rhee, Ekaterina Vylomova, Morgan Weaving, and Melissa A. Wheeler. 2020. "Harm Inflation: Making Sense of Concept Creep." *European Review of Social Psychology* 31 (1): 254–86. https://doi.org/10.1080/10463283.2020.1796080.

Haslam, Nick, and Melanie J. McGrath. 2020. "The Creeping Concept of Trauma." *Social Research* 87 (3): 509–31. https://doi.org/10.1353/sor.2020.0052.

Hightower, Heath, and Morgan Grant. 2024. "Proposing an Individual-in-Contexts Model for Reimagining Suicide Screening, Assessment, and Intervention in Black Communities." *Journal of Human Services* 43 (1): 149–68. https://doi.org/10.52678/001c.124420.

Hughes, Diane, James Rodriguez, Emilie P. Smith, Deborah J. Johnson, Howard C. Stevenson, and Paul Spicer. 2006. "Parents' Ethnic-racial Socialization Practices: A Review of Research and Directions for Future Study." *Developmental Psychology* 42 (5): 747–70. https://doi.org/10.1037/0012-1649.42.5.747.

Jewett, Patricia I., Lindsay A. Taliaferro, Iris W. Borowsky, Michelle A. Mathiason, and Eunice M. Areba. 2024. "Structural Adverse Childhood Experiences Associated with Suicidal Ideation, Suicide Attempts, and Repetitive Nonsuicidal Self-injury Among Racially and Ethnically Minoritized Youth." *Suicide and Life-Threatening Behavior* 55 (1). https://doi.org/10.1111/sltb.13084.

Jones, Serene. 2019. *Trauma and Grace: Theology in a Ruptured World.* 2nd ed. Westminster John Knox Press.

Kendi, Ibram X. 2019. *How to Be an Antiracist.* 1st ed. One World.

Killen, Melanie. 2012. "Kids on Race: The Hidden Picture." *CNN Anderson Cooper 360° Special Report.* https://i2.cdn.turner.com/cnn/2012/images/03/29/ac360.race.study.pdf.

King Jr., Martin Luther. 1968. "The Role of the Behavioral Scientist in the Civil Rights Movement." *Journal of Social Issues* 24 (1): 1–12.

Lancet, The. 2021. "Fatal Police Violence by Race and State in the USA, 1980–2019: A Network Meta Regression." 398 (10307): 1239–55. https://doi.org/10.1016/s0140-6736(21)01609-3.

Menakem, Resmaa. 2017. *My Grandmother's Hands: Racialized Trauma and the Pathway to Mending Our Hearts and Bodies.* Central Recovery Press.

Mental Health America. n.d. "Racial Trauma." Accessed March 3, 2025. https://mhanational.org/resources/racial-trauma/.

O'Connor, Cliodhna, Giulia Brown, Julienne Debono, Lauren Suty, and Helene Joffe. 2024. "How Trauma is Represented on Social Media: Analysis of #Trauma Content on TikTok." *Psychological Trauma: Theory, Research, Practice, and Policy*, September. https://doi.org/10.1037/tra0001792.

Perez-Rodriguez, M. Mercedes, Enrique Baca-Garcia, Maria A. Oquendo, Shuai Wang, Melanie M. Wall, Shang-Min Liu, and Carlos Blanco. 2014. "Relationship Between Acculturation, Discrimination, and Suicidal Ideation and Attempts Among US Hispanics in the National Epidemiologic Survey of Alcohol and Related Conditions." *Journal of Clinical Psychiatry* 75 (4): 399–407. https://doi.org/10.4088/JCP.13m08548.

Pieterse, Alex L., Nathan R. Todd, Helen A. Neville, and Robert T. Carter. 2012. "Perceived Racism and Mental Health Among Black American Adults: A Meta-analytic Review." *Journal of Counseling Psychology* 59 (1): 1–9. https://doi.org/10.1037/a0026208.

Polanco-Roman, Lillian, Regina Miranda, Denise Hien, and Deidre M. Anglin. 2021. "Racial/Ethnic Discrimination as Race-based Trauma and Suicide-related Risk in Racial/Ethnic Minority Young Adults: The Explanatory Roles of Stress Sensitivity and Dissociation." *Psychological Trauma Theory Research Practice and Policy* 13 (7): 759–67. https://doi.org/10.1037/tra0001076.

Rambo, Shelly. 2010. *Spirit and Trauma: A Theology of Remaining.* Westminster John Knox Press.

Smith, Bettye P., and Billy Hawkins. 2011. "Examining Student Evaluations of Black College Faculty: Does Race Matter?" *The Journal of Negro Education* 80 (2): 149–62. http://www.jstor.org/stable/resrep54170.

Stone, Deborah M., Karin A. Mack, and Judith Qualters. 2023. "Notes from the Field: Recent Changes in Suicide Rates by Race and Ethnicity and Age Group–United States, 2021." *Morbidity and Mortality Weekly Report* 72 (6): 160–2. https://doi.org/10.15585/mmwr.mm7206a4.

Tatum, Beverly Daniel. 2003. *Why Are All the Black Kids Sitting Together in the Cafeteria?: And Other Conversations about Race*. Basic Books.

U.S. Department of Education, National Center for Education Statistics. 2023. "Digest of Education Statistics: Integrated Postsecondary Education Data System (IPEDS)." Accessed March 27, 2025. https://nces.ed.gov/programs/digest/2023menu_tables.asp.

U.S. Department of Health and Human Services (HHS), Office of Minority Health. 2025. "Mental and Behavioral Health: Black/African Americans." Accessed March 27, 2025. https://minorityhealth.hhs.gov/mental-and-behavioral-health-blackafrican-americans.

U.S. Substance Abuse and Mental Health Services Administration. 2014. "SAMHSA's Concept of Trauma and Guidance for a Trauma-Informed Approach." U.S. Department of Health and Human Services 14–4884.

U.S. Substance Abuse and Mental Health Services Administration, Center for Behavioral Health Statistics and Quality. 2021 and 2022. "National Survey on Drug Use and Health." Accessed March 27, 2025. https://www.samhsa.gov/data/sites/default/files/reports/rpt42728/NSDUHDetailedTabs2022/NSDUHDetailedTabs2022/NSDUHDetTabsSect6pe2022.htm#tab6.68b.

Uttl, Bob, Carmela A. White, and Daniela Wong Gonzalez. 2017. "Meta-analysis of Faculty's Teaching Effectiveness: Student Evaluation of Teaching Ratings and Student Learning Are Not Related." *Studies in Educational Evaluation* 54 (September): 22–42. https://doi.org/10.1016/j.stueduc.2016.08.007.

Van der Kolk, B. A. 2014. *The Body Keeps the Score: Brain, Mind, and Body in the Healing of Trauma*. Viking.

7

A Laying on of Hands

Confronting Black Women's Suicidality through the Healing Dimensions of Ritual

LaRyssa D. Herrington

It should go without saying that being a Black woman *is hard*, as is living with mental illness. But to place these two realities side by side, *to be a Black woman living with mental illness*, appears paradoxical from the standpoint of researchers in the fields of psychology and public health. Current trends focused on the prevalence of suicidality among US Black populations over the last several decades have come to identify this problem as "the black-white suicide paradox," whereby the age-adjusted rates of suicide among US Blacks are purportedly less than half those of whites despite both groups possessing similar risk factors (Rockett, Samora, and Coben 2006). The conundrum of Black suicide is so pronounced that even Black women (as a research demographic) have been deemed a "suicide paradox," the "paradox" being that Black women are supposedly more immune to the impact of suicide than the rest of the general population for reasons researchers have identified as follows: Black women maintain strong ties to spirituality and religious institutions which "protect" them from suicide; they have developed a specific set of survival skills and level of cultural and social resilience that aids in their ability to persevere due to their historic experiences with racism and oppression; and finally, Black women are highly respected within and among their communities, their clear commitments and responsibilities to these communities making suicide an unviable option for coping with one's pain and suffering (Spates and Slatton 2017).

Columnist Kali Holloway asserts that such oversights and oversimplifications are dangerous, having led to the belief that "suicide is correlated with whiteness, negatively correlated with Blackness, and irrelevant to Black femaleness . . .

[with] Black women's purported immunity to suicide [having] been regarded as . . . an open-and-shut case." Despite the lack of nuance within the research which takes seriously the social phenomenon of intersectionality and its impact on suicidality, Holloway notes that between 2001 and 2017 suicide deaths among Black girls aged 13–19 rose 182 percent, whereas the two decades between 1999 and 2019 saw death by suicide among Black women aged 25–44 increase by 27 percent (Holloway 2023).

Holloway further notes that, although numerically trailing their Black male peers, death by suicide among Black female adolescents aged 15–17 increased by 6.6 percent or twice the rate among Black boys every year between 2003 and 2017. The years between 2003 and 2019 also saw a nearly 60 percent increase in deaths for women aged 15–24 (Holloway 2023). The statistics concerning Black Trans youth and adults are even more alarming. Citing a 2015 survey, the National Black Justice Coalition found that nearly half (or about 49 percent) of all Black Trans respondents reported having attempted suicide. Additionally, respondents reported having feelings of extreme isolation and experiences of violence which often coexist within the matrix of anti-Black racism, misogyny, homophobia and transphobia, poverty, and patriarchy (Henery 2018).

The following has kept countless Black women silent about the reality of mental health and chronic suicidality. It is why in 2022, when news of death by suicide of Miss USA Cheslie Kryst (an accomplished lawyer, TV personality, and model) at the age of thirty after jumping from her 60-story high-rise Manhattan apartment was announced, though heartbroken, I felt an unusual sense of relief; with her death came a level of visibility about the challenges of living with mental illness as a successful, "high-functioning" Black woman. *Oh my God*, I thought. *You mean I'm not the only Black woman who secretly feels this way?* Intrusive thoughts of overdosing on antidepressant medications, leaping from bridges, balconies, and windows, or intentionally crashing my car were forbidden from ever being spoken. Kryst's death is not the only high profile death by suicide to have ever taken the life of a Black woman, her suicide having eerie parallels to the 1996 death of Black German activist, educator, public intellectual, and poet May Ayim who also jumped from her Berlin-Kreuzberg high-rise apartment building which resulted in her untimely death at the age of thirty-six (Florvil 2017).

The notion of a "suicide paradox"—that Black people simply do not ever contemplate let alone die by suicide—only makes sense when understood within the historic realities of medicalized racism and what scholars have come to call *misogynoir*—a term coined by scholar Moya Baily to describe the reality of anti-Black racist misogyny that compounds Black women's experience of oppression and marginalization (Bailey and Trudy 2018)—which, in turn, negatively impacts their physical, mental, spiritual, and emotional health and well-being. In fact, it would be impossible to discuss Black women's suicidality without talking about the trauma of misogynoir, or the racist cultural myths surrounding Black women that have perpetuated the belief that Black women are somehow immune to suffering and pain. Developmental psychologist Pamela Trotman Reid notes:

> There exist at least two myths of African American women; they are either "good" or "bad." The "good" African American woman is strong, maternal, hard-working, devoted to family, and quiet. (Note that quietness is traditionally considered a virtue in children, Blacks, and women.) The "bad" African American woman is ugly, lascivious, lazy, negligent, emasculating, and loud. Both views are based on stereotypes born of a need to justify public policies or societal treatment of African American women; they do not come from data or any close investigation of reality. Thus, when psychologists attempt to address therapeutic needs, obvious anxieties, or behavioral problems, they must ask, "What do we know about African American women?" Too often the answers have been couched in terms of these myths as well as other mistaken notions that may abound. (Trotman Reid 2000, xiii)

The "good" Black woman is strong and hardworking. She takes care of her man/woman, her children, her community, and anyone who asks anything of her. She is unfailing in her faith and trust in God. She is wise and maternal. She knows how to bear heavy burdens. She is selfless with her time and resources, being mentally and physically resilient. What she *is not* is suicidal. Until she is. And it is too late.

Writing as a Black Catholic womanist theologian, I desire in this chapter to reflect on Black women's *very real* experiences with suicidality, utilizing Black Church studies, Black feminist theory and womanist theology, ritual studies, and finally sacramental theology to do so. Specifically, I will examine the ways in which Black women have historically drawn inspiration from the testimony tradition of the Black Church, appropriating this uniquely Afro-religious practice to bring visibility to their experiences and struggles with suicidality. Furthermore, I show how this Afro-religious ritual tradition appears most frequently in the world of Black women's art and literature, testimony functioning like other, more readily recognized, rites of healing present within secular ritual studies, African Indigenous religions, and Christianity. These include Catherine Bell's category of *rituals of affliction*, Patrice Malidoma Somé's *radical ritual*, and the Christian practice of *the imposition* or *laying on of hands*. To do this, the chapter will examine two works of poetry by Black feminist author Ntozake Shange. Serving as a kind of case study, these poems will be used to ground my analysis of the power of testimony and the healing dimensions inherent in religious ritual, specifically the ways this type of religious speech can effect tangible healing and transformation in the lives of its celebrants.

Spirituality Made Manifest: Black Women and the Testimony Tradition

According to *The Blackwell Companion to the Study of Religion*, definitions of "ritual" abound, with most stressing the formality and traditionalism of ritual action. Others have attempted to articulate elusive qualities that can make even the most mundane activities ritualistic. The term "ritual" comes from the Latin *ritus* and *ritualis* and refers to the prescribed ceremonial order for a liturgical service, as well as the book that lays out that order (Bell 2017, 398–9). But, definitions of ritual today tend to place an emphasis on how people *ritualize*.[1] Or, "how they set apart some activities in striking ways and then make those activities distinctive for what is done, for when and where it is done, for how it is done, and by whom it is done" (Bell 2017, 398). Thus, ritual refers not just to religious activity but also to a central *social* activity, contemporary ritual studies shifting the focus from the social origin of religious ritual to the *function* of ritual (Bell 2017, 400).

Based on the following, there are several practices within the Afro-religious tradition[2] that can appropriately be characterized as ritual. These include *rituals of orality* (e.g., singing, specifically the spirituals and the blues; preaching; testifying; and storytelling) and *rituals of movement* (e.g., dancing, specifically the "Ring Shout" or the "Pattin' Juba"/hambone; stomping; shuffling; clapping; and drumming) (Hayes 2012, 22–5, 44–5). Considered one of the four primary pillars of the Afro-religious tradition (Townsend Gilkes 2001, 125), *testimony* or *testifying* can be described as follows:

> Testimony . . . [is] visceral and verbal, emotional and demonstrative, a collective and highly democratic enterprise. . . . When one [stands] up to testify, one

> [offers] a narrative of how one [has] overcome through the work of the Spirit. A woman might stand up and testify, only to hear others respond with cries, laughter, celebration, or even a song. Testifying [is] a highly unpredictable style of worship, as the Spirit [can] be felt at any moment, pulling the entire congregation into a series of communal shouts and dances. Most important, testifying [is] a way [of] mediat[ing] divine presence. When one testi[fies] in the midst of the congregation, God's presence [is] invoked, leading the entire community into experiences of transcendence, deliverance, joy, healing, and so much more. Testifying [is] not merely an individual act. One [doesn't] tell a story solely for some kind of personal cathartic release or relief. This oral practice form[s] the community in love, intimacy, and belonging. . . . Testifying [is] a communal act; it forge[s] a truly democratic community drawn together by filial bonds of love, care, and accountability. We [trust] that God [will] speak through our sisters and brothers as they testif[y] to God's goodness, mercy, and grace. We [utter] our stories in hopes that we [will] experience the power of the Spirit to be healed and made whole. (Day 2021, 1–2)

Sociologist of religion Cheryl Townsend Gilkes notes that during the period of slavery, testimony served as a mechanism of psychological survival for enslaved persons since it allowed the believing community to transform private troubles of distressed individuals into the public issues of a covenant community (Townsend Gilkes 2001, 137). Deemed the "bearers of [Black] culture" due to their passing down of folk stories, songs, memories, and the prayers of their people (Hayes 2016, 103),[3] Black women were arguably the best testifiers in the community since they carried forward the slaves' determination to survive.

Moreover, testimonies provide connections between situations of biblical characters and the contemporary experiences/problems of the gathered community, further providing believable examples of faith that motivate individuals to attempt new strategies for coping with those problems. Thus, it was not uncommon for Black women to creatively appropriate the biblical text to assert truths and process their own suffering. These included the stories of Hagar, Tamar, Jephthah's daughter, and liberationist accounts like the Exodus story. For many, testimony became a form of protest against the constraints of being female, operating as a means of lament over the brokenness experienced in their relationships, especially those with men (Townsend Gilkes 2001, 129, 131, 137). Furthermore, recent investigations of slavery and its aftermath suggest that Black women were not only central to the development of a uniquely African American spirituality but were important actors in the process out of which the Black religious experience grew. Known as "troublers" not only within their respective communities but larger society, Black women functioned as prophetic critics who worked to initiate movements for social change.

Hence, the prophetic is an indispensable feature of testimonial driven action. While it is true that testimony involves bearing witness to one's own and another's suffering—specifically the ways in which God through the work of the Spirit is able to create conditions of healing in the midst of brokenness—testifying also demands that the community be transparent about the ways they have been complicit and complacent in the perpetuation of sinful structures and/or the suffering of others. Day explains that testifiers who operate within the realm of the prophetic are equally called by God to remind the community of their continued need for genuine repentance or *metanoia* (Day 2021, 2–3). In the cry of the prophetic, the community bears witness to God's past and continued acts of faithfulness in the midst of ongoing oppression, marginalization, and suffering; they are continually called into ongoing conversion by the Spirit, being empowered by God's grace to resist sin and grow in holiness; and finally, they are oriented toward the future eschatological promise of renewal and restoration that God has promised in Jesus Christ. Thus, testimony allows the community to participate fully in the drama of salvation history.

Confronting Black Women's Suicidality through the Healing Dimensions of Ritual

While one is more likely to experience the ritual act of testimony within a Black religious service, testimonies are not solely confined to institutional religious spaces. This also necessarily means that their potential to evoke healing and mediate the presence of the divine is not bound by the specific dogmas, doctrines, and rites of the Christian Church. Being a unique Afro-religious practice that ties the experience of suffering to a dynamic and imaginative spirituality that is always examining the ways in which God is—to borrow a phrase from the Black Church, "making a way out of no way"—testimonies have spilled over into other areas of Black sociocultural life, including Black women's folk traditions, music, art, and literature.

To demonstrate this, we will examine two works of poetry by Black feminist playwright and poet Ntozake Shange from her acclaimed 1975 choreopoem,[4] "For Colored Girls Who Have Considered Suicide/When the Rainbow Is Enuf." The play tells the story of seven African American women who are only identified by colors of the rainbow (i.e., the lady in red, blue, green, brown, yellow, purple, and orange), specifically their experiences with various traumas that are the result of racism which continue to marginalize them as Black women. These include reflections on domestic violence, rape, abandonment, abortion, grief, self-hatred, and poverty, to name a few. Being a survivor of several suicide attempts herself, Shange's poetry (which is inspired by true events from her own life) offers some of the best examples of testimony within the African American literary world.

Poem #1 – "dark phrases"

The show opens with the prologue "dark phrases," offered by the lady in brown who begins to weave a tale of both contemporary and historic traumas seemingly intrinsic to the experience of Black womanhood. *Dark phrases of womanhood, of never having been a girl.* I cringed the first time I read these words. In them, I heard the echoes of my own story speak loudly as silent tears began to fall down my face. Memories of my own childhood and the various experiences of abandonment, abuse, and neglect that forced me to grow up too quickly. That robbed me of my innocence. A seemingly "happy" child whose smile and zeal for life conveniently hid how truly lonely and misunderstood she was. *Don't tell nobody, don't tell a soul* that to cope she developed an eating disorder and began to engage in non-suicidal self-injury and other addictive behaviors. *It's funny, it's hysterical, the melody-less-ness of her dance* which never betrayed to her family, friends, and colleagues the truth that she was dead inside. A strong and successful Black woman without a voice, longing to be reborn and handled warmly for the first time in her life.

But the individual trauma of one always exists within a larger, collective story. For me, it is the story of a people who were kidnapped from their homelands, brought to a new world, separated from their families and loved ones, and eventually enslaved. It is the story of institutionalized racism, legalized segregation, misogynoir, and the ensuing intergenerational trauma that continues to persist in our communities today. Thus, my story, Shange's story, and the countless stories of Black women in the diaspora cannot be told without telling this larger story. Roman Catholic womanist theologian M. Shawn Copeland states that it is the Black woman who stands at the "crossroads of two of the most well developed ideologies in America, that regarding women and that regarding [race]" (Copeland 2010, 24). The ambivalence of race and gender politics surrounding Black women was initially felt in the seizure of their bodies during what scholars now call the *Maafa* ("The African/Black Holocaust")—a term referring to the transatlantic slave trade, traditionally referred to as the "Middle Passage"—which rendered them as objects of *property*, *production*, *reproduction*, and *sexual violence* (Copeland 2010, 29).

For enslaved women, beatings, overwork, excessive childbearing (often being used as breeders since breeding was a cheaper way of obtaining more slaves than buying them on the slave market), and various forms of sexual abuse were everyday occurrences on the plantation. Moreover, *miscegenation*—the forced practice of racial mixing—frequently took place between white slave masters, overseers, and their Black female slaves, several slave narratives attesting that many young mulatto (mixed-race) women were especially targeted by men for continual sexual abuse. J. C. Furnas writes in his 1956 book, *Goodbye to Uncle Tom*, that in some slave markets, mulattos and quadroons often brought higher prices due to their use as sexual objects. Additionally, their proximity in color to the ideal of white feminine beauty made them more desirable to the white gaze, often being held over and against darker-skinned Black women who, in comparison, were seen as repulsive and vulgar. While all slave women, men, and children were vulnerable to sexual violence, mulattos in particular afforded white men the ability to sexually abuse persons who were physically near-white but legally Black with impunity (cited in Pilgrim 2000).

The sexual exploitation of enslaved people would eventually lead to warped social narratives and the creation of grotesque stereotypes concerning Black sexuality. Specifically, this included the belief that Black men and women were hypersexual by nature, possessing sexual appetites that were insatiable and out of control. Racialized-sexualized images which began to emerge included the asexual "mammy" and the sexually deviant "jezebel" for women, and the "Uncle Tom," "coon," "sambo," and "brute" for men ("Jim Crow Museum of Racist Memorabilia," n.d., in Pilgrim. 2000).[5] Eventually, these images would take on pornographic dimensions that were carried forward to argue for the necessity of segregation after slavery. To overcome this heritage of concubinage, many Black men and women during the postbellum period attempted to adopt the cultural norms and practices of what historians have come to call the *cult of domesticity*, better known as the *cult of true womanhood* and manhood, respectively. A prevailing value system rooted in the upper and middle classes of Victorian society, women especially were expected to adopt four basic virtues inherent to their nature: *purity*, *domesticity*, *piety*, and *submissiveness* (Collier-Thomas 2010, 42–3).

Within Black social-cultural circles, the ideal Black woman was, in fact, the mixed-race Black woman, "the earliest and most pervasive image of the female protagonist in Afro-American literature [at the time being] . . . the tragic mulatto" (Pilgrim 2000),[6] "[who was] the epitome of True Womanhood. Not only is she pious and pure, but she is also beautiful and more refined than most white women" (Kaiser 1995, 98).[7] Unfortunately, as Laurie Kaiser notes, "in their attempts to shed the stereotype of the sinful sexual woman [often depicting them as sexual martyrs or saints], these writers sometimes robbed their characters of their sexual identity, making them pure, passionless, almost holy-Virgin Mary figures" (Kaiser 1995, 97). Due to the mulatto's mixed racial lineage and subsequent proximity to whiteness, many Black men and women desired to adopt aspects of this trope in their daily lives. Moreover, Kaiser points to the surrounding sociopolitical reality driving Black attempts at assimilation: increased instances of racial violence and the institution of legalized segregation, that is, "Jim Crow" (Kaiser 1995, 97–8).

Not surprisingly, the enduring legacy of racial violence and misogynoir would eventually give rise to the social phenomenon called "passing," something that was especially prevalent during the early to mid-twentieth century. Because Jim Crow did not allow Black people the ability to enter the highest stratums of society, many social barriers could not be penetrated unless lighter-skinned Black people passed as white. Unfortunately, this meant having to cut ties with one's family and community. Passing would eventually bring with it the internalized form of racial oppression called *colorism*. The consequence of both passing and colorism would be the eventual cultural humiliation of Black people within literary, media, and other popular forms of representation. Being deemed "visually deviant" by the larger white society, African Americans came to violate every dimension of American gender norms and standards of beauty (Townsend Gilkes 2011, 81, 90).

Sadly, what resulted was "one of the deepest sources of conflict and turmoil within the African-American community" (Townsend Gilkes 2011, 81–2), the prevalence of low self-esteem and self-hatred among Black people. Several studies have demonstrated that the experience of racism, whether explicit or implicit, can contribute to feelings of self-loathing in African American youth. Furthermore, trends in neuroscience, biology, and psychology have suggested that racial trauma not only has the potential to be passed down intergenerationally but can also "live" in the body, manifesting as somatic or psychiatric disorders like anxiety, post-traumatic stress-like disorders, and depression; or as chronic illnesses like high blood pressure, heart disease, obesity, and cancer. For Cheryl Townsend Gilkes, self-hatred is not merely low regard for the self but literal "damage and brokenness to [one's] inner visions" which makes impossible sharing one's unique "liberating visions" (Townsend Gilkes 2011, 81)—visions of Black pride and dignity as one made in the image and likeness of God.

Therefore, we can read Shange's "dark phrases" not only as testimony, but what ritual theorist Catherine Bell identifies as a *ritual of affliction*. These types of rituals seek to "rectify a state of affairs that has been disturbed or disordered; they heal, exorcise, protect, and purify" (Bell 1997, 115). The dynamics of the ritual attempt to redress what the community determines as an anomaly or imbalance, this taking the form of purging the individual or social body of all impurities which have disrupted the mind-body holism from its natural state; or, by seeking the intercession of powerful beings that can correct the imbalances which transcend the body of a single individual (Bell 1997, 115). In Shange's "dark phrases," the disordered situation attempting to be righted is the enduring presence of societal forces which exacerbates Black women's suffering. In recognizing the anomalous imbalances present within the lived experiences of these women, Shange desires for those who bear witness to these stories to participate in the purging of those impurities—impurities like misogynoir—from the social body of the Black community and the individual bodies of Black women.

Like testimonies, which double as "litan[ies] of the social problems affecting black women [including] abandonment, assaults, aging, poverty, violent crime, single-parenthood, and their children's futures" (Townsend Gilkes 2001, 138), rituals of affliction reflect "people's persistent efforts to redress wrongs, alleviate sufferings, and ensure well-being . . . [further] illustrat[ing] complex cultural interpretations of the human condition and its relation to a cosmos of benign and malevolent forces" (Bell 1997, 119). By bringing radical visibility to her own experiences with suicidality, Shange opens her readers to a larger story where Black women have had to endure without question the various disruptions impacting their mind-body holism, disruptions that have not only left them with broken "inner visions" but thoughts of taking their own lives.

Poem #2 – "a laying on of hands"

Despite trauma being a key aspect of the framing of "For Colored Girls," trauma does not get the last word in Shange's play. Rather, the final piece, "a laying on of hands," finds the women coming together to offer each other one final benediction before they depart. Being a short invocation for divine help, along with mutual blessing and guidance, this benediction opens with the assertion that the women are missing something critical, something promised to them; the healing touch of another's hands. *I was missing something.* For years I silently drifted through a sea of anxiety and depression, unaware that anything was wrong. Plagued by nightmares and bouts of crippling insomnia, I told myself this was just my lot in life. Somehow, I was deserving of every terrible thing that had ever happened to me. It was the will of God; otherwise, why would God ignore my cries for deliverance? *Something so important*, like the love of my mother and father, along with the family into whose care I was eventually entrusted. *Something promised*, like healing and restoration. A sense of peace and the assurance that I was not only loved, but that my life was not a mistake or that I was better off dead. *A laying on of hands.*

The *imposition* or *laying on of hands* is an ancient Judeo-Christian practice, being one of the most frequently mentioned rites in both the Old and New Testaments, as well as early Christian liturgy. The actual rite involved placing one's hands on the head of the recipient, an act which typically involved the transmission of power or the conferring of a blessing (The Catholic University of America 2003, 364–5). To lay one's hands upon another did not only mean to confer a blessing but also petition for divine favor (Ferguson 2014, 161). This is significant because in the Jewish imagination, the hand was not merely an instrument but an extension of the entire self, specifically its power. Hence, the phrase "hand of God" in various Old Testament passages (e.g., Isa. 45:12) stands for the power of God, "hand" being nearly equivalent to the personal pronoun, "It was I [God], my hands" (The Catholic University of America 2003, 364–5). In short, to lay on hands was to enact or embody prayer, a prayer that spelled out the grace which God was being asked to bestow. Moreover, it was considered to effect that for which the prayer was uttered (Ferguson 2014, 161).

In the New Testament, the act of laying on hands was evident in the healing ministry of Jesus, and in passages where Christ confers a blessing on the apostles such as Lk. 24:50. What is interesting about the conferring of the blessing by Christ in this passage is its proximity to the promise of the coming gift of the Holy Spirit in later passages. This would seem to suggest that the imposition of hands is somehow connected to the apostolic rite of giving the Holy Spirit. During the apostolic age, the act of laying on hands was introduced for Christian ordination and used for the impartation of the postbaptismal gift of the Holy Spirit (The Catholic University of America 2003, 364–5). This practice of laying on hands would later evolve and come to be associated with the sacramental practice of anointing of the sick; it was not uncommon for early Christian communities to commend the sick to the care of a presbyter and the mercy of God through the use of prayer, the laying on of hands, and anointing with blessed oil, as evidenced in James 5:14-15. The practice, however, would not formally be considered "sacramental" until the Second Council of Lyons in 1274 (Kasza 2015, 558–66).

Each woman's recognition that she is "missing something, something so important, something promised," along with her subsequent request to receive "a laying on of hands" from her fellow sisters, suggests that she expects in the reception of this blessing the restoration and healing of her mind, body, and soul. Because the act of laying on hands cannot be separated from the impartation of the Spirit, it operates similarly to healing traditions coming out of African Indigenous religions. A primary example of this includes what Patrice Malidoma Somé calls a *radical ritual.* Within these healing rites, the community gathers in the hopes of experiencing a "dramatic interaction with Spirit for the purpose of removing from the psyche something that has been seriously troublesome to a person in the [community]" (Somé 1999, 150). By gathering the community to feel the call of the Spirit while simultaneously expressing publicly whatever emotions and petitions need to be conveyed, the rite is able to create, alongside others, an unrehearsed and deeply moving response to the Spirit. This not only heals the participant by reminding them of who they are, along with their true purpose within the context of the community, but also calls the community to safeguard this sacred knowledge by protecting that purpose, awakening in the individual memories of their unique gifts (Somé 1999, 143).

Thus, in the act of requesting and in return receiving a "laying on of hands," each woman is able to experience restoration to her fragmented psyche. In fact, this act of healing brings with it the graced awareness of what exactly was previously missing: the recognition that each woman is fearfully and wonderfully made in the image of God, and that she already possesses divinity (via the gift of the Holy Spirit which was conferred through the blessing bestowed upon her in the imposition of another's hands) within herself. Hence, the bold declaration that "[she] found god in [her]self & [she]loved her/[she] loved her fiercely."

Moreover, Shange's testimony via "a laying on of hands" reveals a deeper truth concerning notions of Christian salvation: salvation not only includes our entire selves (i.e., our spiritual *and* bio-psycho-social reality),[8] but is a communal reality that begins in this present life, having ties to our final sanctification and destiny of eternal life in Christ. We can see this lay-driven and communal work of healing in several passages in the New Testament, including the story of Mary and Martha who entrust their brother Lazarus to Jesus' care in Jn 11:1-44, and the story of the paralytic man in Lk. 5:17-39. Specifically in the story of Jesus healing the paralytic, a man is brought by several of his friends to see Jesus. Due to the crowds, they are unable to enter the home where Jesus is teaching. To circumvent this, they remove the roof of the house and lower their friend down to see Jesus directly. When Jesus sees the faith (the *pistis*—or belief/trust in Christ's identity as the Messiah) of the man's friends, he then turns to the man and says, "Your sins are forgiven." It is the belief of the paralyzed man's community that not only results in his spiritual salvation (i.e., the forgiveness of his sins), but his eventual physical salvation after Jesus commands him to take up his mat and walk.

Additionally, our participation in communal acts of healing and salvation primarily begins when we bear witness to ourselves and our own experiences of suffering, including the ways in which God's grace has restored us through the power of the Holy Spirit. We can see this witnessing unto the self—where one's own faith results in their respective healing—in the biblical story of the woman with the issue of blood. The Matthean text says that "a woman who had been suffering from hemorrhages for twelve years came up behind him [Jesus] and touched the fringe of his cloak, for she said to herself, 'If I only touch his cloak, I will be made well.' Jesus turned, and seeing her he said, 'Take heart, daughter; your faith has made you well.' And instantly the woman was made well" (Mt. 9:20-22, NRSV).

The word translated as "well" in this passage is the Greek verb *sōzō* ("Lexicon," n.d.), meaning *to save* or *to keep*. Strong's Greek lexicon further defines it as "to rescue from danger or destruction"; "to save one from peril or injury"; "to save a suffering one (from perishing), i.e. one suffering from disease"; and "to make well, heal, or restore to health (including spiritual healing, as in James 5:15)." In each account where the verb appears—Mk 5:34 and Lk. 8:48—it is translated in the present perfect tense, suggesting that the action of saving is completed here and now. While the woman's faith resulted in her complete bodily healing (i.e., salvation), it was not merely physical in nature. Thus, like other passages in the New Testament, salvation seems to imply a process which begins in this life (i.e., deliverance from sin, suffering, and/or disease; or the experience of the soul being reconciled to God) but is ultimately destined to achieve its perfected end upon the soul's union with God at death.

And this is for colored girls who have considered suicide but are moving to the ends of their own rainbows. In the Bible, rainbows are often tied to themes of covenant and promise, specifically God's faithfulness to the people of Israel. I do not believe it is a coincidence that Shange asserts through her characters that one's healing can only be found at the end of the rainbow. Indeed, the affirmation that "the rainbow is enuf" is the exact same affirmation the apostle Paul receives in 2 Cor. 12:9: "My grace is sufficient for you, for power is made perfect in weakness." Despite the apostle's present experience of suffering which the Lord continues to allow within the mystery of God's permissive will, the grace of Christ is somehow still sufficient for him. Thus, the rainbow not only becomes a metaphor for God's grace, but also the graced knowledge and awareness that although complete healing may not occur in this life nor result in the immediate cessation of our suffering, restoration of God's entire creation is a reality promised to all those who love God and have been called according to God's purposes.

Conclusion

The prevention of Black women's suicide demands we familiarize ourselves with the current and historical structures that make the persistence of Black suffering possible. Although suffering is not something that will be totally eradicated in this life due to the reality of finitude and human sinfulness, what rites of healing reveal is that God's grace is *indeed sufficient*; and, when our experience of suffering is mysteriously united to Christ's own in the depths of the paschal mystery we, too, are able to experience healing and wholeness through the recontextualization of our pain within the light of God's grace. As M. Shawn Copeland suggests in her womanist political theology, just as we are charged with upholding the dangerous memory of Jesus Christ to whom we all belong as members of his body, so too are we charged with lifting up the dangerous memories of those most exploited members of that same body which, in this case, are Black women (Copeland 2010). Black women like Cheslie, May, Lincoln University administrator Antoinette "Bonnie" Candia-Bailey, Isabella "Izzy" Tichenor, and Ashawnty Davis whose lives mattered but were mercilessly stolen away by the sting of suicide.

What would becoming witnesses to these ritualized testimonies and the dangerous memories of Black women do for us as a community of Christian believers? How might holding these memories in tension with the dangerous memory of Christ circumvent Black women's struggles with mental illness and suicidality? The testimonies of Black women are prophetically calling all those who bear witness to their stories of trauma and survival into penitent acts of confession and contrition. We must allow these testimonies to reveal the places within our own lives still in need of God's mercy and grace.

Notes

1 "Ritualized" behavior can refer to a cultural production that takes an unpredictable practice and makes it predictable and patterned with repetition. It maintains some structure yet retains a level of spontaneity. Kimberley H. Belcher. *Rituals for Crisis and Healing*, Lecture, 2020.

2 A development that emerged out of Antebellum Slave Religion, the Afro-religious tradition, colloquially referred to as the "Black Church," consists of "the religious, cultural, and social experience[s] of Black people. With its roots on the continent of Africa and the Middle Passage, the Black Church provided structure and meaning for African people and their descendants in the Americas who struggled to survive the ravages and brutality of slavery and racial oppression. . . . [Moreover, it] functioned as the center of Black life, culture, and heritage for much of the history of the African American experience in North America" (Floyd-Thomas et al. 2007, xxiii).

Due to the diversity of denominational identities, Barbara A. Holmes states that the Black Church exists as more of a spiritual entity unbounded by time and space, Delores Williams stating that "the black church does not exist as an institution. Regardless of sociological, theological, historical and pastoral attempts, the black church escapes precise definition. . . . Some believe it to be rooted deeply in the soul of the community memory of black folk. Some believe it to be the core symbol of the four-hundred year-old African American struggle against white oppression with God in the struggle providing black people with spiritual and material resources for survival and freedom. Others believe it to be places where black people come to worship God without white people being present. I believe . . . [it] is the heart of hope in the black community's experience of oppression, survival struggle and its historic efforts toward complete liberation" (Holmes 2017, 5). See also Williams (1993, 204–5).

3 Citing Bernice J. Reagan, Hayes says that "[women] were the heads of their communities, the keepers of the tradition. The lives of these women were defined by their culture, the needs of the community and the people they served. . . . These

women, . . . became central to evolving the structures for resolving areas of conflict and maintaining, sometimes creating, an identity that was independent of a society organized to exploit natural resources, people, and land" (Hayes 2016, 103; see also Reagan 1987, 169).

4 A dramatic art form that blends poetry, dance, music, and song to create a theatrical experience, focusing on emotional expression rather than traditional plot or character development.

5 The "mammy" caricature is the most well-known and endearing racial caricature of African American women. Historically, she was portrayed as a happy, contented slave with a jovial and loyal disposition who primarily served the political, social, and economic interests of mainstream white America. She is often depicted as an old, obese, and maternal figure who has great love for her white "family." The mammy was further constructed to suggest ugliness (and detract from the sexual abuse of female slaves) by being portrayed as dark-skinned, often pitch Black in a society that regarded Black skin as ugly/tainted. This de-eroticism meant that the white wife—and by extension the white family—was safe. In contrast, the "jezebel" (another enduring stereotype of African American women) sees Black women as inherently lascivious, her behavior often being described as seductive, alluring, worldly, beguiling, tempting, lewd, and so on. By being painted as a "promiscuous predator-whore," society was able to reinforce the portrayal of white women as models of self-control, self-respect, and modesty, especially sexual purity.

The "Tom" caricature portrayed Black men as happily faithful, submissive servants who were eager to serve their white masters. "Tom" was seen as docile and nonthreatening to whites, often presented as old, physically weak, asexual, and psychologically dependent on whites for approval. On the other hand, the "coon" was portrayed as a lazy, easily frightened, chronically idle, and inarticulate buffoon. Unlike Toms, coons were depicted as acting childish and being unhappy with their status as slaves, often accused of being too lazy or too cynical to change this lowly position. Eventually, the coon came to be associated with young urban Blacks who disrespected whites and did not "know their place." Like the coon, the "sambo" was also seen as a submissive, childlike buffoon. Rather than being unhappy with their status, sambos were portrayed as devoted house servants with an all-consuming love for their master. Such portrayals presented sambos as loyal, contented slaves who were in essence "perpetual children"; they were indolent and improvident, yet humorous and musical (a congenitally docile clown). Finally, the "brute" portrayed Black men as innately savage, animalistic, destructive, and criminal. Such portraits reinforced the idea that Black men were inherently sociopathic predators, serial rapists whose primary victims were helpless white women ("Jim Crow Museum of Racist Memorabilia," n.d., in Pilgrim 2000).

6 The "Tragic mulatto" is a trope that first appeared in literary sources in 1842 ("The Quadroons") and 1843 ("Slavery's Pleasant Homes"). She is often depicted as a light-skinned woman who was the offspring of a white slaveholder and his Black female slave. Her character is often naïve and ignorant of both her and her mother's "true" race as she believes herself to be white. If her white father died, her "Negro blood" would often be discovered casting her down into the stratum of slavery where she would die both a victim of slavery and white male violence (Pilgrim 2000).

7 See also Smith Foster (1985, 34).

8 (Larson-Miller 2007, 5–6). Lizette Larson-Miller notes that in the theological developments surrounding the sacrament of anointing of the sick (which cannot be separated from larger conversations on Christian soteriology or salvation), there was an assumption that "illness of one kind affects the other dimensions of an individual. To be emotionally sick is perhaps also to be physically sick, to be spiritually sick is to risk the whole person. So the oil on which the blessing prayers were focused was to be a healing agent for the whole person; spiritual, physical ailments, and emotional problems were dealt with together" (Larson-Miller 2007, 5–6).

Bibliography

Bailey, Moya, and Trudy. 2018. "On Misogynoir: Citation, Erasure, and Plagiarism." *Feminist Media Studies* 18 (4): 762–8. https://doi.org/10.1080/14680777.2018.1447395.

Bell, Catherine. 2017. "Ritual." In *The Blackwell Companion to the Study of Religion*, 397–411. John Wiley & Sons, Ltd. https://doi.org/10.1002/9781405168748.ch23.

Bell, Catherine M. 1997. *Ritual: Perspectives and Dimensions*. Oxford University Press.

The Catholic University of America. 2003. "Imposition of Hands." In *New Catholic Encyclopedia*, edited by Thomas Carson and Joann Cerrito, 2nd ed., vol. 7, 364–6. Gale Virtual Reference Library. Gale Group Inc.

Collier-Thomas, Bettye. 2010. *Jesus, Jobs, and Justice: African American Women and Religion*. 1st ed. Alfred A. Knopf.

Copeland, M. Shawn. 2010. *Enfleshing Freedom: Body, Race, and Being*. Innovations. Fortress Press. Http://Id.Loc.Gov/Authorities/Names/No2008030569, Http://Viaf.Org/Viaf/sourceID/LC|no2008030569.

Day, Keri. 2021. *Notes of a Native Daughter: Testifying in Theological Education*. Theological Education between the Times. William B. Eerdmans Publishing Company.

Ferguson, Everett. 2014. "Laying On of Hands: Its Significance in Ordination." In *The Early Church at Work and Worship*. James Clarke & Co. 160–72.

Florvil, Tiffany. 2017. "Remembering Afro-German Intellectual May Ayim – AAIHS." *Black Perspectives.* AAIHS. September 6. https://www.aaihs.org/remembering-afro-german-intellectual-may-ayim/

Floyd-Thomas, Stacey, Juan M. Floyd-Thomas, Carol B. Duncan, Stephen G. Ray Jr., and Nancy Lynne Westfield. 2007. *Black Church Studies: An Introduction.* Illustrated ed. Abingdon Press.

Hayes, Diana L. 2012. *Forged in the Fiery Furnace: African American Spirituality.* Orbis Books.

Hayes, Diana L. 2016. *No Crystal Stair: Womanist Spirituality.* Orbis Books.

Henery, Celeste. 2018. "Black Women's Suicide and a Call for Radical Friendship." *Black Perspectives.* AAIHS, February 27. https://www.aaihs.org/black-womens-suicide-and-a-call-for-radical-friendship/.

Holloway, Kali. 2023. "The Crisis Killing Black Women." *The Nation*, February 3. https://www.thenation.com/article/society/the-crisis-killing-black-women/.

Holmes, Barbara Ann. 2017. *Joy Unspeakable: Contemplative Practices of the Black Church.* 2nd ed. Fortress Press.

"Jim Crow Museum of Racist Memorabilia." n.d. Accessed March 29, 2023. https://www.ferris.edu/HTMLS/news/jimcrow/index.htm.

Kaiser, Laurie. 1995. "The Black Madonna: Notions of True Womanhood from Jacobs to Hurston." *South Atlantic Review* 60 (1): 97–109. https://doi.org/10.2307/3200715.

Kasza, John C. 2015. "Anointing of the Sick." In *The Oxford Handbook of Sacramental Theology*. Oxford Handbooks in Religion and Theology. Oxford University Press. https://doi.org/10.1093/oxfordhb/9780199659067.013.5.

Larson-Miller, Lizette. 2007. "'Healed to Life': The Historical Development of Anointing of the Sick at the Heart of the Church's Healing Ministry." *Liturgy* 22 (3): 3–12. https://doi.org/10.1080/04580630701273942.

"Lexicon :: Strong's G4982—Sōzō (RSV)." n.d. In *Blue Letter Bible.* Accessed November 2, 2021. https://www.blueletterbible.org/rsv/gen/1/1/s_1001.

Pilgrim, David. 2000. "'The Tragic Mulatto Myth'—Anti-Black Imagery." Jim Crow Museum of Racist Memorabilia, Ferris State University, November. https://www.ferris.edu/HTMLS/news/jimcrow/mulatto/homepage.htm.

Reagan, Bernice J. 1987. "African Diaspora Women: The Making of Cultural Workers." In *Women in Africa and the African Diaspora*, edited by Rosalyn Terborg-Penn, Sharon Harley, and Andrea Benton Rushing. Howard University Press. 167–80.

Rockett, Ian R. H., Julie B. Samora, and Jeffrey H. Coben. 2006. "The Black-White Suicide Paradox: Possible Effects of Misclassification." *Social Science & Medicine* 63 (8): 2165–75. https://doi.org/10.1016/j.socscimed.2006.05.017.

Shange, Ntozake. 1975. *For Colored Girls Who Have Considered Suicide/When the Rainbow Is Enuf: A Choreopoem.* First Scribner Poetry ed. New York: Scribner Poetry.

Smith Foster, Frances. 1985. "Adding Color and Contour to Early American Self-Portraittures: Autobiographical Writings of Afro-American Women." In *Conjuring: Black Women, Fiction, and Literary Tradition*, edited by Marjorie Pryse and Hortense Spillers. Indiana University Press. 25–38.

Somé, Malidoma Patrice. 1999. *The Healing Wisdom of Africa: Finding Life Purpose Through Nature, Ritual, and Community*. 1st trade pbk. ed. J. P. Tarcher/Putnam.

Spates, Kamesha, and Brittany C. Slatton. 2017. "I've Got My Family and My Faith: Black Women and the Suicide Paradox." *Socius* 3 (January): 2378023117743908. https://doi.org/10.1177/2378023117743908.

Townsend Gilkes, Cheryl. 2001. *If It Wasn't for the Women ...: Black Women's Experience and Womanist Culture in Church and Community*. Orbis Books.

Townsend Gilkes, Cheryl. 2011. "The 'Loves' and 'Troubles' of African-American Women's Bodies: The Womanist Challenge to Cultural Humiliation and Community Ambivalence." In *Womanist Theological Ethics: A Reader*, edited by Katie G. Cannon, Emilie Maureen Townes, and Angela D. Sims, 1st ed. Library of Theological Ethics. Westminster John Knox Press. Http://Id.Loc.Gov/Authorities/Names/N91099329, Http://Viaf.Org/Viaf/sourceID/LC|n91099329.

Trotman Reid, Pamela. 2000. "Foreword." In *Psychotherapy with African American Women: Innovations in Psychodynamic Perspectives and Practice*, edited by Leslie C. Jackson and Beverly Greene. The Guilford Press. xi–xv.

Williams, Delores S. 1993. *Sisters in the Wilderness: The Challenge of Womanist God-Talk*. Orbis Books.

8

Solidarity across the Water

Suicide, Caste, and Racism

Jamall A. Calloway

Every powerful empire subjugates at least one powerless community beneath its feet. Part of the domination includes propagating lying narratives about these powerless communities struggling to break free. This is the seemingly never-ending story of humankind—the crux of the fall of the human collective. Humankind has never known, nor is it ever likely to learn, how to coexist peacefully with an equal distribution of access to power and resources, and without notions of "peace" and "civility" becoming weapons against those who desire freedom, equality, and justice. From the United States of America to South Africa, from Palestine to India, and in every powerful society flourishing on this earth, oppression of one group functions as the catalyst of prosperity and comfort for another group.

In the United States, it is racial and economic injustice. In South Africa it is still the effects and debris of Apartheid. And in India this clash of collectives is the maintaining of an ancient oppressive hierarchy known as the caste system that disenfranchises, disempowers, and denigrates 167 million Dalits, while also discriminating against and demeaning the 104 million people who belong to tribal communities. Every form of oppression in this world is disseminated through pervasive patriarchal logic that leave girls and women vulnerable to economic and sexual violence. Sometimes this oppression can be so brutal, so calculated, and so heavy that it has the power to cause people to take their own lives to alleviate the pressure. This is what I call homicide by suicide.

Catching my attention are the horrible cases of death by suicide occurring in the United States and India, from Sandra Bland in Texas to Rohith Chakravarthi Vemula in India. These occurred within six months of each other: Sandra

Bland died on July 13, 2015; Rohith Vemula on January 17, 2016. Considering the differences and similarities in their contexts, this chapter asks whether their deaths may be viewed through a combination of what sociologist Émile Durkheim theorized as "anomic" and "fatalistic" suicides (Durkheim 1897). As a theologian, judging Durkheim's text on the merits of sociology is beyond the scope of my argument and ability. Rather, I intend to view Durkheim's argument through the lens of philosophy, seeing it as a constructive, if limited, device to analyze the larger backgrounds behind suicide.

Durkheim argues that there are various circumstances, reasons, and categories of suicide that expand our understanding of it from an individual decision to a social fact. I will explain Durkheim's theories first and then use his work to explain how I read both Bland and Vemula's tragedies. Durkheim says with unique sensitivity and clarity:

> Suicide is like madness: for the average person, the latter is a single state, always the same, which can only vary externally with circumstances, while for the psychiatrist, on the contrary, the word indicates a number of different nosological types. In the same way, most people see the victim of suicide as a melancholic type for whom life is a burden. In reality, the actions by which a man gives up living cover a range of different kinds whose moral and social implications are not at all the same. (Durkheim 2006, 307)

According to Durkheim, suicides are deeply misunderstood. They are usually portrayed as a singular decision made by a melancholic soul whose despondence was so overwhelming that they could no longer bear the difficulties of life. This was the result of so much religious propaganda that asserted suicide was sinful and morally criminal. Durkheim disagrees. Suicide is more than its typical misunderstandings. It exceeds its constant reductive portrayal. To Durkheim, it is, unfortunately, a social fact. And a social fact to Durkheim is defined, as he wrote in the preface to his second edition of *Rules of Sociological Method*, as "manners of acting or thinking, distinguishable through their special characteristic of being capable of exercising a coercive influence on the consciousness of individuals" (Durkheim 1982, 43). In other words, suicides appear as the resolution of the disheartened, but they are better understood as the clandestine results of societal pressure. Suicides are socially engineered as much as they are personally selected. People feel forced in their helplessness; they feel they have no other choice. And the confusion and misunderstanding of the sentiment that precedes the ordeal are easily understandable. They come across to many people, especially the brokenhearted, as the result of a person who decided they would rather discontinue with their life than persist, but he sees much more than its misconstrued phenomena.

For Durkheim, suicides, and their reasons for occurring, vary across social contexts, geographies, class statuses, and reasons. And though the act of ending one's own life is the same in terms of the painful conclusion, the *decision* to do so is tremendously complicated. This chapter challenges, through Durkheim, the notion of decision and seeks to find another term that would get us closer to sensitively describing what transpires—what collapses—when oppression and domination particularly function as the sources of a person's reason to say no more to this life. Thus, I prefer use of the term "acquiesce." Survivors of domination who take theor own lives, I suggest, are more or less giving in, acquiescing to Anomic-Fatalistic suicide.

Despite the limitations of Durkheim's trailblazing study, it is helpful in allowing us to see the complexity of the situation, parsing through the various contours of the contexts in which suicide occurs. I assert that those who self-transitioned in light of oppression, because of racism and casteism, did not necessarily think they were making a personal decision as much as they were succumbing to a cosmic decision that has been made for them. This falls within the category of what Durkheim describes (and dismisses) as "Fatalistic suicide." I want to expand this term and combine it with the Anomic to take seriously what Durkheim did not.

For Durkheim there are three major types of suicides. They are categorized as Egoistic, Altruistic, and Anomic. Egoistic suicide occurs because of societal alienation, through a sense of not belonging, of feeling disconnected from one's own community. It is preceded by an inability to overcome the detachments, what Paul Tillich would describe as estrangement from one's neighbor (Tillich 1952, 51). Altruistic suicide is the opposite of egoistic in that it is the result of placing the group's purpose ahead of one's own; it is the consequence of seeing one's demise as valuable for the group's mission. It is the suicide where "one does not belong to himself, or else is merged with something other than himself, and where the pole star that guides his behavior is situated outside of himself, that is to say in one of the groups to which he belongs" (Durkheim 2006, 239). Durkheim describes these two as opposites: Egoistic is the result of too little integration into the society while altruistic is a result of being overly integrated into the society to the point that the individual aspect of one's existence is quelled.

Anomic suicide transpires during sudden change, perceived as an upheaval impossible to endure, an alteration in life so sudden that the person finds no way of escaping. There is some connection to the fatalistic suicide but the distinctions between them are clear. Overall, Durkheim spends ample time analyzing variations, religious groups, gender and class distinctions, employing a host of sociological data to understand these types of suicides. Yet fatalistic suicide is reduced to a footnote, dismissed as more theoretical than actual. He asserts that "it affects so few people today and, apart from the cases that we have just mentioned, it is so hard to find examples of it, that it seems unnecessary for it to detain us further" (Durkheim 2006, 305). He then says, "is this not the kind of suicide of slaves that is said to be common in certain circumstances?" (Durkheim 2006, 305). What Durkheim sets aside is what I will focus on now.

For clarity, my goal in this chapter is not to shame nor chastise the people I am highlighting, nor am I trying to shame suicide itself. Though my hopeful intention is that this chapter will serve as an informative argument against the domination that causes suicide, and that it will compel international dialogue, nonviolent political resistance, and coalition building, I am not making any moral judgments about suicide itself. And though I am using the categories outlined by Durkheim, I am aware of the various mysterious factors that also play a role in one's decision to do so that he did not understand. We live in a world of so much pain, destruction, harm, and evil, that it would be foolish to believe that someone or anyone living and being here who is enduring some unimaginable anguish has not considered suicide as a possibility. Thomas Joiner is clear that the factors that play a role in suicides are both particular but common (Joiner 2005). Sometimes we feel we are burdening our loved ones; sometimes we feel isolated. That is why I am approaching this chapter not objectively but with compassion.

Now, to reiterate, here is my claim: in a world ravaged by injustice, domination, and oppression, there are people of several sectors of societies who are marginalized, who live on the edge of the worthwhile, who are trying to make it—by any means with integrity—to find their way, and are constantly encountering troubles that are the result of their identities and inclusion within the marginalized group. Many within the marginalized group experience the conditions that Durkheim unconvincingly describes as fatalistic suicide. In contrast, I am suggesting that there are people on the edge who are more prone to succumb, to acquiesce, to anemic suicide. In other words, there are members of marginalized groups—especially men—who are more prone to dying because of something gone awry, because of some painful and terrible unexpected occasion, because they already live a life that exerts so much pressure and injustice on top of them.

My hope is that this perspective on politically induced suicides across continents will inspire and cause international solidarity. I am arguing for an international combining of forces, a continuation of intercontinental solidarity started by freedom fighters long before us. I am arguing for a continued connection of ideas and empathy between Black Americans, Dalits, and indigenous peoples—along with and all oppressed communities—across the globe. This is not a new idea. This is an idea realized and crafted by a combination of Black and Indian strategic ancestors (Pandey 2013). They knew fundamentally that in order to rid ourselves from the multifaceted components and logics of oppression that trample human beings for the fruit of capital, we have to struggle and work together. There have been too many suicides that are caused by acquiescing to sociopolitical pressure. Both Bland and Rohith Vemula are examples of this. I will begin with Bland before turning my attention to Vemula.

Sandra Bland

One tragic story that caught the nation's attention in 2015 was the suicide of Sandra Bland. Sandra Bland was a 28-year-old Black woman from Illinois who was driving from Illinois to Texas in preparation for her new job at her alma mater, Prairie View A&M University. While driving on the road through Texas, she was pulled over by State Trooper, Brian Encinia, for changing lanes without properly signaling. Such a minor traffic violation is typically overlooked by officers of the law. Yet Encinia was notorious for not only conducting a significant amount of traffic stops, but he was also known for his sheer number of pretextual stops. In other words, Brian Encinia was noted for his tactics.

Brian Encinia was no stranger to using minor and insignificant violations as pretexts for searching for hidden and more serious crimes. It seems, however, that he did not find a more serious crime or transgression when he pulled over Sandra Bland. Instead, the trooper decided to fabricate the moment of encountering one. While Bland was understandably annoyed with his overaggression, matching his aggression with her rights and dignity, Encinia reported that he felt his life was endangered. The report stated that he felt threatened by Bland, insinuating that he thought she was going to harm him and so he met force with force. Encinia brandished his taser. He ordered her to step out of her vehicle for not disposing of her cigarette. And after she rebuffed him too much, he screamed with all the hatred in his voice that he was going to "light her up" before throwing her to the ground. He lodged his knees deeply into her back, forced her arms together to place handcuffs on them, and arrested her for assault. A claim the FBI would eventually declare a lie after reviewing dash camera footage and Bland's personal video recordings.

Bland was taken to Waller County Jail. She was placed in jail attire. They took her fingerprints; they took her mugshot; they placed her into a cell alone—across from a cell where other women were keeping each other's spirits high—because she was considered high-risk and an unhinged danger to others. In a private voicemail to a friend, she questioned how a minor violation, something as small and insignificant as a simple traffic stop, could escalate into a violent arrest where weapons were drawn and harm could transpire. She felt like her arm was broken. She was in pain. She was distraught. She was lonely. And while alone in her cell—one she claimed repeatedly that she did not deserve to be in—she succumbed to suicide, an act that impacted the nation and beyond.

This idea that black bodies, that black flesh, is a threat that needs to be subdued, held hostage, incarcerated if not eviscerated, is inherent in what Kelly Brown Douglas theorizes as the myth of Anglo-Saxon exceptionalism that undergirds police interactions with Black people (Douglas 2015). Using the Trayvon Martin case and tragedy to study the theology of "Stand Your Ground" laws, Douglass outlines how white superiority and Black dehumanization go hand in hand in the United States. The state trooper did not see a person when he looked at Sandra Bland, but black flesh that was unruly and needed to be controlled for the sake of society. Bland was legitimately no threat. But in the eyes of white supremacy, her "breathing" was nothing less than a nuisance.

Her family asserted foul play. They could not wrap their minds around their loved one yielding to suicide. They accused the police of wrongdoing, of murdering Sandra Bland and concealing all evidence of doing so. It was concluded by every state agency that all evidence proved contrary to their allegations. Yet I am asserting a different interpretation of the event, one that suggests that the family is not fully incorrect in alleging homicide; but that the broader social context makes their case. Bland's videos and content that showed a focus on racism, police brutality, and the deaths of Black people in the United States at the hands of law enforcement reveal an understanding and attention to racism, racism that was experienced and studied, until an unnecessarily violent encounter with an officer pushed her to acquiese to suicide.

Within the tension between anomic and fatalistic suicide is the understanding that one already and always lives a life on the edge of the insurmountable, that there are groups of people in this world, so dominated and oppressed that a turn of events could cause suicide. But the decision is one of acquiescence. It is one of consent. One already feels the cosmos against them. One already tries to live and maintain and preserve. And then there is one event that is tied to the oppression that forces one to give in to what they feel they are already constantly cosmically pressured into.

Unfortunately, there is a severe rise in suicides among African American youth. The Pew Charitable Trust reports as 144 percent increase among Black youth suicides from 2007 to 2010. According to Akkas and Corr (2024):

> As Black youth suicide rates continue to climb, additional research is needed to better understand the risk factors and protective factors—circumstances that increase or protect against suicide risk—specific to this group. Authors of the 2019 report to Congress called for increased federal funding and resources for studies on risk factors such as stigma, protective factors such as a strong sense of cultural identity and connectedness to the community, and mental health care access and engagement among Black youth.

Young lives are in danger. What was initially thought of as a problem unique to white Americans has become a significant problem in Black and other marginalized communities. Research shows that lives are at stake. Sandra Bland's death and mistreatment by law enforcement brought the #SayHerName campaign to the national stage. Attention was given to Black women's violent encounters with police. Before delving more into the theological and theoretical implications of this tragedy, I turn now to Rohith Vemula's death in India to continue building my claim.

Rohith Vemula

Rohith Vemula was a doctoral student at the University of Hyderabad, India, in 2016. He was a dedicated student and a brilliant scholar with promise. He was also an active member of the Ambedkar Students Association (ASA), where he challenged caste oppression on campus and especially advocated on behalf of

Dalit rights. Reports agree that he was loved by his friends and respected by his peers; however, he was despised by the administration, which did not want to address the subject of caste privilege. Unlike racism and the awareness of its history and presence across the world, caste privilege and oppression operate without much international attention in South Asian societies—of course India, but also Sri Lanka, Nepal, Bangladesh, and not to mention the South Asian diaspora. Caste discrimination influences every aspect of society, yet its quietness allows for the upper caste to claim its society is structured fairly with caste as some forgone ancient problem.

The lack of awareness of caste oppression allows it to survive. The origin of caste derives from the ancient Hindu text *Laws of Manu*, which mandate *dharma*, the natural structure and order of the world. Caste hierarchy, based originally on the *varna* system which proscribes various social requirements and professions—transmogrified into the inflexible and dogmatic *jati* system, which is the localized and doctrinal practice of ensuring people are in their rightful place in society according to their caste. This dangerous and unjust structure is basically divided into four social varnas: Brahmins, Kshatriyas, Vaishyas, and Shudras. If one is not a member of any of these varnas, they are considered Dalits, pejoratively referred to as Untouchables.

Dalits were considered insignificant, backward people. They were and are mistreated to this day as worthless people, people who were at the bottom of South Asian societies. Hinduism had doomed Dalits, lower caste, and people from tribal communities to a life of perpetual servitude and domination. And to this day they are still fighting for rights beneath a Hindustan that subdues them and produces their agony. Caste oppression is alive and forceful, which is why Rohith Vemula was so dedicated to eliminating its presence on campus. Too many students face caste issues in their universities. Too many children are growing up in world where caste dictates their opportunities and futures.

Allow me to pivot to the unfolding of Rohith's story. Many across India, especially progressive activists and intellectuals, believed that Yakub Memon—the man held responsible for financing the 1993 bombings in Bombay—did not receive a fair trial or punishment and therefore should not receive the death penalty. Though Memon cooperated with Indian intelligence agencies and was the only one caught for his involvement, the government still opted to punish him by hanging. Progressives saw this as politically motivated and unfair. Conservatives saw it as national justice. And when Rohith and the Ambedkar Students Association decided to hold a forum for Yakub Memon, the Akhil

Bharatiya Vidyarthi Parishad Student Union—a right-wing Indian nationalist group—accused them of having an antinational funeral prayer.

These actions set off a chain of events in which Rohith's university stipend of 25,000 rupees per month was unfairly withheld. Vemula was then accused of attacking Nandanam Susheel Kumar, a right-wing activist of the Akhil Bharatiya Vidyarthi Parishad (ABVP). A suspension of the Ambedkar students was next. Afterward, they were eventually expelled. A couple weeks after the expulsion, Vemula was found dead with a note in a friend's room. Like Sandra Bland's death and its national impact on discussions of race and police violence, Rohith's death brought caste oppression back to the forefront of South Asian society and introduced it to others.

Though close in time but far away geographically, both examples of suicides exhibit some similarities and differences. Both Sandra and Rohith were educated. They were intelligent and ambitious. They were navigating the professional class in their respective countries. At the same time, they were not rich. Sandra could not afford bail easily. And after several months of having his income withheld, Rohith had nothing. This also means the forms of oppression they endured attacked their ability to provide. They were more than likely on a positive trajectory toward financial health, meaning they were on their way to improving their lives economically, until white supremacy and what B. R. Ambedkar labeled "Brahmanism" sought to derail it (Ambedkar 2016). Moreover, both were actively public about their sentiments. Sandra Bland recorded videos for YouTube where she discussed racism and white supremacy. Rohith Vemula was very active with the ASA and explicitly challenged the Hindutva character of the college. Both remained committed to social justice and equality. Lastly, both became victims of suicide because of encountering something they conceived as insurmountable. We assume this for Sandra Bland through secondary sources. We come to this conclusion for Rohith because of his suicide note.

According to the note Vemula left, he chose suicide because he felt "empty and unconcerned" about himself. And although I believe that despair foregrounded the suicide and the note he penned, it is not a letter of despair. It is not a proclamation of inconsolable anguish. It is not a letter of rage. Rather it is a note that exposes a deep unmitigated disappointment with a world so "unlike the stars," a world so unlike the coherence and aesthetics of the science and nature in which he delighted.

Some have argued that this painful event has nothing to do with caste; after all, Vemula never explicitly mentions caste; he never clearly states he is a Dalit;

he never directly writes a word about the Hindu right or Brahmanical culture. Others have argued that because ABVP student activist Kumar is himself a part of an OBC caste that the initial allegations of casteist foul play against Vemula must be untrue and sparked by leftist political propaganda. In connection to that there are those who have argued that it was because of Vemula's needless involvement in leftist politics that instigated this horrendous occasion in the first place.

All three arguments—drenched in condescension—miss the essential elements that color this entire catastrophe. The issue with their rebuttals is that caste never has to be mentioned; like race, caste is always implicit in the structure of the culture itself. Vemula never had to mention caste; caste is always and already announced. Like race, caste exists independently of its citation. Like race, caste is a permanent feature of the sociocultural logistics of South Asian society. Therefore, the effects of caste oppression, bullying and discrimination was highlighted by Vemula when he wrote that his "birth" was his "fatal accident." That is also why BSP chief Mayawati called this ordeal "government terrorism."

Second, like the structures of white supremacy, caste operates independent of the presence of an upper-caste person. The absence of upper-caste people in no way suggests the absence of Brahmin supremacy. Again, these are logics that exists in spaces, practices, and structures that are accepted and imbibed without awareness. That Kumar and Vemula were both lower castes, in fact, is proof of the permeation of caste oppression.

Lastly, Vemula's activism, the activism of the Ambedkar Students Association, the activism of the Black Lives Matter movement, the activism of The Dalit Women's Self-Respect movement, the activism of the #SayHerName campaign, the activism of the old but never forgotten Black and Dalit Panthers cannot be reduced to ideological cliques of leftist politics. That is too shallow a way of qualifying the raison d'etre of these movements. These movements are about saving lives and preventing murders of the flesh and soul, and nothing less. Therefore, it is my contention that it was not the activism or the leftist politics that distracted Vemula from his studies. In fact, I believe, it was his activism, his outspoken commitments to changing the hierarchy in South Asian culture, that actually kept him alive more than anything.

Vemula's activism was about saving lives and changing the structure of Indian society. That is why his suicide note was more than a letter about his impending death. It was a letter about ensuring that his loved ones' financial needs were taken care of after his departure. It was about consoling those who would be hurt after he was gone. Vemula's suicide note was, in fact, if you read it closely, about performing the duties of being a decent human being seconds before death. Do not misunderstand me; I in no way wish to glorify Vemula's suicide or his letter. It is tragic. It is terrible. But I do want to honor Vemula by showing how even in the face of death he was still caring for his people. There is an integrity in the tragedy that cannot go overlooked, that should not be missed. His death, although because of caste, does not mean he was defeated by caste. His death, at the heart of it all, is a radical indictment of caste, and how it caused his suicide.

Currently, there is a small, but growing, consensus that Dalit suicides in India should be a public health problem. Over the last decade, there has been elevated attention to its constant occurrence, and though Rohith Vemula is a primary example, and the primary example that grounds this chapter, he is growing to become only one among many. India already has a high suicide rate, ranking 49th globally.[1] And Dalit suicides do not normally play as high percentage, until recently. It is growing. And they must be addressed.

What Sandra and Rohith Share

But is there a solution? What do I propose we do in the face of what existentialist Albert Camus refers to as the Absurd (Camus 2018)? Camus believed that the question of suicide is the ultimate philosophical question in the modern world. Once one discovers for themselves that there is no meaning in the universe, they must face the question of whether or not life is worth living. I am not asserting that life is devoid of purpose, meaning, God. My Tillichian leanings compel me to see that we all—one way or another—have an Ultimate Concern (Tillich 1952). But what does one do when one feels that the universe is conspiring against them? Is it worth constantly battling and combating an ultimately adverse life? Black philosophical theologian William R. Jones asked the question directly, "What if God is a white racist? What if God, the deity of the universe, is indifferent to black and brown pain and anguish? Is there any reason to persist? To continue on?" I believe returning to Reinhold Niebuhr is helpful because he argues that we, all of us, need to believe in progress at all costs to live in the face of immoral nations and empires.

Reinhold Niebuhr states, "As individuals, men believe they ought to love and serve each other and establish justice between each other. As racial, economic, and national groups they take for themselves, whatever their power can command" (Niebuhr 2013, 9). For Niebuhr, the human individual has the capacity to be good. They have the ability to do good. They are endowed with a certain level of compassion, empathy, and understanding that is natural to them in their daily lives; but it, unfortunately, vanishes in the context of their group. For Niebuhr, the social group, regardless of who they are, will always be governed by their own self-interest. Yet the individual, the singular person in time and space, has the capacity and moral fortitude to transcend self-interest, they are seemingly powerless, overwhelmed, and morally corrupted by the wants and needs of their group. Niebuhr focuses on the nation—like the United States and India—as the perfect example of group relations that have little trouble with organizing the world around their own needs and benefits.

Niebuhr believes, rightfully so, that "the will-to-live is the will-to-power" (Niebuhr 2013, 18). The nation dominates while the individuals allow it, even at the expense of the poor. This structure of the world makes justice both a necessity and an impossibility—necessary in order to prevent war from destroying the world and killing countless people, an impossibility because the world functions on group power relations. Niebuhr argues the way for the minority groups of the world to attain justice is through force and coercion, even if that means through violent tactics. Overall, these groups must believe in the illusion of the possibility of justice, of victory, in order to maintain the encouragement necessary for such a fight. Niebuhr (2013, 221) states:

> The naïve faith of the proletarian is the faith of the man of action. Rationality belongs to the cool observers. There is of course an element of illusion in the faith of the proletarian, as there is in all faith. But it is a necessary illusion, without which some truth is obscured. The inertia of society is so stubborn that no one will move against it, if he cannot believe that it can be more easily overcome than is actually the case.

It is the *necessary illusion*, the illusion of one day attaining freedom and liberty from those who prevent it for their own good and grandeur, according to Niebuhr, that animates moments of resilience, that demands justice at whatever cost. The belief in illusions must be held in tension with reason in order to prevent what Niebuhr sees as inevitable fanaticism. He believes that fanaticism is channeled through one's illusions and emotions. But on the other hand, he hopes that reason does not relinquish the emotions and illusions before the fight for justice ends. Reinhold Niebuhr is correct. One has to believe, at all costs, in the possibility of ridding the world from the group powers, from white supremacy, Brahminism, and all forms of oppression and domination. He leaves room for violent resistance. Without being a full advocate of nonviolence, I assert that nonviolence is the most responsible foundation of resistance against colossal international powers that engineer social injustice and inequity.

For Dr. B. R. Ambedkhar, the annihilation of caste meant the annihilation of Indian (and the rest of caste infected South Asian) culture that employed the deaths of lower-caste people for its productivity. It did not mean ignoring caste as a topic of discussion in order to deny its current prevalence and violence (Ambedkar 2016). Vermula's suicide is a testament to India's failure in heeding Ambedkhar's words.

Like economic and racial injustice in the United States, caste is an evil too large, too sanguinary, too ingrained in the mechanics of the society to be overcome and defeated without help. It is a historical contention between international freedom thinkers that our countries are too big, too self-interested, too politically malicious and morally bereft to alter their ways of abusing the powerless in their societies; therefore, it will take global solidarity, international coalitions, widespread, extensive empathy that travels across oceans between the oppressed in order to join hands and minds to eradicate the systems that kill us.

We need each other's help to fight and eradicate these systems because these systems are killing us into killing ourselves. The sharp truth of the matter is that the United States has too much invested in the benefits of economic and racial injustice to do all that is necessary to restructure its current way of life. The sad truth of the matter is that India has too much stock, too many assets in maintaining the abusive configurations of caste to decide to expunge it from its culture without pressure.

What we need, and what it has come down to, is the demand for internationally organized nonviolent political anarchy. What it has come down to is the need for aggressive, disruptive demands from the citizens of this world who seek justice. What it has come down to is the need for inaugurating a brand-new world and the destruction of the current way of the world as we know it. If that sounds too rancorous, too extreme, then you are unaware and unfortunately oblivious to just how violent and vicious normal, polite society truly is. There is blood everywhere. Just look down, there, underneath you.

Note

1 Changing pattern of suicide deaths in India. *Lancet Regional Health* – Southeast Asia https://www.thelancet.com/journals/lansea/article/PIIS2772-3682%2823%2900125-7/fulltext.

Bibliography

ABC News. 2015. "Sandra Bland's Voicemail from Jail: 'I'm Still Just at a Loss.'" *ABC News*, July 23. https://abcnews.go.com/US/sandra-blands-voicemail-jail-im-loss/story?id=32624003.

Akkas, Farzana, and Allison Corr. 2024. "Black Adolescent Suicide Rate Reveals Urgent Need to Address Mental Health Care Barriers." Pew.org, April 22. https://www.pewtrusts.org/en/research-and-analysis/articles/2024/04/22/black-adolescent-suicide-rate-reveals-urgent-need-to-address-mental-health-care-barriers.

Ambedkar, B. R. 2016. *Annihilation of Caste: The Annotated Critical Edition*. Verso.

Ashon Crawley. 2016. *Blackpentecostal Breath: The Aesthetics of Possibility*. Fordham University Press. https://doi.org/10.1515/9780823274574-001.

Camus, Albert. 2018. *The Myth of Sisyphus and Other Essays*. Vintage.

Douglas, Kelly Brown. 2015. *Stand Your Ground: Black Bodies and the Justice of God*. Orbis Books.

Durkheim, Émile. 1982. *The Rules of Sociological Method*. Edited by Steven Lukes, translated by W. D. Halls. Free Press. https://doi.org/10.1007/978-1-349-16939-9.

Durkheim, Émile. *On Suicide*. Translated by Robin Buss; introduction by Richard Sennett; notes by Alexander Riley. Penguin Classics. London: Penguin Books, 2006. Originally published 1897.

Durkheim, Émile. 2006. *On Suicide*. Translated by Robin Buss. Penguin UK.

Hassan, Adeel. 2019. "The Sandra Bland Video: What We Know." *The New York Times*, May 7. https://www.nytimes.com/2019/05/07/us/sandra-bland-brian-encinia.html.

Joiner, Thomas. 2005. *Why People Die by Suicide*. Harvard University Press.

Landrin, Sophie. 2023. "India's Elite Schools See a Wave of Suicides among Dalit Students." *Le Monde*, September 27. https://www.lemonde.fr/en/international/article/2023/09/27/india-s-elite-schools-see-a-wave-of-suicides-among-dalit-students_6140378_4.html.

Lewis, Taylor. 2015. "FBI Investigating Circumstances Surrounding Sandra Bland's Death." *Essence*, July 17. https://www.essence.com/news/sandra-bland-death-fbi-investigating-circumstances/.

Niebuhr, Reinhold. 2013. *Moral Man and Immoral Society: A Study in Ethics and Politics*. Westminster John Knox Press.

Pandey, Gyanendra. 2013. *A History of Prejudice*. Cambridge University Press. https://doi.org/10.1017/CBO9781139237376.
Pickering, W. S. F., and Geoffrey Walford, eds. 2000. *Durkheim's Suicide: A Century of Research and Debate*. Routledge. https://doi.org/10.4324/9780203459270.
Tillich, Paul. 1952. *The Courage to Be*. Yale University Press.

9

Agency Enhanced through Communal Support

A Potential Remedy to Suicidal Tendencies

Christopher J. Krall, S.J.

Making any decision can be difficult. Decisions involving suicide are seriously complex and taxing. Every person faces forks in the road, moments where life presents multiple options and when only one action is possible. Decisions made at such junctures often have lasting consequences. The question addressed in this chapter is, "How much freedom do people have in making conscious, willed, and intentional decisions?" If decisions made along life's path lead ultimately to the threshold of suicide, one may question what factors, so-called "Influences of Intentionality" (IOIs), might be at play along the way toward the brink. Based on neurological research and theological reasoning, I argue that despite the many internal and external IOIs—including the confluence of neurological, epistemological, philosophical, and theological factors—many persons still retain the ability to make decisions, but their intentionality may become compromised. The decisions that lead to suicide are complex and yet each human life is precious. Therefore, this intentional examination of the artistry of decision-making attempts to shed light on people's capacities for freely directing the course of their lives, while also admitting the restrictions and pressures outside of anyone's control that influence decisions.

Robert Frost's poem "The Road Not Taken" describes facing a choice: "Two roads diverged in a yellow wood / And sorry I could not travel both / And be one traveler, long I stood" (Frost 1951, 270). While standing at this fork in the path, Frost's traveler seeks a "right" path assuming it will lead to the greatest good. Thomas Aquinas offers a method in his discourse on human persons by identifying a person as "the master of his actions through his reason and will" (*Summa Theologiae* 2.1.1). Human reason and the power of the will are drawn to that which is right and good. Intentionality can be defined as the human capacity to translate internal desires into external actions. It allows persons to confront each juncture along the path of life by using clear reasoning and right willing. Intentionality is possibly the most remarkable capacity of any living creature. And yet, Aquinas's notion of mastery does not account for the many IOIs that challenge, block, and prevent reason and the will from acting in full capacity, intentionally, and with clarity.

Reason-guided and willed intentionality is neither simplistic nor easily practiced. In his *Letter to the Romans*, Paul sought intentionality in his decisions yet faced the weakness of his carnal and mortal nature in frustration: "I do not understand my own actions. For I do not do what I want, but I do the very thing I hate" (Rom. 7:15, NRSVUE). The direct movement from "I want" to *doing* the desired act is intentionality. Paul is the first to admit that he performs actions he hates doing. Why would he choose to resist what he knows he ought to do? The bombardment of Internal and external IOIs impel people to act one way not the other, even to the point of suicide.

In this chapter, I address the "science of decision-making" by considering implications of culpability, moral discernment, addictive behaviors, and the weight of divine grace. I first consider four internal and four external IOIs. This section involves technical/scientific concepts which may seem obvious. The point of conducting an intentional examination is to name specifically the elements that influence human decisions which can be taken for granted. At the same time, the reader should feel free to skim or skip this section so as not to become bogged down in technical details and move to the theoretical/theological concepts in the second half on the art of decision-making. In the second section, titled "Theological and Ethical Considerations Involved with the Decision of Suicide," I explore four elements involved with decisions that compound as a person enacts suicide. First, there is a method to decision-making. Second, there are the sources of human freedom. Third, there are potential strengthening remedies when facing a loss of freedom. Fourth, through faith-based integrated self-consciousness, there is possibility to endure with the strength of agency to preserve life.

Internal IOIs

Genetics

In a 2015 meta-analysis of 2,748 twin studies conducted over the last fifty years, investigators established that more than 17,804 human traits are genetically inherited 49–69 percent of the time (Polderman et al. 2015, 703–9). Moreover, "The ten most investigated traits were temperament and personality functions, weight maintenance functions, general metabolic functions, depressive episode, higher-level cognitive functions, conduct disorders, mental and behavioral disorders due to use of alcohol, anxiety disorders, height and mental and behavioral disorders due to use of tobacco" (Polderman et al. 2015, 703). Most of these traits could, if stressed, trigger suicidal ideation. The influence genetics has on behavior is arguably extensive. From facial shape to personality, to genetic illness or a proclivity to diseases, to higher levels of cognitive mannerisms, the IOI of genetics envelopes human persons, influencing the decisions we make and the attractions we have. The path one chooses to follow in life, and those that one avoids are in large part pre-determined by genetics prior to any conscious decision-making activity. Traits are woven into us at the double-helix structures within every fiber of our physical being.

Probing into the cellular composition of the human body, within the gaps (synapses) between neurons in the brain—of which there are an estimated six-hundred trillion—are the potent locations where chemical neurotransmitters are emitted by the electrically excited neuron. These chemical neurotransmitters (especially the amino acid glutamate), which are emitted through the chain reactions caused by the impulse of the electrical signal in the pre-synaptic neuron, intend to spark another electrical signal to surge through the postsynaptic neuron by means of special receptors on the postsynaptic cleft. This intricately complex process is how thoughts and signals are constantly communicated throughout the central nervous system. The neurotransmitters oozing across the synapse are received and taken up by the postsynaptic receiving neuron through "gatekeepers," called EAATS (excitatory amino acid transporters). Currently, scientists know of five different types of EAATS, each of which uptake particular types of neurotransmitter chemicals at distinct rates and times. Genetics determines the presence of each of the five types of EAATS, the arrangement of the EAATS across the postsynaptic neuron, and the number of each type of EAATS. These factors combine to affect the rate at which neurotransmitters are taken up by the postsynaptic neuron which then has an important influence on the cognitive processing across the billions of synapses throughout the brain. Genetic influence on the decisions each person makes at forks in the road is enormous because of these microscopic modifications in a person's billions of synapses.

Compiled with the genetics of neuroscience is the tendency to favor right brain over left brain perception. Iain McGilchrist explains in *Master and His Emissary* the unique ways in which the left and right hemispheres cause changes in thinking patterns and functionality. The right hemisphere tends to favor sustained, broad, open, evolving, interconnecting, implicit thinking capable of empathy, concern for other living entities, attention to transcendent understandings, and big picture, teleological perspectives. When details are missing, the right brain tends to fill in with broad sweeping and safe generalizations. The left hemisphere maintains vigilance on the fine details, narrowly focused, fixed concepts, static data, and sharply focused attention. The side or type of thinking that each person favors is outside of conscious control and is determined largely by genetics.

There are also theological considerations to genetic influences on human intentionality. According to the Roman Catholic Church, Scripture, using figurative language, identifies guilt which humanity bears from a primeval event represented by the original fault of the first parents that is passed genetically through human lineage (*CCC* §§385-421). Paul recognizes the spread of sin through all of humanity in his letter to the Romans, "Therefore, just as through one man sin entered into the world, and death through sin, and so death spread to all mankind, because all sinned—for until the Law sin was in the world, but sin is not counted against anyone when there is no law. Nevertheless, death reigned from Adam until Moses, even over those who had not sinned in the likeness of the violation committed by Adam, who is a type of Him who was to come" (Rom. 5:12-14, NAB). Concupiscence is the appetitive instinctual and inescapable desire for carnal goods contrasting from the divine good. In contrast, God's mercy also is passed from generation to generation. Moses taught the people of Israel, "Know, then, that the Lord, your God, is God: the faithful God who keeps His covenant of mercy to the thousandth generation toward those who love him and keep his commandments" (Deut. 7:9). Genetics, woven within every bodily function, influences behavioral intentionality in life's decisions.

Biology

A second category of internal IOIs is biological. Recent studies show compelling evidence that the human body is "a super-complex ecosystem containing trillions of bacteria and other microorganisms that inhabit all our surfaces, skin, mouth, sexual organs, and especially intestines" (Montiel-Castro et al. 2013, 1). Rather than the bacteria causing detrimental or destructive effects on the human body, medical scientists recognize beneficial qualities of the microorganisms within and on the body. The gastrointestinal track is a bustling colony of bacteria, archaea, viruses, fungi, and protozoa advantageous to human survival. "Acting as a *probiotic*: a live microbe with a beneficial effect on the host via modifications of host-associated microbial communities, enhance[es] the host's response toward disease, its nutrient-exploitation capacity, or improving its environment" (Montiel-Castro et al. 2013, 1). As scientists understand important qualities of the gut-microbiome, probiotic foods such as sourdough breads (natural yeast), fermented tea (kambucha), kimchi (fermented cabbage) and dairy products are beneficial for their ability to re-colonize microorganisms within the gastrointestinal tracts. While bacteria offer many bodily aids, they also influence thoughts, actions, and behaviors.

Neurological studies confirm bidirectional signaling between the gastrointestinal track and the brain mainly through the myelinated branch of the tenth cranial nerve known commonly as the Vagus nerve. This elaborate nerve system reaches from the medulla oblongata in the center of the brainstem to branches wrapping the heart, lungs, and digestive system in the stomach and intestines. The cranial nerve functionality involves the autonomic parasympathetic system and stimulates actions that involve mood, speech, facial expression, swallowing, taste, breathing, heartrate and blood pressure, digestion, urine output, and skin and muscle sensation. The bacterial culture within the intestines sends signals through the Vagus nerve and into the "microbiota-gut-vagus-brain axis," which establishes and maintains homeostasis, metabolic regulation, and mental functioning. Neuroscientists hypothesize that due to the mutualisms formed between hosts and commensal bacteria, the influence of the bacteria culture could "shape higher cognitive functions at the individual level, and work as a selective force promoting socialization and social structures, with an influence on the psychobiological basis of gregariousness, social perception, mate choice, and sexual behavior" (Montiel-Castro et al. 2013, 2). Gut-based decision making or "intuitive" decisions, neuroscientists find, are rooted in biological influences. Thus, the motivation behind a person's intentional decisions has sources of influence within subconscious perception. The strong influence of biological organisms within the human body has a major impact on the intentionality of decision-making.

Habits

Neuroscientists are finding decision-making occurs physically in the corticobasal ganglia and loops to the operation of the cerebral cortex. Within this neuro-loop is the neostriatum that gathers glutamatergic input from many cortical regions as well as from the midbrain dopamine neurons which is involved in reward processing. The brain uses habits for energy conservation and cognitive efficiency. Rather than developing new firing patterns for each new action caused by unique dopaminergic transmissions, training, or habit-making, is the brain adapting with neuroplasticity for quick adjustments for goal-directed actions with less neuron-firing in the cerebral cortex and less dopamine dependency. In other words, going back to Robert Frost's poem, the traveler who walks through the same woods the second day, even though Frost doubted that he would ever return to the same fork in the road again, the likelihood that the person walking through the woods would take the same road less-traveled by is higher, because he would not have to discover a new route home. Choosing a new route would require more brainpower and the dopaminergic reward is already perceived when looking down the familiar road.

Neuroscientists Eike Buabang and his colleagues at Trinity College carefully analyzed real-world habits and identified them as either stimulus-response associations or goal-directed action-outcome (Buabang et al. 2025). They define habits as, "behaviors triggered by contextual stimuli, developed through frequent repetition, that often persist regardless of current beliefs and goals" (Buabang et al. 2025, 42). Actions that persist regardless of beliefs or goals are "Influences of Intentionality." Because of internal and external IOIs, a person acts out of habit, with less brain investment, and thus mindlessly, rather than acting with careful intentionality (Dahl, Wilson-Mendenhall, and Davidson 2020).[1] Stimulus-response actions involve behaviors triggered by familiar contexts, cues, or memories of past experiences. People may hold beliefs and have goals, yet in certain contexts (such as opening a cellular phone) the stimulus of dopaminergic charges from the images on the phone triggers an automatic response of opening an application which leads to the habitual pattern of hours of scrolling through social media posts. Even though the person may have strong intentions for accomplishing specific goals, the habit caused by the stimulus-response overrides any goal-directed actions.

Goal-directed actions require energy for the formation of new neuropathways. Habitual actions, like scrolling, are efficient, energy conserving, and minimally taxing on the brain. Goal-directed behaviors are driven by what Buabang and his colleagues explain as action-outcome expectancies. The goal-directed behavior fueled by higher-order beliefs and value-systems, works intentionally, mindfully, and with disciplined focus to obtain a specific outcome. Actions willingly enacted to achieve a goal, such as the hours of disciplined training required to run a marathon, the years of focus to complete a doctoral degree, the lifetime of struggle and labor for composing a symphony or a book, require willed discipline and focus and refusing to become distracted by triggers or bodily cravings of negative habits. Goal-directed action is the willingness to expend excess energy for the sake of forming new and intentional paths, to resist the temptations caused by distracting triggers that stimulate negative habitual thinking, and to forego instant gratification while holding out for the desired goal.

Nevertheless, as stimulus-driven habitual behavior is reinforced and enacted consistently, "Neurons representing stimuli and responses fire simultaneously and thereby form connections" (Buabang et al. 2025, 4). When goal-directed actions are weakened and the stimulus-response exhibits hyperactivity, neuroscientists find that there are disturbances to frontostriatal circuits, often resulting in OCD tendencies. The opposite is also true, in what Buabang and his colleagues call the law of exercise. When goal-directed actions are practiced, given focused attention, and reinforced with rewards, the less any stimulants tempt or distract.

Some habits prompted by stimulus behavior are beneficial. An efficiency method the brain adopts called "chunking" is "the integration of multiple actions into a sequence [. . .] shown to be dopamine-dependent" (Buabang et al. 2025, 11). Actions like driving a car with a manual transmission and working through the multiple gears while using the clutch or brushing one's teeth and moving directly into flossing are examples of chunking habits. Ideally, beneficial stimulus behaviors are compounded with other healthy actions that allow for growth and strength with increasing efficiency. Stimulus behavior patterns are the kinds of actions that when not performed on one day due to abnormal circumstances cause an out-of-place or not "right" feeling. Dependency on drugs, alcohol, or pornography can cause such unease when not used as can a day without exercise, healthy eating, or brushing one's teeth. Habits are reinforced when a person performs the same action in multiple environments and contexts regardless of the triggering cues. At that point, they become goal-directed, and thus intentional and desired, rather than stimulus-response, which are unconscious or unintentional.

Habitual actions caused by internal and external triggers thrust influential forces into decision-making. Decisions resort to unconscious efficient processing that potentially harm self and others. Harmful habits are rigid, numb to consequences, and un-freeing, as if the person is stuck in a rut with no way to escape from the drive to persistently perform the seemingly required act. Alternatively, healthy habits are willed acts that are a rhythm of life lifting a person to freedom through an intentional goal-directed enthusiasm. Recognizing the ease in which habitual actions form and the influence the stimulus-response has on decision-making allows for greater intentionality and careful discernment.

Intellectual Mindset

Biases, or intellectual lenses through which people view the world, can skew decision-making without conscious recognition. Twentieth-century philosopher, theologian, and epistemologist Bernard Lonergan defined bias as a limited consciousness and comfortable but narrow worldview with ties to neurological conditions and psychic blocks. More specifically, he described "a flight from understanding [which] blocks the occurrence of the insights that would upset its comfortable equilibrium" (Lonergan 1992, 6). Lonergan named four ways biases are manifest. Dramatic bias is the neurotic condition of refusing to accept the truth, which may have manifestations in fear about a required action for growth or indications necessitating a change of course. This is often an unconscious repression at the psychic level of the feelings or images that may suggest a new and enhanced way of living. Change is hard, and if a person is convinced that no change is needed, then any suggested provocation of change is ignored and repressed. Addicts caught in the patterns of their addiction cannot recognize that a different and more healthy way of life is possible.

Second, there is individual bias, which takes the form of egoism. Lonergan explained that egoism, "is an incomplete development of intelligence. It rises above a merely inherited mentality. It has the boldness to strike out and think for itself. But it fails to pivot from the initial and preliminary motivation provided by desires and fears to the self-abnegation involved in allowing complete free play to intelligent inquiry" (Lonergan 1992, 245–6). The failure to allow for the expansion of consciousness because of the dominance of self-absorbed interests and satisfactions is a flight from understanding and a failure to ask further questions for intelligent understanding and reasonable judgments. Modern social media reinforces the egoistic mindset with reminders for how much one is "liked," how many followers one has acquired by posting news of oneself, and the obsession encouraged to post pictures of oneself.

Third, group bias is rooted in the manipulative competition for power between groups of people in the social order of society. Group bias is large-scale communal blindness as groups seek success but fail to allow intelligence to expand to recognize the need to enhance the well-being of the whole population. Lonergan explained, "The attitude of the dominant groups determines the attitude of the depressed groups. Reactionaries are opposed by revolutionaries. Progressives are met by liberals. In the former case the situation heads toward violence. In the latter case there is a general agreement about ends with disagreement about the pace of change and the mode and measure of its execution" (Lonergan 1992, 250). The proliferation of the Nazi party after the First World War is a shocking instance of how a regime can influence the decisions, actions, and world perspectives of large numbers of people, manipulating them to embrace racist tendencies and actions of persecution. In his "Letter from Birmingham Jail," Martin Luther King wrote, "We can never forget that everything Hitler did in Germany was 'legal' and everything that Hungarian freedom fighters did in Hungary was 'illegal'" (King 1963, 3). Again, bias is a large-scale flight from intelligent understanding and authentic living.

Fourth, general bias is complacency with common-sense thinking. Rather than progressing into higher levels of intelligence through self-reflection or expanding one's consciousness through questions, learning, and new experiences, general bias is "concerned with the concrete and particular. It entertains no aspirations about reaching abstract and universal laws. It easily is led to rationalize its limitations by engendering a conviction that other forms of human knowledge are useless or doubtfully valid" (Lonergan 1992, 251). This bias is an obsession with one way of thinking. The ancient desert fathers and mothers used the term *logismois* to describe the way the mind can fixate on just one thought, such as anger, and to ruminate within this thought until it becomes all-encompassing for one's worldview, even to the point of self-identification: "I am an angry person." As a person gets lost in this mental whirlwind, any collateral insights, values, beauty, or wider perspectives are blocked. The person is blinded to all other possibilities for alternative perspectives. All these forms of bias create an internal influence strongly affecting the human intentional decision-making process.

External IOIs

Along with the internal IOIs are the external forces that inhibit free decision-making and which dictate life's direction. As with the internal, the external are limited to four examples.

Environmental

The environment in which children grow influences their adult life and the lenses through which they will view the world. From an overly protective home where the child is sheltered from discomfort and blocked from seeing harsh realities, to places where children experience domestic violence, weapons, and no tenderness, the environmental factors forge memories and shape neural patterning. The Adverse Childhood Experiences Inventory (ACE), which was developed in the mid-1990s, surveyed a group of over 17,000 participants in California about their experiences with childhood maltreatment, family dysfunction, and current health status and behaviors. Strikingly, a direct correlation was established between childhood trauma and adult onset of chronic disease, incarceration, and employment challenges (Cronholm et al. 2015).

Children who experience trauma have deep wounds etched into the fibers of their bodies and psyches which will influence how they see the world, live their lives, make their decisions, and choose their paths. A leader in "trauma informed care," Bessel van der Kolk, in *The Body Keeps the Score*, explains, "These experiences leave traces on people's biology and identity and have devastating social consequences—medical illnesses, problems with school and work performance, drug addiction and a variety of psychiatric illness. In fact, the Centers for Disease Control and Prevention calculate that childhood trauma is our single largest public health issue—more costly than cancer or heart disease" (van der Kolk 2015). The decisions made while enduring physiological, psychological, and even spiritual wounds are not free from the influence of environmental factors.

The environmental context which is considered "home" sets the bounds or limits for meaning in life. The expressions "the apple does not fall far from the tree," or "like father/mother, like son/daughter" emphasize that the context people absorb impacts future decision-making. The neurological transformations of environmental factors of especially maternal actions were explored by Frances Champagne and Michael Meaney (Champagne and Meaney 2001). They state, "Through the activation of the hypothalamo-pituitary-adrenal (HPA) axis and corticotropin-releasing hormone (CRH) pathways, prolonged or exaggerated responses to stress have profound effects on physiological and cognitive functions" (Champagne and Meaney 2001, 287). The environmental impacts, for health or for harm, have generational effects. Champagne and Meaney elaborate, "The neural basis of this inheritance pattern appears to reside in the central oxytocin system which determines features of maternal behavior. Through these various adaptive neural mechanisms, the environmental demand on the mother is reflected in the quality of maternal care to her offspring" (Champagne and Meaney 2001, 287). These researchers looked at the ways mother mice either engaged or neglected licking and grooming of their pups. The care the pups received determined how they would treat their future pups. Neglect in one generation breeds neglect and impresses a context of trauma on future generations. Alternatively, an environmental context of care, love, and support is also transferable.

Relationships

Relationships form the social webs in which every person is inevitably enmeshed and thus profoundly influence intentionality. Parental indoctrination, peer pressure, inspirational teachers, fear-instilling coaches, the good, bad, beautiful, ugly, the manipulators and the caretakers, the haters and the compassionate all make their marks. The fitness of survival and the procreative drive for offspring depend on non-agonistic relationships which fuel attraction to other people. Neuroscientists attempt to investigate the neurobiological and endocrinological alterations due to engagement in relationships or separations, yet recognize the complexity involved in these studies. Claudia Manca and Karen Bales, social psychologists at UC Davis, explain, "that oxytocin as well as vasopressin may influence basic emotional mechanisms that regulate social approach and social aversion. According to this hypothesis, oxytocin, acting on the hindbrain parasympathetic system should stimulate pro-social behavior, while vasopressin acting on sympathetic pathways should stimulate withdrawal and/or aggression" (Manca and Bales 2024, 44). Note the language of "should stimulate" used, indicating that research is speculating about the factors determining human behavior. Neuroscientists attribute strong influence on hormones circulating through the synapses of the brain to the decisions that people make and the behaviors that people exhibit. Hormonal influences are largely subconscious impressions sparked by the many personally experienced interactions. Depending on the prevalence of the hormones and their receptors, even rational and carefully discerning persons are impelled to connect to particular people and avoid others. The types of relationships that a person is habitually attracted toward, whether agonistic or altruistic, through the neurological reward pathways will influence decisions.

Extensive research shows that "Positive social relationships are vital for healthy psychological functioning and serve as a buffer against psychological disorders, such as depression and anxiety, while poor social relationships can be more harmful than excessive drinking and smoking" (Dahl, Wilson-Mendenhall, and Davidson 2020). At the same time, relationships can cause distress. Social pain, due to break-ups, arguments, threats, or loss, have similar effects in brain-activation as physical pain (Eisenberger 2015). There are both top-down and bottom-up actions in brain activity during interactions with others. Premeditated actions like empathy, generosity, or harsh critique toward others show correlations of brain activity in the mental areas of the medial prefrontal cortex, temporoparietal junction, temporal pole, and precuneus. While instinctual judgments toward others of disgust, attraction, or rash emotional reactions have activation in the insula, amygdala, and the autonomic networks for reward or distress, social interactions stir a strong IOI that can impact life-decisions significantly.

Cosmic Forces

The classic rebuttal of Cassius to Brutus in Shakespeare's *Julius Caesar*, "The fault, dear Brutus, is not in our stars but in ourselves that we are underlings," challenged the common perception from Roman times to the modern era that our "stars," or the many forms of fate, have an influential impact on our living and acting. Lunar cycles, astrological signs, sun bursts, dark energy, gravitational pulls, tidal shifts, temperature fluctuations, barometric pressure changes, plate tectonics, galactic spins, cosmic microwave background radiation, cellular transmissions, or just plain luck; the universe is chaotically full of clashing forces. Humans are sensitive and vulnerable creatures caught in whirlwinds of external influences. Many scientists recognize that life in the chaotic universe is evidence for fine-tuning. External forces somehow set conditions just right to allow for precious and fragile life to spring forth. Starting with dark energy, the physicist Alan Lightman writes:

> [A] little larger, and the universe would have accelerated so rapidly that matter in the young universe could never have pulled itself together to form stars and hence complex atoms made in stars. And, going into negative values of dark energy, a little smaller and the universe would have decelerated so rapidly that it would have re-collapsed before there was time to form even the simplest atoms. (Lightman 2014, 18)

Universal fine-tuning suggests that beneficial or harmful arrangements and determinants are set which human conscious capacities cannot fathom. Extrapolating from and speculating about finely tuned dark energy, could all moments of each person's life have finely tuned cosmic determinants that give rise to the opportunities we have come to know as life?

Sam Harris, a modern philosopher and neuroscientist, argues that luck rather than free will is the driver of human choices. Any selection from among choices is merely an illusion because the option chosen was determined by lucky confluences of internal and external factors long before any choice was offered. Luck, the random, yet seemingly determining, force that guides every aspect of life, seemingly determines much of human action. We are lucky if we are born with a healthy body, a caring family, or desires to succeed. We are unlucky if we are sickly, living in a dangerous environment, or have a mind full of hate. Harris writes, "You can change your life, and yourself, through effort and discipline—but you have whatever capacity for effort and discipline you have in this moment, and not a scintilla more (or less). You are either lucky in this department or you aren't—and you cannot make your own luck" (Harris 2012, 38). Luck, and any other cosmic external forces that we may or may not perceive, certainly influence our decisions.

Spiritual Forces

Pascal's classic wager makes the contrast between the naturalist view, which holds that materiality is all that exists, and the supernaturalist perspective, which holds that existence extends beyond the material. If nature exists by random chance, then it will eventually dissolve into randomness, and any speculation of supernatural existence, including meaning, purpose, or value, is pointless. However, if supernatural realities exist, then the order that science finds in the universe has a basis and teleological fulfillment is logical. With the supernaturalist perspective, religion, in its many iterations, elaborates how supernatural beings are revealed within the natural order.

Christianity, specifically, holds that the supernatural creator is the source of goodness, love, and truth. The second person of the Trinity God took on flesh and dwelt in human form. The power of the Holy Spirit, the third person of the Trinity God, continually enters human hearts and minds. The challenge that theologians through the ages grapple with is the determinacy of divine forces on human decisions. One postulation is that supernatural grace has two distinct effects in humans, operative and cooperative. Peter Lombard, in the twelfth century, explicated, "Grace is operative inasmuch as it causes this efficacious good will, making what already was a will into a good and right will. It is cooperative inasmuch as it aids good will to execute good intentions" (Lonergan 2000, 12). Augustine of Hippo described his conversion in similar ways, operative in that it "called and shouted and broke through his deafness" and cooperative in the continual growth into virtue. Much later, in the twentieth century, Bernard Lonergan summarized Aquinas by writing, "God operates to initiate us in the spiritual life, and he cooperates to bring us to perfection; alone he works to give us good desires, and together with our good desires he labors to give us good performance" (Lonergan 2000, 5). The operative grace of God flooding a person's heart with unmerited love (Romans 5:5) is a religious conversion while cooperative grace is found in the daily decisions made to overcome bias and choose good habitually, which is moral conversion.

According to the Roman Catholic Church, a person guided by cooperative grace is still free to assent to God's encouragement or not. By cooperating with divine grace, the person intentionally decides to embody charitable actions habitually. Choosing not to love is a violation of the two great commandments, or separation from God. The challenge that Aquinas and theologians face is whether human freedom is preserved with the IOI of supernatural forces or if, like luck, grace determines human actions.

Theological and Ethical Considerations Involved with the Decision of Suicide

This section addresses the challenges and strengths of human intentionality as it relates to the act of suicide. It contains three short subsections that address the epistemological complexity of human decision-making as well as the philosophical and theological implications of free decisions. The first section examines the method of decision-making that can impel a person to consider suicide, the second examines the sources of human freedom, and the final section considers a faith-based perspective that can offer freedom from despair and suicidal ideation.

The Method of Decision-Making

To be clear, agency refers to the capacity individuals retain amid the forces of IOIs to act intentionally and to make decisions. The making of a decision consists of several important steps which have become an art or science. The Air Force fighter pilot John Boyd formulated in the 1970s what he called the "OODA Loop" consisting of "observation, orientation, decision, and action." This decision-making method involves an iterative process of gathering information from the surrounding environment, continually observing feedback, establishing an hypothesis, testing whether the observations are accurate, and moving to decided-upon actions (Osinga 2007, 2). Bernard Lonergan also articulated a very similar decision-making method, the "General Empirical Method (GEM)" which is a culmination of a self-appropriating process of sublation from attentively experiencing, to rationally understanding, to reasonably judging, to responsibly deciding. Lonergan explains how experiential attentiveness is driven by a desire for understanding. With proper understanding an intentional decision is enacted. The GEM allows for a consistent translation from knowledge acquired to action executed. Lonergan writes, "The rational subject as carrying out an obligation is not just a knower, but also a doer, and his rationality consists not merely in excluding interference with cognitional process but also in extending the rationality of his knowing into the field of doing. But that extension does not occur simply by knowing one's obligations. It occurs just inasmuch as one wills to meet one's obligations" (Lonergan 1992, 638). The interference between the subject and the action decided upon are the internal and external IOIs discussed above. The driving force of the will to meet one's obligations empowers translation from intentions to actions. Lonergan continues, "judgment is concerned to complete one's knowledge of an actuality that already exists, while decision is concerned to confer actuality upon a course of action that otherwise will not exist" (Lonergan 1992, 636). Conferring actuality is how life is advanced or diminished through the power of intentional decision-making.

As people intentionally will actions to confer actuality and obtain desired outcomes, they assume that in an ordered and predictable universe their willed action results in the desired outcome. However, involuntary, unplanned, or unwilled acts occur frequently. Many bodily movements are reflexive, caused by stimulus rather than conscious intentionality. Seizures, cramps, cancer, autoimmune actions, or autonomic nerve response systems are a few examples of the body acting involuntarily even to the detriment of the person's survival. When considering the moral implications of human actions, if a person acts involuntarily, thus, without willful intention, the person is not responsible or culpable for the action, for either praise or blame. Alternatively, voluntary actions are "free" or intentional, consciously executed, premeditated, or desired by a person using reason. Based on the first section of this chapter, both internal and external IOIs are powerful forces that can undermine even seemingly deliberate and willed actions.[2]

Now that the internal and external IOIs are appreciated and the method of decision-making is established, we can finally address the difficult question of whether suicide is voluntary. Is a person who is wrestling with the action of suicide making a willful and intentional decision or do IOI's slowly crush the intentional process of knowledge and will to irrational or instinctual action? Rather than identifying suicide as one big sudden decision, this chapter has shown the importance of examining the many parts involved in the science of decision-making. I offer the consideration of "slow suicide," or many small decisions made over time in the process of following the paths of life with many forks that culminates in the decision to pursue suicide. Thomas Joiner, a psychologist and specialist on suicide ideation, emphasizes suicide is not an instinctual reaction. He writes, "we have no death instinct, but we have an irrepressible draw toward life; many suicidal people have tried to tame this force with their proverbial pitchforks, and while some tragically do so, many are gainsaid by this force that can 'come back upon' them" (Joiner 2024, 50). If the default mode of humanity is survival, then to override this life-instinct takes willed and intentional decisions, in little choices, over time.

For many who are at the brink of suicide, will and reason are overrun with strong influences on their agency, or capacity for intentionality. Outi Benson, Susanne Gibson, and Sarah Brand developed an important study analyzing the experience of agency while facing feelings of being suicidal. They interviewed 124 men and women who were self-reported as suicidal asking specifically about the feelings they experienced. They found, "Our participants described suicidal feelings as a bodily experience that was also a restructuring of their experience of self, world, and others . . . 'becoming suicidal' constitutes a fundamental change in the person's experiential background such that no thought, perception, or emotional response is left completely unchanged" (Ratcliffe 2014, 52). The participants of their study described their mode of existence as intolerable. Some felt disintegrated as a person, involved in a battle going on inside themselves, caught in a "glass coffin" (Ratcliffe 2014, 59), or out of balance where the only way to restore the balance is through suicide. These feelings, which the authors analyzed from the interviews, powerfully restructured a person's entire orientation toward life and the realities of the world. "The world is thus variously described as inaccessible to the self, or with changed meaning, in the sense of having lost or altered in its significance for the self" (Ratcliffe 2014, 59). Many influences compound and cause a person to experience these intensely encompassing feelings.

The "slow suicide" happens over the course of weeks or even years while pressured by compounding IOIs with micro-decisions. The choices of each decision, at the time a decision is made, may seem good and life-giving. However, increasingly, decisions become narrowed to a single category which becomes all-consuming. Consciousness is consumed on that category, whether it is a job, a relationship, a financial matter, and so on. The person's identity becomes absorbed into this category. When issues with this category arise, decisions become desperate, and the category is seen through catastrophic biases which gives the impression that nothing is going right, and nothing can change the awfulness of life. The narrowing horizon of intentionality is Catastrophic Categorical Thinking (CCT) and has detrimental consequences. As small, good, life-directed decisions are made over time, they seem natural. However, the decisions, pressured by IOIs and focused through CCT, become confining and increasingly more restrictive. Freedom to pull out from the category is seemingly impossible and a person *feels* trapped. The decision of suicide, in many cases can involve a slow, seemingly natural decision-making process that is heavily influenced by many IOIs channeling a person into CCT.

Sourcing Human Freedom

If IOIs can cause people to tumble into the horrendous feelings of imprisonment and internal battles, from where can the experience of freedom come? Wisdom from the Judeo-Christian tradition offers three sources that impel persons toward the liberating power of relationship in communal connectedness: (1) the foundational goodness of a person's identity, (2) the disciplining of desire to make the achievement of goodness first possible and then effortless, and (3) the act of giving love rather than seeking to receive it. Understanding the sources of human freedom may not be possible for a person who is entrenched in suicidal tendencies to recognize. As much as humanity's intentionality has roots in the mental capacities of reason and will-power, brain scans (such as fMRIs) are revealing that traumatic experiences cause significant silencing of components of the brain associated with logical thinking, executive function, deductive reasoning, and language production. Even when a person may want to reason their way out of suicidal thinking and will their feelings into happiness, van der Kolk's research has found that "the emotions, sounds, images, thoughts, and physical sensations related to the trauma take on a life of their own" (van der Kolk 2015, 66). The survival mentality instinctually resorts to flight, fight, or dissociative freeze responses as a means of coping. Flashbacks to traumatic events are often triggered resulting in a state of numbness and disconnectedness. The capacity for free and coherent decisions is dramatically limited when a person is enveloped in suicidal related feelings. Nevertheless, for a friend to remind a traumatized person of the sources of freedom or for someone who is moving toward the brink of suicide to catch him or herself with these deep realities can offer healing, awakening, and expansion out of CCT.

The first source of freedom stems from philosophical and theological principles and is tucked in an obscure question of Thomas Aquinas's *Summa Theologiae*. He states, "Every being, as being, is good. For all being, as being, has actuality and is in some way perfect; since every act implies some sort of perfection; and perfection implies desirability and goodness" (*Summa Theologiae* 1.5.3). Far from mere theological abstraction, this principle, when transposed into anthropological and psychological practice, is the basis of human hope. Human persons are existing creatures active in the world and each person's existence exudes goodness and desirability. A person who recognizes his or her fundamental goodness relieves the perceived misunderstanding of burdensomeness as discussed in the "Interpersonal Theology of Suicide"(Van Orden et al. 2010). Grasping one's personal foundation of goodness in existence is a first-level freedom.

After one's foundational identity is grounded in goodness, the second level of freedom comes from the direction toward which one's life is oriented. A person who directs his or her words, thoughts, and actions toward goodness is freed from the many lures of unfree attachments and evil dispositions. When the disposition toward good and virtuous ends becomes habitual and second nature, the person is free at a second level. The struggle of learning a new language can serve as an example of this second level source of freedom. At first, a novice Spanish-speaker does not grasp the meanings of words, stumbles through verb-tenses, and fails to formulate sentence structures. But over time, through the discipline of practice and training, the "good" of conversation and communication of ideas through the Spanish language becomes easier until fluency, at which point the person freely expresses ideas in Spanish naturally. Likewise, with aspects of morality, self-worth, or the goodness of life, the discipline required for growing in the mastery of goodness is the means by which freedom is gained.

A last source of freedom is the awakened capacity within a person for self-giving love, in Greek, *agape*. The bias of self-centeredness or pridefulness closes people off from each other, especially the needy and vulnerable of society. St. Paul spoke about and exhibited this third level of freedom as recorded in the *Acts of the Apostles*. "I have never wanted anyone's silver or gold or clothing. You knew well that these very hands have served my needs and my companions. In every way I have shown you that by hard work of that sort we must help the weak, and keep in mind the words of the Lord Jesus who himself said, 'it is more blessed to give than to receive'" (Acts 20:33-35). Many who are struggling with a sense of perceived burdensomeness or failing to recognize self-worth, which are some of the sources of suicide ideation, when given the chance to serve others who are suffering or impoverished, begin to recognize the gift of life. When freed *from* the tendencies of selfishness and self-focus and motivated by the freedom *for* giving to the suffering or vulnerable, there is liberation from the restrictions of IOIs.

Faithful Responses to Despair

Despair is still a reality despite having the sources of freedom. The French philosopher/mystic/philanthropist Simone Weil wrote in detail about despair. "*Malheur*," the French word used by Weil, fails to fully translate to English. Affliction may offer a close resonance to what Weil is trying to convey about the depth of suffering, but Weil's translator, Emma Craufurd, offers that *Malheur* is affliction doused with inevitability and doom. Weil describes how *Malheur* is not a free choice or a willed movement through God's intervention, but a supreme tearing of the soul away from God in agony that causes a distance or the abandoned feeling of the absence of God. *Malheur* is the "uprooting of life, a more or less attenuated equivalent of death, made irresistibly present to the soul by the attack or immediate apprehension of physical pain" (Weil 2021, 118). Weil's vivid and intense description of *Malheur* reveals her personal witness and experience of the torturous existence. Weil described *Malheur* in *Waiting for God*, "the great enigma of human life is not suffering but *Malheur*. . . . It *is* surprising that God should have given *Malheur* the power to seize the very souls of the innocent and to take possession of them as their sovereign lord. At the very best, he who is branded by *Malheur* will keep only half his soul" (Weil 2021, 120).

Malheur develops because freedom is restricted or seemingly absent. Tragedy, injury, or loss constrict the categories of meaning and the roles of a person's life to one category and within that one role or category, there is a sense of inevitability, doom, and catastrophe. Despair is overwhelming. There are seemingly no viable choices from which to decide and ending life seems inevitable, the only free choice.

Malheur may be best described by an example. In 2004, the First Marine Regiment of the First Marine Division was involved in operation "Phantom Fury" in the second battle of Fallujah during the Iraq war. This battle is now considered one of the most iconic battles of the Marines and the most intense urbanized combat since the "Battle of Huê City" in Vietnam in 1968. Over the course of two weeks of intense combat in Fallujah, thirty-three Marines died while hundreds were wounded from the gunfire, shrapnel, mines, and artillery, some severely, all awarded the Purple Heart. In the years since that battle, thirty-one more Marines who survived the combat in Fallujah could not survive the *Malheur* in their own hearts and minds and they decided on suicide. Possibly similar to Weil's experiences during her service to soldiers and communities through the Spanish Civil War of 1936 and through the Second World War, the atrocities of war for the Marines triggered *Malheur*, the existential seizing of their souls, the perceived loss of freedom, the thwarted belongingness from families, communities, and the human race, and the perceived burdensomeness that what they had seen or the injuries they endured, or inflicted on others, were a burden to their families, communities, and the rest of society. CCT deflated their sense of worth, meaning, value, and freedom to one inevitable decision, that they could not exist.

Strength in the Face of Despair

This last section considers remedies for catastrophic categorical thinking (CCT). While there is no clear-cut solution, quick fix, or magic pill used for healing all suicide ideation, there are methods that can help people become aware of the strong pressures of IOIs which fuel CCT. Becoming aware of IOIs and seeking support in releasing the pressures allows a person to find safety, freedom, and strength.

"Self-complexity," or what Lonergan identified as creative self-appropriation, is a wholistic approach to personal freedom and growth of the personal, social, and spiritual dimensions of personhood. While categorical thinking is useful in practical matters, it is detrimental when considering one's personal source of meaning. For example, when a teacher returns home to her family after a day of teaching, writing, and working with students, she instinctually compartmentalizes, sets aside the concerns of work to engage with her family and enter the joys and struggles of family life. Here, compartmentalization is healthy. If, however, residual anxiety lingers from a faculty meeting and is brought home, she may direct frustrations and anger to her children or spouse. The compartments of life collide. If taken to a traumatic level, like the marines fighting in Fallujah, the intense combat they experienced was seared into their bodies, memories, hearts, and minds. Coming home, they cannot compartmentalize the experiences as their "marine job" and return to their "family compartment" or "friend compartment." Rather, Fallujah becomes their only perspective. This compartment entraps them to perceive the world as dangerous, full of enemies who kill their friends.

Any remedy is certainly not easy; however, psychology, neuroscience, and the ancient Judeo-Christian tradition offer a multilevel relational integration. By appreciating the physical, psychological, spiritual, and communal dimensions of personhood, one's horizons broaden from CCT. What concretely does this look like? An effective method of assisting a person in *Malheur* is to help the person discover his or her agency. Despite IOIs, encouraging the person to make conscious and intentional decisions gives the person autonomy, a glimpse of controlled agency in even small aspects of life. In the face of *Malheur*, instinctual reactions can include defense, defiance, revenge, protection, separation, or escape.

Weil found that *Malheur* reaches an intensity that drains a person's energy and narrows the consciousness to the point of collapse. At the moment of extreme CCT and when suicide seems inevitable, the body is exhausted, the mind dissociates, and the soul is exposed. Weil explained through a lens of faith that at this tragic moment each person still has a choice; to decide to persevere in love or decide to resort to despair. This choice, in the face of trauma and the depths of *Malheur*, is the manifestation of the freedom, will-power, and intentionality of human reason and faith. To love, even in total desperation, vulnerability, and emptiness, is the faith-based conversion into freedom. The agency shown in the choice to love is the act of opening the categories of thinking and relationships by recognizing one's need for support. To not love is instinctually locking into the category of despair and succumbing to the darkness of CCT. Weil says God's absence becomes final and the person has lost agency due to the pressures of IOIs and CCT.

Conclusion

Agency is a powerful force even when facing the despair and the slow decisions leading to suicide. The rational, intentional will to decide a course of action at each fork the road of life inevitably presents is the freeing capacity human persons possess. Internal and external Influences of Intentionality (IOIs) inevitably restrict and sway decision-making. Yet, taking the time to recognize and name the impact IOIs make are important steps as they mitigate the narrowing of Catastrophic Categorical Thinking (CCT). However, maintaining personal agency with self-complexity involves bravely facing the fears directly and making the choice to persevere in love even at the point of *Malheur*. The agency to respond to life's challenges while supported by loving relationships is the strength of human persons. Flourishing is possible as people develop multi-categorical relational integration and intentionally choose life.

Notes

1 According to Dahl, Wilson-Mendenhall, and Davidson (2020), "The ability to be aware and attentive has important implications for healthy psychological functioning. A large-scale study of more than 5,000 people from 83 countries revealed that, on average, people spend an estimated 47% of their waking life in a state of distraction and that states of distraction are typified by lower levels of well-being."

2 There is an historical and still active debate between those who say free will exists and those who argue that it does not. For the opponents of free will see Harris (2012); Sapolsky (2023), or Haidt (2001). Alternatively, for proponents of free will, see Grisez and Shaw (1988) and Tancredi (2007).

Bibliography

Aquinas, Thomas. 2012. *Summa Theologiae: Complete Set.* Emmaeus Academic.

Buabang, Eike K., Kelly R. Donegan, Parnian Rafei, and Claire M. Gillan. 2025. "Leveraging Cognitive Neuroscience for Making and Breaking Real-World Habits." *Trends in Cognitive Sciences* 29, no. 1 (January): 41–59.

Caldwell, Heather K., and H. Elliott Albers. 2024. *Neuroendocrinology of Behavior and Emotions: Environmental and Social Factors Affecting Behavior*. 1st ed. Vol. 16. Masterclass in Neuroendocrinology. Springer International Publishing.

Catechism of the Catholic Church. 2003. Libreria Editrice Vaticana. https://www.vatican.va/archive/ENG0015/__P1C.HTM.

Champagne, Frances, and Michael J. Meaney. 2001. "Like Mother, Like Daughter: Evidence for Non-Genomic Transmission of Parental Behavior and Stress Responsivity." *Progress in Brain Research* 133: 287–302.

Cronholm, Peter F., Christine M. Forke, Megan H. Bair-Merritt, et al. 2015. "Adverse Childhood Experiences: Expanding the Concept of Adversity." *American Journal of Preventive Medicine* 49, no. 3 (September): 354–61.

Dahl, Cortland J., Christine D. Wilson-Mendenhall, and Richard J. Davidson. 2020. "The Plasticity of Well-Being: A Training-Based Framework for the Cultivation of Human Flourishing." *Proceedings of the National Academy of Sciences* 117 (51): 32197–206. https://doi.org/10.1073/pnas.2014859117.

Eisenberger, Naomi I. 2015. "Social Pain and the Brain: Controversies, Questions, and Where to Go from Here." *Annual Review of Psychology* 66 (1): 601–29.

Frost, Robert. 1951. *The Road Not Taken: An Introduction to Robert Frost*. Henry Holt and Company.

Grisez, Germain, and Russell Shaw. 1988. *Beyond the New Morality: The Responsibilities of Freedom*. University of Notre Dame Press.

Haidt, Jonathan. 2001. "The Emotional Dog and Its Rational Tail: A Social Intuitionist Approach to Moral Judgment." *Psychological Review* 108 (4): 814–34.

Harris, Sam. 2012. *Free Will*. Simon & Schuster Press.

Ignatius of Loyola. 1992. *The Spiritual Exercises of St. Ignatius*. Translated by George E. Ganss, S.J. Loyola Press.

Irenaeus of Lyon. 1992. *Against the Heresies*. Edited by Dominic J. Unger, John J. Dillon, Michael Slusser, and M. C. Steenberg. Ancient Christian Writers 55. Paulist Press.

John Paul II. 1998. *Faith and Reason: Encyclical letter Fides et Ratio of the Supreme Pontiff John Paul II to the bishops of the Catholic Church on the Relationship between Faith and Reason*. Veritas. http://w2.vatican.va/content/john-paul-ii/en/encyclicals/documents/hf_jp-ii_enc_14091998_fides-et-ratio.html.

Joiner, Thomas. 2024. *The Varieties of Suicidal Experience*. 1st ed. New York University Press.

King, Martin Luther. 1963. "Letter from Birmingham Jail." https://www.csuchico.edu/iege/_assets/documents/susi-letter-from-birmingham-jail.pdf.

Lightman, Alan. 2014. *Accidental Universe*. Constable & Robinson.

Lonergan, Bernard J. F. 1992. *Insight: A Study of Human Understanding*. Edited by Robert M. Doran and Frederick E. Crowe. Collected Works of Bernard Lonergan 5. University of Toronto Press.

Lonergan, Bernard J. F. 2000. *Grace and Freedom: Operative Grace in the Thought of St. Thomas Aquinas.* Edited by Robert M. Doran and Frederick E. Crowe. Collected Works of Bernard Lonergan 1. University of Toronto Press.

Manca, Claudia, and Karen L. Bales. 2024. "Chapter 2: Adult Social Relationships in Primates." In *Neuroendocrinology of Behavior and Emotions: Environmental and Social Factors Affecting Behavior*, edited by Heather K. Caldwell and H. Elliott Albers, 27–56. Springer.

McGilchrist, Iain. 2019. *The Master and His Emissary: The Divided Brain and the Making of the Western World.* New Expanded ed. Yale University Press.

Montiel-Castro, Augusto J., Rina M. González-Cervantes, Gabriela Bravo-Ruiseco, and Gustavo Pacheco-López. 2013. "The Microbiota-gut-brain axis: Neurobehavioral Correlates, Health and Sociality." *Frontiers of Integrated Neuroscience* 7 (October): 70–85.

Osinga, Frans. 2007. *Science, Strategy, and War: The Strategic Theory of John Boyd.* Routledge.

Polderman, Tinca J. C., Beben Benyamin, Christiaan A. de Leeuw, et al. 2015. "Meta-Analysis of the Heritability of Human Traits Based on Fifty Years of Twin Studies." *Nature Genetics* 47, no. 7 (July 1): 702–9.

Ratcliffe, Matthew, and Achim Stephan, eds. 2014. *Depression, Emotion and the Self: Philosophical and Interdisciplinary Perspectives.* 1st ed. Imprint Academic.

Sapolsky, Robert. 2023. *Determined: A Science of Life without Free Will.* Penguin Books.

Tancredi, Laurence R. 2007. "The Neuroscience of 'Free Will.'" *Behavioral Sciences and the Law* 25 (2): 295–308.

Tetlow, Joseph A. 2021. *Spiritual Exercises of Ignatius Loyola.* Crossroad Publishing.

Van der Kolk, Bessel A. 2015. *The Body Keeps the Score: Brain, Mind, and Body in the Healing of Trauma.* 1st ed. Penguin Books. https://www.besselvanderkolk.com/resources/the-body-keeps-the-score.

Van Orden, Kimberly A., Tracy K. Witte, Kelly C. Cukrowicz, et al. 2010. "The Interpersonal Theory of Suicide." *Psychological Review* 117, no. 2 (April 1): 575–600.

Weil, Simone. 2021. *Waiting for God.* 1st ed. Routledge Classics. Routledge.

10

Love, Justice, and Healing

Reimagining Christian Ethics in the Context of MAID and Suicide

Kimberly L. Penner

I am a person of Swiss and German descent, able-bodied, cis-gendered, financially stable, Canadian settler, pastor of a predominantly white, queer-affirming, Mennonite church,[1] and an academically trained theological ethicist. I begin by locating myself in this way for the sake of accountability. I have been shaped by the social systems of privilege and disadvantage that relate to the social locations that I embody. Through an intersectional feminist approach to Christian ethics, I seek to unlearn the systems of privilege I have been complicit in, benefited from, and am meant to remain unaware of.[2] Using an intersectional approach, I assume that all matters of ethics are contextual and shaped by intersecting relationships of power (i.e., the ability to effect change). I am committed to understanding how power functions to oppress, marginalize, or disempower to work toward healing, well-being for all, and grace as love and justice (I expand on these norms shortly). To do this, I begin where the suffering and pain is. Those who experience harm are well positioned to understand the harmful power dynamics at hand and to articulate, sometimes with the help of others, what is needed for healing.

I did not set out to be a pastor and an academic. Now that I am both, I see how these two callings are different, yet mutually beneficial. My intersectional feminist ethics are put into practice in pastoral ministry as I walk with folks who face the very moral dilemmas and theological questions that I have considered through research and writing. Equally important, my method for doing ethics and my understandings of the divine are shaped and nuanced in relationship with those with whom I minister to and with. While theology is an academic discipline, it is also understandings of God that are felt, experienced, lived out, and shaped in our relationships as human beings with all our eco-social relations.

As a pastor, I have the privilege of being present with people when they are at their most vulnerable—in dying, death, and grief. Each situation is unique to its context. Some deaths and losses are more traumatic than others.[3] Sometimes a death is experienced as traumatic not only because of the manner or timing of death, but because of the theological rhetoric that might judge that particular death as "sinful" or the result of "sin." As this edited volume highlights, this can be the case with death by suicide. In this chapter, I engage two fictionalized stories of pastoral care experiences: (1) about medical assistance in dying (MAID), and (2) about suicide. I address both MAID and suicide because the theological/moral arguments in each case overlap regarding perceptions of the choice to end or hasten the ending of a life, theological interpretations of that choice, and social systemic factors contributing to health and well-being and who accesses MAID or chooses suicide.

I consider experiences of suffering in relationship with other potential sources of authority for Christian ethics. In this chapter, these include the authorities of reason (e.g., statistics), tradition (feminist strands within the Mennonite tradition), and scripture (intersectional interpretations of scripture regarding sin and God's love and justice). The norms of justice are the criteria by which I analyze these sources for what is authoritative. These norms are "rightly ordered relations of mutuality in the total web of our (eco-) social relations" (Harrison 1985, 253), which include gender justice, racial justice, Indigenous justice, and eco-justice, for example; peace (rooted in the biblical understanding of *shalom* as justice and well-being);[4] and love (rooted in the example of Jesus, who revealed God's love by affirming the inherent value of each person and modelling relationships of mutuality rather than the hierarchy of oppressive Empire).

In engaging these sources, with these norms, using social analysis, I find that MAID and suicide are not inherently moral issues—neither moral nor immoral. Related moral issues can and do emerge, however. For example, I look at a possible connection between systemic injustice and traumatic stress, mental health, and well-being. From a Christian perspective, I claim that neither MAID nor suicide is inherently "sinful." With an understanding of sin as injustice (individual and social), I encourage Christian communities to respond to MAID and suicide contextually and with a commitment to systemic justice and liberation from inequality and oppression, including supportive, culturally appropriate, and accessible health care and access to healing from trauma for all. Individual health and healing require social change since our social context and the relationships of power that shape it have an impact on our individual well-being. With an understanding of sin as injustice, I view grace as Divine love, unearned and freely given, that includes a sense of God's justice for the oppressed (the "kin-dom" of God) and inspires us to show that same love and justice to others.

Case: MAID

Chelsea is the pastor of a mostly white, middle-class, Mennonite church in the Canadian prairies. One day, she receives an email from Kathy, a congregant. It reads: "Pastor Chelsea, the cancer I had previously is back and there's nothing the doctors can do. I have been cleared by my doctor to choose a medically assisted death if I would like. What do Mennonites believe about MAID? If it's considered okay, would you be there with me if I choose it?"

Pastor Chelsea is taken aback. She is close with Kathy as her pastor and cares for her. It is hard to learn the news that Kathy's cancer has returned and is now terminal. On top of that, she feels the weight of Kathy's question about MAID. Pastor Chelsea has never thought about the potential theo-ethical significance of someone pursuing MAID. She feels the seriousness of Kathy's question. She asks herself the following questions: "What is at stake for Kathy if I say no? What is at stake for Kathy if I say yes? Will it change Kathy's decision if I say no? If I say no, and Kathy does not choose MAID, will Kathy die a long painful death? In that case, will I have added to her physical suffering and to her spiritual/emotional suffering since I, as her pastor, and representative of the church, did not support her choice? If I say yes, Chelsea's death will be hastened, and I will choose to be present to her at her death to offer spiritual support to her. How will this impact her family, friends, and church?" Chelsea also thinks about what Kathy has been through already with cancer, and what she is going through now. She knows that Kathy would not be considering MAID unless she had put a lot of prayer and thought into it. Considering this, she feels in her gut that there is significant reason to consider the possibility that MAID is an ethical option for Kathy.

Chelsea feels keenly aware of her authority as a clergy member. Mennonites often talk about having a flat church polity, where all members of a congregation are considered equals in terms of their ability to interpret scripture and the leading of the Holy Spirit. In this case, though, Kathy is seeking the theological opinion of her pastor. What Chelsea says will have a significant impact on Kathy's well-being and choices. Chelsea feels the weight of the authority and trust that has been granted her through her professional role. She also knows that her answer is not hers alone, but a reflection of the theological values of their church.

The church they are part of has a strong commitment to love, justice, and peace. "How would the congregation respond to Kathy's question?" Chelsea wonders. The church believes in a God of peace, this is part of the church's history as a peace church. Chelsea wonders, is hastening death violence? Alternatively, is asking someone to continue to suffer a form of violence? Looking to scripture, Chelsea does not find a clear answer one way or another. Turning to some of the scriptures that her church frequently turns to, what Chelsea does find are examples of God's love and presence with those who suffer unjustly (from ailments they did not choose) and God's preference for liberation and healing. She turns to gospel stories of Jesus ministering to and with the sick. These are not stories of redemptive suffering. Jesus weeps with those who weep. And while there will always be pain and suffering, the "kin-dom" of God that he preaches about seeks to alleviate as much of that pain and suffering as possible through more love and more justice.

Taking these things, including Kathy's experience of suffering, her medical assessment, the church's understanding of who God is, and understandings of God in scripture, into prayerful consideration, Chelsea shares with Kathy what she knows for sure is that God loves Kathy and grieves her suffering along with her. Pastor Chelsea tells Kathy that she would be honored to be present with Kathy for her death as a sign of God's presence and love if Kathy chooses to access MAID. She would also be honored to be present with Kathy on her journey if Kathy does not choose to access MAID.

Case: Mental Health and Suicide

In a Mennonite church in North America, the news has spread that an adult in the congregation, Aspen (they/them), has died by suicide. Most people in the community were aware of Aspen's challenges with mental illness. Church members supported them as best they could over the years, but it was difficult. Aspen's mental illness made it difficult for Aspen to realize that they needed help. Aspen's mental illness was further complicated by their gender nonconformity in terms of the care they received (or did not). When they were admitted to the psychiatric ward, they were worried about their safety because of their gender. These experiences added to their distrust of the health care system and their unwillingness to access care. Faced with Aspen's death, the congregation is left with intense grief, as well as anger at the injustices that affected Aspen's mental health in the first place, as well as how difficult it was to get Aspen the help they needed from the health care system.

Social Analysis: MAID

Pastor Chelsea's thought process in response to Kathy's question about MAID reflects an approach to ethics and theology that values the experiences of those who suffer as possible sources of authority for ethics. Chelsea begins with Kathy's experience of her pain and desire to use MAID. Chelsea considers her relationship with and knowledge of who Kathy is and what is at stake for her. She then considers Kathy's question about whether or not MAID is an ethical choice alongside other sources like reason (in the form of the insights of the medical professionals who have determined that Kathy is cleared to choose MAID), tradition (the Mennonite church's history as a peace church), and scripture (finding nothing specifically for or against MAID, but choosing to focus on stories of God as one who resides with those who suffer), and using norms that are central to the faith of their congregation: peace, love, and justice. For Pastor Chelsea and her congregation, MAID is inherently neither moral nor immoral.

There are many cases like Kathy's. Many people choose MAID to ease unavoidable suffering associated with a terminal illness. Many people like Kathy go about their decision-making process in a way that is mindful of self and others. From a pastoral perspective, it is important to pay attention to and be mindful of the feelings and spiritual questions of the friends and family of the person seeking MAID. Sometimes friends and family find it even more difficult to process their grief around MAID than the person who is dying and choosing MAID. In any case, the use of rituals, prayers, and open conversation about what is happening and how God is present can help ease some of the fears of those involved. Rituals and prayers can also give shape to the time immediately before, during, and after the person's death so that it is trauma-informed and gives loved ones an opportunity to experience agency and meaning-making through the experience. MAID is medical assistance in dying and not inherently a moral issue. The experience of MAID or walking with a loved one who chooses MAID is not necessarily at odds with a person's or church's faith or understanding of who God is.

Other times, MAID becomes embedded in matters of morality and injustice. A September 2024 news article from the Canadian Broadcasting Corporation cites a report from Inclusion Canada that "there has been an alarming trend where people with disabilities are seeking assisted death due to social deprivation, poverty and a lack of essential supports." Here MAID becomes connected to larger social justice issues. The article reports that disability rights advocates are launching a "Charter challenge against a part of Canada's law on medical assistance in dying." They would like to see Track 2 of the MAID law changed or eliminated. Track 2 allows people to apply for assisted death when their natural deaths are not reasonably foreseeable, but their condition leads to intolerable suffering. Another Canadian news article, "How poverty, not pain, is driving Canadians with disabilities to consider medically assisted death," considers the challenges of living impoverished and with/as a result of disability. In some cases, this leads such people to consider MAID (Leffler and Dimain 2022). The article includes the perspectives of Toronto palliative care physician Dr. Naheed Dosani. Dr. Dosani says that the kind of poverty and stress that people with disabilities experience is making people sicker and driving a lot of Canadians with disabilities to consider ending their lives (Leffler and Dimain 2022). He wonders, "When people are living in such a situation where they're structurally placed in poverty, is medical assistance in dying really a choice or is it coercion?" MAID becomes a moral issue when it is considered in the context of an ableist society where people with disabilities experience greater levels of poverty and can and do seek MAID as a solution for their preventable suffering.

What about people whose primary diagnosis is mental illness? Should they be able to access MAID? In 2027, Canadians suffering solely from a mental illness will be able to apply for MAID, whereas currently mental illness cannot be the primary diagnosis for people eligible for receiving MAID (Government of Canada 2025). This makes some people working with those who suffer from mental illness very uncomfortable. Mara Grunau, Robert Olson, and Crystal Walker from the Centre for Suicide Prevention in Calgary, Alberta, state that unlike people who suffer because of a terminal illness, "People in suicidal crisis are in deep psychological pain—they don't want to die—they want the pain of living to end" and that this can be treated, and people can recover (Centre for Suicide Prevention, n.d.). Much like people living with disabilities and in poverty, they find that what is called for is support for living. Resources for recovery from suicidal crisis, rather than assistance in dying, are needed. In this case, access to MAID can become a moral issue tied to the following questions, for example: Who is worthy of access to social supports and quality of life? Whose life is dispensable? From my perspective, MAID is not the issue, as much as it highlights the issue. Quality of life, not to mention traumatic stress, are connected to social factors such as racism, sexism, ableism, classism, and cis-heteronormativity. What is needed, then, is social transformation toward more peace, justice, and love, which can improve quality of life.

Social Analysis: Mental Health and Suicide

The social context of suicide in Canada is likewise full of intersecting relationships of power that are relevant for determining if and how suicide is a moral issue. According to information on the Government of Canada website from 2024, higher risk populations for suicide include: men and boys; people serving federal sentences; survivors of suicide loss and survivors of a suicide attempt; some First Nation and Métis communities, especially among youth; all Inuit regions in Canada. They also found that women have higher rates of self-harm (self-harm can be a risk factor for suicide). Thoughts of suicide and suicide-related behaviors are also more frequent among Two Spirit, lesbian, gay, bisexual, transgender, queer, and additional sexual and gender identities (2SLGBTQ+) youth in comparison to their non-2SLGBTQ+ peers. Age was a major factor, as was household income. While the pandemic was an equalizer in many cases, inequality is a factor otherwise in suicidal ideation.

Data on rates of psychological distress and suicide attempts among indigenous peoples living off-reserve indicates that socioeconomic inequalities were a significant factor. In their article, "Socioeconomic Inequalities in Psychological Distress and Suicidal Behaviours among Indigenous Peoples living Off-reserve in Canada," Mohammad Hajizadeh, Amy Bombay, and Yukiko Asada (2019) share their research findings:

> The results of our study are consistent with those of an analysis in Saskatchewan, which showed higher household income to be a protective factor against lifetime suicidal ideation among Indigenous peoples. Our results are also consistent with the findings of previous studies examining associations between income and mental health outcomes among non-Indigenous populations.

For example, they refer to a 2005 study involving 200 low-income African Americans, which found that life hassles (defined as work and time pressure), social and cultural difficulties, finances, and social acceptability and victimization were all independently significant risk factors for suicide attempts. In sum, psychological distress and rates of suicide attempts can be linked to socioeconomic factors. The most significant factor the article highlights is food insecurity. Within the field of trauma studies, this is explained in terms of there being more stress on the brain when there is inequality or suffering. This increased stress can increase the likelihood of or exacerbate traumatic stress and mental/brain illness.[5] If we want to reduce deaths by suicide, we need to work at healing and maintaining good health in people's brains medically and socially. In these ways, suicide is both a public health issue and a social justice issue.

Sadly, mental health supports are stretched thin in most places in Canada. The Canadian Association of Mental Health reports on their website as of 2025 that "while mental illness accounts for about ten percent of the burden of disease in Ontario, it receives just seven per cent of health care dollars. This shortfall, totalling almost $1.5 billion, creates an ever-widening gap in the system's ability to deliver timely intervention and adequate long-term care." And as my case study with Aspen illustrates, laws regarding involuntary patients can make it difficult for people to get the help they need. In Ontario, an involuntary patient is "a person who is detained in a hospital without their consent and cannot leave without permission" (Government of Ontario 2024). A person can become an involuntary patient when assessed by a psychiatrist and found to have a mental health illness that could likely result in harm to oneself or others. There are various lengths of time that a person can be detained as an involuntary patient, beginning with no more than two weeks, but with options for longer under Certificate of Renewal. If a person with a mental illness is not a danger to themselves, but given the nature of their illness struggles with understanding their illness, it can make it difficult for them to seek and receive help (as in the example in the case study). Each of these challenges and more can make it difficult for people to access the health care they need and further contribute to their mental health crisis. Again, mental health and suicide are not moral issues. They become moral issues in so far as they are correlated to social/systemic inequality, interpersonal and/or social systemic violence, and lack of access to health care.

Theo-ethical Analysis: MAID and Suicide

Sin

While not all things about Christian theo-ethical arguments framing suicide and MAID as sin are the same, the theme of sin is a point of overlap. For this reason, I approach the theo-ethical analysis of sin in the two cases, of MAID and of suicide, together. Rather than delving into arguments that claim suicide and MAID are sinful—for example, because in choosing suicide or MAID humans take on the authority of God to take away life and therefore disobey God—my work here is primarily constructive. If a theology of sin is helpful or necessary for Christianity, I argue that it needs to be a theology of sin as injustice—socially, systemically, and interpersonally as shaped by those systems. I use theologian Reinhold Niebuhr's doctrine of sin as a starting point and move toward an intersectional understanding of sin informed by Womanist theologian Delores Williams.

In *The Nature and Destiny of Man*, Niebuhr, a Protestant theologian influenced by the atrocities of the Second World War, explains how sin (specifically choices that go against God and God's ways for us to live) can be understood along both vertical and horizontal axes. The vertical dimension of human sinfulness is about the self in relation to God. Niebuhr describes this dimension as human rebellion against God. Given freedom of choice, humans can choose pride, idolatry, and placing oneself in the center, thus seeking to usurp God, and thus choose sin. The horizontal dimension, which follows, is injustice because, as Niebuhr writes, "[t]he ego which falsely makes itself the centre of existence in its pride and will-to-power inevitably subordinates other life to its will and thus does injustice to other life" (Niebuhr 1941, 179). Or, as the feminist expression goes, we are always also "selves in-relation." It follows, that our individual choices are always choices that have effects, implications, assumptions, about others. To be created "in the image of God" is to be created for right relationship with God and right relationships with self and others (i.e., for social responsibility and justice-making). In this way, faith becomes a pursuit of justice.

Applying an intersectional analysis of power further complicates Niebuhr's basic articulation of sin as vertical and horizontal. The articulation of the vertical is further complicated if we understand that power dynamics shape individual experiences and thus open the possibility that sin for one person might look different from sin for another person, based on their social location.

For example, in situations where a person represents the status quo, yes, sin would be pride, greed, continuing to benefit from our privilege uncritically, and trusting ourselves rather than God. However, in a context in which a person is the oppressed, the marginalized, the disempowered, sin would be to let that positionality shape one's understanding of oneself such that one believes they are lesser than. In this context, what is needed is self-love; that is, a self-love that locates oneself in the image of God and thus affirms oneself as created and loved by God.

Womanist theologian Delores Williams has been and continues to be integral in promoting such an approach to sin. With Black women's experiences of racism and sexism as her starting point, Williams begins with lived realities and impacts of social sin. As she does so, she recognizes the need to locate Black women, their embodied selves, their gender, race, sexuality, within the image of God. She also writes that any depletion of Black women's self-esteem is sinful and thereby names the elevation and healing of Black women's self-esteem as what constitutes salvation. Individual sin, according to Williams, is participating in systems that "devalue Black women's womanhood (humanity) through a process of invisibilization—that is, invisibilizing the womanist character of Black women's experience and emphasizing the stereotypical images of Black women that prevail and are perpetuated by the larger society" (Williams 1993, 146). Sin in this case looks like feeding narratives of inequality that degrade self-worth. As Williams illustrates, context and power are integral for ethics. In a Christian context, context and power are integral for considering what choices are at odds with God's ways and which are congruent with God's ways.

Williams' theology of sin is beneficial for considering the experiences of people who suffer from similar forms of injustice (racism, sexism, heteronormativity, classism, ableism) that can lead to increased risk of mental illness, higher rates of suicide, or a decision to seek MAID because there are no other social supports available to them. What is sin and salvation here? The social sin is the lack of health care, the queer phobia, the anti-trans violence, the poverty, the racism, the ableism, and intersections of all of these (and more) injustices that deplete well-being and contribute to higher rates of suicide among these populations. In this case, similar to what Williams describes for Black women, salvation is elevating each person's self-esteem, working to heal traumatic stress, and seeking well-being through social change. In this case, suicide is the result of injustices and inequalities—social sin. The interpersonal or communal sin would be, again as Williams proposes for Black women in a racist and sexist society, perpetuating the myth that this is an individual problem, rather than a social systemic one, and making the individual to blame.

In sum, in cases where suicide and MAID are predominantly the result of medical or biological issues (e.g., terminal illness for those seeking MAID, or genetic brain health conditions), talk of "sin" is largely irrelevant. Many people who seek MAID do so because they are terminally ill. Not precluding the fact that these circumstances also take place within contexts shaped by relationships of privilege and disadvantage, it is possible that a conversation about sin (even social systemic sin) is largely irrelevant to a Christian's experience with either suicide or MAID. In this case, it is important that the community of faith, including the pastor, avoid making sin (individual or social systemic) a concern in these circumstances. At the same time, social and theological analysis that begins with people's experiences of suffering and injustice reveal that there are also many ways in which suicide and MAID are shaped by unjust relationships of power and potential abuses of power and thus require ethics.

Peace, Suffering, and MAID

In the story about Kathy, Pastor Chelsea considers the weight given to the value of peace in her Mennonite church's theology in relation to the morality of MAID. Does MAID go against a commitment to peace and non-violence? Some might claim that ending life is always a form of violence as it ends a life given by God that should end according to "God's timing." However, Chelsea understands how definitions of violence vary. Using Kathy's experience as her starting point for understanding what peace and violence look like here, Chelsea finds that the violence occurring in this case might be the ongoing suffering that Kathy is experiencing. Kathy's suffering does not seem to have a point. It does not seem "redemptive."[6]

Theologians committed to liberation for all from oppression, including Mennonite feminists such as Susanne Guenther Loewen, Hilary Jerome Scarsella; womanist theologians such as Delores Williams, Kelly Brown Douglas; and Black theologians like James Cone, are critical of atonement theologies for their understandings of suffering as redemptive. Intersectional relationships of power shape people's experiences of suffering, including Jesus' own suffering, and need to be examined. When relationships of power and privilege are examined, it is possible to see the difference between suffering that is chosen versus suffering that is not chosen and the difference it makes for ethics.

Martyrdom narratives and their significance for Christians can also contribute to the valorization of suffering for Christian discipleship. Martyrdom narratives are prominent in Anabaptist-Mennonite history. A particular genre of writing, these narratives speak about early Anabaptists of the Radical Reformation willing to be martyred for their faith for their belief in such things as adult baptism and not swearing oaths to the state. These narratives give meaning to the suffering and death that these people of faith experienced and have continued to shape notions of Mennonite identity and discipleship ethics since then. It is easy to see how this narrative that values suffering, like Jesus' suffering on the Cross, could be used as justification for not seeking MAID and for viewing suicide as failure or sin. However, this emphasis on martyrdom and suffering is not the only way to frame discipleship. In fact, in making it the only way, Mennonites have overlooked how it can inadvertently uphold the status quo by encouraging the oppressed to remain oppressed. Again, context and power dynamics play an important role in determining whether willingness to suffer could possibly be considered an honorable or moral act of discipleship.

Is suffering freely chosen? Does it resist oppressive relationships, systems, and ways of knowing/acting to work toward liberation? If a person's decision to receive MAID is because of the injustices they experience as an impoverished disabled person, then MAID is not an ethical option—it only adds to the idea that some lives are less valuable than others. If, on the other hand, continuing to die slowly and painfully from cancer does nothing to undo the status quo, and if receiving MAID does not uphold a status quo of inequality, MAID could be an ethical option (considered in consultation with medical professionals). Does dying from mental illness by suicide indicate anything other than, potentially, the brokenness of health care systems, and the existence of systemic injustices related to who "belongs" and has what they need to survive and thrive in our society? If not, then it is not a moral issue in terms of the individual's actions, but a moral issue socially.

The defining question for ethics that emerges here is: does the continued suffering uphold the status quo, or does it lead to transformation toward justice, peace, and love? If it upholds the status quo, or reflects the status quo, then something needs to change—social systemic sin needs to be addressed, and individual choices regarding death considered unrelated to sin. There is no reason to consider that kind of suffering as redemptive or moral.

Figuring out whether the status quo is changed, reinforced, or irrelevant to an experience of suffering requires an awareness of context and power dynamics, which again, points to the significance of the experiences of those who suffer as potentially authoritative for ethics. The difference in one sense is choice. What is at stake for each person? The difference is also theological. What is God like and what does God want for us? God with us, Emmanuel, suffered the unjust consequences of a broken world. These injustices continue today in the form of social and systemic inequality and the oppressive ways of Empire.

Conclusion

I want to leave you with three suggestions for creating faith communities that are focused on healing and less likely to cause theological or spiritual trauma regarding MAID and suicide. First, I invite you to educate people about mental illness, suicide, and MAID. In addition to medical information, talk about how rates of suicide, traumatic stress, health and well-being, and relationships to health care, can be shaped by inequality, injustice, and social systemic failures. Second, preach a theology of love for all people with an awareness of power dynamics related to race, class, sexuality, gender, age, or ability and consider this love as a guiding norm or commitment for Christian ethics. Third, take actions to seek social justice and material change that improve well-being and decrease the likelihood of illness, trauma, and suffering. There is so much suffering and injustice in this world. Christian approaches to MAID and suicide should seek to reduce suffering and injustice rather than contribute to them, inspired by the example of Jesus who preached Good News to the poor and the oppressed.

Notes

1 Mennonites find their beginnings in the Anabaptist Movement of the Radical Reformation in sixteenth-century Europe. This movement was a reaction to several key features of existing Catholic and Protestant churches. Early Anabaptists were concerned with maintaining a clear separation of church and state. They chose to baptize each other as adults to separate citizenship in the kingdom of God from citizenship to the state (at the time, infant baptism was tied to political citizenship). A few central features of Early Anabaptism, which continue to define many Mennonite churches today, are adult baptism, refusal to take up the sword (i.e., pacifism or nonviolence), and an emphasis on both an inner faith and an outer

discipleship ethic rooted in Jesus' teachings in the Sermon on the Mount (Mt., chs. 5–7). Mennonite churches in North America are diverse in their theological perspectives and social locations/identities such as race, class, gender, sexuality, age, and ability.

2 Intersectional theological ethics names the ways in which theology is always contextual, shaped by time and place, and recognizes the ways in which systems of oppression and inequality are interlocking, individual as well as social systemic (e.g., sexism, racism, classism, ageism, and ableism—often under the umbrella term of "patriarchy"). It seeks to name and dismantle them simultaneously, beginning with the experiences of those who suffer (assuming God's solidarity with the oppressed) and living into a vision that supports the well-being of all of creation. Intersectionality as a term was coined by lawyer Kimberlé Crenshaw in 1989. Crenshaw gave a name to how Black women's experiences of overlapping identities (e.g., gender and race) shape their experiences within social institutions, such as work and law. That said, notions of overlapping and converging identities and social institutions have been part of Black feminist thought since much earlier (e.g., Sojourner Truth, 1851; Anna Cooper, 1892; Ida Wells, 1890s). The roots of intersectionality are also in the advocacy and writing of women around the world. For example, intersectionality is used in the work of Savitribai Phule (1831–97) in nineteenth-century colonial India. She looked at caste, gender, religion, and economic disadvantage or class (Collins and Bilge 2016, 4).

3 "Traumatic" here refers to that which can cause traumatic stress. Traumatic stress is about how a person experiences/reacts to stress or a traumatic event and/or theology. I take a holistic approach to trauma, recognizing the ways that emotions, physiology, thinking, acting, the individual and the social, are interconnected. With Staci Haines, I find that trauma is, "an experience, series of experiences, and/or impacts from social conditions, that break or betray our inherent need for safety, belonging, and dignity" (Haines 2019, 74).

4 My understanding of peace is also informed by John Paul Lederach's understanding of peace as centered and rooted in "the quality of face-to-face interactions and the ways in which we structure social, political, economic, and cultural relationships" as those which increase understanding, equality, and respect (Lederach 2003, 20–1).

5 The common connection between social insecurity, inequality, injustice, and traumatic stress is articulated and considered in the work of Staci Haines, Jennifer M. Gómez, Robyn L. Gobin, Carolyn Yoder, and Strategies for Trauma Awareness and Resilience workshops and resources out of Eastern Mennonite University in Harrisonburg, Virginia. In terms of intergenerational trauma and the connection between social systemic inequality and traumatic stress, see, for example, the work of Maria Yellow Horse Braveheart, Renee Linklater, and Stephanie C. Edwards.

6 An understanding of "redemptive suffering" within Christianity comes from an interpretation of Jesus' death on the Cross as redeeming humanity from its sins. This suffering serves a purpose. The "Suffering Servant" passages in the Hebrew scriptures (specifically, Isaiah 53) also shape Christian understandings of suffering as possibly redemptive.

Bibliography

Canadian Association for Mental Health. 2025. "The Crisis Is Real." https://www.camh.ca/en/driving-change/the-crisis-is-real.

Canadian Broadcasting Corporation. 2024. "Disability Rights Groups Launching Charter Challenge against MAID." Accessed September 26. https://www.cbc.ca/news/politics/maid-charter-challenge-1.7334653.

Centre for Suicide Prevention. n.d. https://www.suicideinfo.ca/.

Collins, Patricia Hill, and Sirma Bilge. 2016. *What is Intersectionality?* Polity Press.

Government of Canada. 2024. "Suicide in Canada." September 16. https://www.canada.ca/en/public-health/services/suicide-prevention/suicide-canada.html.

Government of Canada. 2025. "Medical Assistance in Dying Legislation in Canada." https://www.canada.ca/en/health-canada/services/health-services-benefits/medical-assistance-dying/legislation-canada.html#a2.

Government of Ontario. 2024. "Information Guide: Involuntary Patients." https://www.ontario.ca/files/2024-05/moh-information-guide-involuntary-patients-en-2024-05-2.pdf.

Haines, Staci. 2019. *The Politics of Trauma: Somatics, Healing, and Social Justice*. North Atlantic Books.

Hajizadeh, Mohammad, Amy Bombay, and Yukiko Asada. 2019. "Socioeconomic Inequalities in Psychological Distress and Suicidal Behaviours among Indigenous Peoples Living Off-Reserve in Canada." *CMAJ* 191 (12): E325–E336.

Harrison, Beverly Wildung. 1985. *Making the Connections: Essays in Feminist Social Ethics*. Beacon Press.

Lederach, John Paul. 2003. *Little Book of Conflict Transformation*. Good Books.

Leffler, Brennan, and Marianne Dimain. 2022. "How Poverty not Pain Is Driving Canadians with Disabilities to Consider Medically Assisted Death." *Global News*, October 8. https://globalnews.ca/news/9176485/poverty-canadians-disabilities-medically-assisted-death/.

Niebuhr, Reinhold. 1941. *The Nature and Destiny of Man: A Christian Interpretation. Volume One: Human Nature.* Charles Scribner's Sons.

Williams, Delores. 1993. "A Womanist Perspective on Sin." In *A Troubling in My Soul: Womanist Perspectives on Evil and Suffering*, edited by Emilie M. Townes, 139–49. Orbis Books.

11

Models for Interpreting Suicide in Catholic Social Teaching

A Contribution from *Gaudium et Spes*

Julia Fleming

When I assigned a long section of *Evangelium Vitae* to my undergraduate class in Catholic Social Teaching several years ago, I expected a lively discussion over abortion, end-of-life care, or capital punishment. Yet I never anticipated that the chapter passage that would draw the most student comments would be its general discussion of suicide:

> Suicide is always as morally objectionable as murder. The Church's tradition has always rejected it as a gravely evil choice. Even though a certain psychological, cultural and social conditioning may induce a person to carry out an action which so radically contradicts the innate inclination to life, thus lessening or removing subjective responsibility, suicide, when viewed objectively, is a gravely immoral act. In fact, it involves the rejection of love of self and the renunciation of the obligation of justice and charity towards one's neighbor, towards the communities to which one belongs, and towards society as a whole. In its deepest reality, suicide represents a rejection of God's absolute sovereignty over life and death. (*EV* §66)

In retrospect, I regret my pedagogical and theological tunnel vision in not expecting their response. Although my students were in their early twenties, many of them had already been touched by suicide. For them, this was an issue that struck close to home. Later, reflecting upon their insights and experiences, I asked myself why I had never thought of suicide, the eleventh leading cause of death in the United States between 2018 and 2022, as a topic for Catholic social ethics (Centers for Disease Control 2024a). As a moral theologian, I associated questions about *suicide* with medical ethics at the end of life—the broader context for *Evangelium Vitae's* discussion. But surely that focus is too narrow. What resources does Catholic Social Teaching (hereafter CST) provide—or what resources could it provide—for interpreting and responding to suicide in a wider context?

After explaining two important limits to the analysis, this chapter will examine three interpretive models for suicide that have already left a mark upon CST, as broadly rather than conventionally construed. The first focuses on the act, interpreting suicide as an unjust taking of innocent human life. A second, centered upon the agent, views suicide as a tragic consequence of mental illness. The third, emphasizing historical/cultural context, invokes suicide as a sign of social/communal dysfunction or injustice. These models are not mutually exclusive, although their relationship raises important analytical and practical questions. Finally, we will explore a potential fourth perspective drawn from the opening lines of *Gaudium et Spes*, approaching suicide as a reminder of shared humanity and finitude.

The Boundaries of the Present Discussion

The term "suicide" encompasses a class of actions united by their outcome but divided by their motives. Suicide can represent a way to escape from psychological agony, when the agent sees no alternatives, or from external threats, including torture, imprisonment, or public shame. People take their lives to avoid suffering at the end of life. Some suicides are meant to protect others (i.e., the captured resistance member who fears betraying his/her colleagues) or to convey a political message. We read of *murder-suicides*, *suicide bombers*, *suicide clusters*, *suicide cults*, and *suicide-by-cop*. Mass shootings sometimes end with the suicide of the shooter. Of course, two people with the same motive for taking their lives can differ in age, mental health, and physical health, while acting within disparate historical, cultural, social, and personal circumstances. Among this range of possibilities, our discussion will focus on suicide intended as an escape, in situations other than the end of life, in which the agent acts alone, and only the agent dies.

Catholic Social Teaching (CST) refers to a body of papal, conciliar, and episcopal documents concerned with the social order. The encyclical *Rerum Novarum*, issued in 1891, inaugurated its modern phase (Himes et al. 2005, 3–5). However, this corpus was shaped by earlier Roman Catholic ethical traditions, so examining an issue from the perspective of CST often requires work with earlier sources as well. In addition, the distinction between CST and other areas of Catholic teaching and practice can be somewhat artificial, especially in the analysis of concrete issues like suicide. Various forms of suicide raise questions of medical ethics, pastoral practice, and even canon law, as well as social issues regarding the relationship between morality and civil law, the character of a just society, distributive justice, and the preferential option for the poor. Thus, it is reasonable to consider texts beyond those typically included within CST when addressing suicide. This discussion will consider suicide in CST as broadly construed.

However, the present analysis is by no means comprehensive and has two important limitations. First, it addresses only selected universal church documents and texts from the United States. Suicide is strongly shaped by cultural/historical circumstances, so suicide raises different analytical or ethical questions in different societies. In the United States, but not in other parts of the world, for example, the phrase *suicide survivors* generally refers to those mourning another's suicide, not to those still alive after an attempted suicide (Cerel et al. 2014, 592). Similarly, firearms have become the most common method of completed suicide in the United States, a development that raises ethical issues less relevant for societies with restricted gun access (Centers for Disease Control 2024b). Such variations justify limiting the focus of the current discussion.

Second, this analysis will not consider assisted suicide/medical aid in dying, even though this seems to be the context of suicide most frequently referenced in CST (Antus 2020, 398).[1] In July of 2024, for example, the "Topics" page on the United States Conference of Catholic Bishops' website listed *assisted suicide* and *euthanasia* as subheadings under *End-of-Life issues*, but offered no general heading for *suicide* (https://www.usccb.org/topics).[2] Certainly, there are overlapping issues between suicide within and outside of a medical context (see, for example, USCCB 2017). Yet there are good reasons for limiting the present discussion to suicide beyond the medical realm. First, assisted suicide raises distinct and complex ethical issues (e.g., the role of health care professionals and institutions and the limits of autonomy) less relevant to interpreting suicide in other circumstances. Second, most suicides in the United States do not occur in a medical context. Elissa Koslov and her colleagues identified more than 5,200 completed cases of medical aid in dying from 1998 until 2020 (2022, 3042). Yet the last year of that period alone (2019) saw more than 47,000 suicides in other contexts (Ehlman et al. 2022, 306).[3] Thus, excluding assisted suicide will highlight what CST has to say about more common experiences of suicide in the United States.

Suicide as Unjust Taking of Innocent Human Life

Apart from its references to psychology and culture, *Evangelium Vitae*'s major arguments on suicide were systematized by Thomas Aquinas more than seven centuries ago in the *Summa Theologiae*. Taking one's own life, Aquinas explains, is a not only a sin against the love that one should have for oneself, but also a sin against justice toward the community to which one belongs, and toward God, who alone has power over life and death. Aquinas also distinguishes capital punishments imposed by civil authority from imposing a death sentence upon oneself—illicit even for magistrates, since no one can be his/her own judge. Suicide, Aquinas's argument suggests, is a usurpation of authority—God's, over life and death, and the State's, over capital punishment. It substitutes a greater evil for some lesser evil—even the chance that one will yield to temptation—and deprives the person of the opportunity for repentance (II-II q. 64, art. 5). "'Evils must not be done so that goods may come,' or that [other] evils may be avoided, especially lesser or less certain [evils]," asserts Aquinas, citing Romans 8:3 (ad. 3).[4] In his argument that suicide is worse than whatever one is attempting to escape, Aquinas echoes Augustine, who had developed the point at length in *De Civitate Dei* (1.16-27), in response to sexual assaults upon consecrated virgins during the sack of Rome (Barbagli 2015, 41–5; Barry 1995, 467–71, 476–80).[5]

One final parallel links *Evangelium Vitae*'s treatment of suicide with Aquinas's. Each considers the issue within a broader analysis of the legitimacy of taking life. In Aquinas's case, this review extends from killing plants and animals for food to capital punishment, suicide, self-defense, and responsibility for accidental homicide (II-II q. 64, arts. 1-8). Several articles focus on the killing of wrongdoers (by public authority, clerics, and private persons). By contrast, although *Evangelium Vitae* addresses capital punishment (in §56), its central concern is with the killing of the innocent through direct abortion and euthanasia. Suicide emerges in reference to the latter. Yet for each analysis, the broader context of taking human life provides the context for a discussion of suicide.

Thus, for CST, earlier authorities provided not only a long-standing evaluation of suicide, but also an ethical framework within which to consider it. Evidence for the power of that framework appears in the word *suicide* itself, which, Barbagli points out, first appeared in 1642. Prior to that time, and even for centuries afterward, authors continued to use *homicide* or its linguistic equivalents (*self-homicide, self-slaughter, homicide de soy-mesme, sui ipsius homicidium*) rather than embracing a distinct term for taking one's own life. Killing oneself was simply one form of homicide (Barbagli 2015, 83–4). For many centuries in Christian Europe—Orthodox and Protestant, as well as Roman Catholic—draconian legal punishments, affecting the body and the property of the deceased and the welfare of his/her family, reinforced this characterization (Barbagli 2015, 29–40, 45, 55, 70, 99–100; Watt 2004, 4–5). Early Modern Catholic casuistry typically focused on distinguishing suicide per se from licit acts that would foreseeably result in the agent's death, such as jumping from a burning ship to escape the flames or refusing an excessively expensive or painful medical treatment (Caramuel 1664, 7–8; Fleming 2008). It was the boundaries of suicide, rather than suicide itself, that dominated the discussion. This was the legacy of ethical thought on suicide that Catholic Social Teaching inherited.

Yet Catholic moral thought also asserted that without sufficient knowledge and freedom, persons were not culpable for their actions (Slater 1908, 1:18–20, 23–4). Mental illness could obviously limit both. Well before *Rerum Novarum* appeared, acceptance of a medical model for interpreting suicide had become widespread in the West (see Barbagli 2015, 87–101, 103; Watt 2004, 8). *Evangelium Vitae* reflects this development when it acknowledges that "psychological, cultural, and social conditioning" could lessen or remove subjective responsibility for suicide, yet the encyclical primarily focuses upon its objective character as "a gravely immoral act" (§66).

A variation of these arguments appears in the *Catechism of the Catholic Church*, which analyzes suicide within its treatment of the Fifth Commandment (§§2280–3). Beginning with God's sovereignty over life and death, and persons' responsibilities as stewards of life, the text describes suicide as "gravely contrary" to just love of self, an offense against love of God and neighbor, and an act of scandal, if the person intends to set an example for others. Voluntary cooperation in another's suicide also violates moral law (§§2280–2). Yet immediately afterward, the *Catechism* observes: "Grave psychological disturbances, anguish, or grave fear of hardship, suffering, or torture can diminish the responsibility of the one committing suicide." Its final paragraph emphasizes that Christians should not "despair of the eternal salvation" of those who have taken their lives, for God can offer them the chance for repentance in ways beyond human understanding (§2283).

Thus, the *Catechism* offers the same basic assessment of suicide per se as *Evangelium Vitae*, yet two elements in the first text create a rather different tone. First, the reference to diminished responsibility appears in the culmination of the *Catechism*'s argument, rather than as a possibility acknowledged in passing. Second, its reminder of divine grace shifts the focus from human agency to God's mercy. Interestingly, many discussions of contemporary church teaching on suicide per se—sometimes, even within church documents—rely more explicitly on the *Catechism* than on *Evangelium Vitae* (see, for example, Griffin 2020, 65–8; Antus 2020, 395–6; Rohlheiser 2018, 38; USCCB 2023, 17; California Catholic Conference 2018, §6). The *Catechism*'s formulation seems to create a more pastoral rendering of the traditional model for interpreting suicide.

Suicide as the Tragic Consequence of Mental Illness

As the previous discussion indicates, the unjust-taking-of-innocent-human-life model is not necessarily inconsistent with an acknowledgment that mental illness can limit someone's moral responsibility for suicide. Yet that recognition raises several important questions. How often do people who take their own lives have sufficient knowledge and freedom to be morally responsible? Are there cases where knowledge, freedom, or both are so lacking that the suicide is less a chosen act than a tragic consequence of the disease? Explaining why it is often appropriate to speak of *victims of suicide*, for example, Ronald Rolheiser asserts, "They were claimed by a disease that they didn't choose. The act that ended their lives was not a freely chosen one" (2018, 39). Similarly, when discussing his daughter's suicide, Ed Shoener compares mental illness to cancer, an illness treatable for many, but eventually lethal for others, no matter how hard they struggle to survive and how good the care they have received (2020, 21). From this perspective, suicide often says less about the persons who die than about the relentlessness of their disease.

Not surprisingly, the influence of this model appears when CST considers mental illness, although that topic, Nussbaum argued in 2018, has received comparatively little explicit attention from Catholic bioethics or magisterial documents, and even less from those devoted to social questions (67–8, 71).

But in 2021, following the Angelus on World Mental Health Day, Pope Francis called for prayers for "our brothers and sisters affected by mental disorders and also the victims, often young, of suicide" (Francis 2021). Discussing hope in a later message for World Youth Day, the pope invoked young peoples' high rates of suicide around the world as a "dramatic sign" of how hardships have left them "gripped by despair, fear and depression," and feeling as if they "are in a dark prison, where the light of the sun cannot enter" (Francis 2023b).

A more extensive illustration of such ideas appears in a document from the United States. In 2018, the California Catholic Conference's "Hope and Healing" devoted a section to those affected by "the heartbreaking tragedy of suicide." Noting the "staggering" number of suicides in the United States each year, the bishops acknowledge that most such deaths are associated with "severe mental illness," which can be "difficult to treat or impossible to cure." Despite everyone's best efforts, "sometimes mental illness proves fatal" (§6). "Hope and Healing" explains:

> Such illnesses can . . . constrict a person's thinking—even to the point where the person feels entirely trapped and cannot see any way out of his or her mental anguish. Mental illness can impair a person's capacity to reason clearly; it can adversely impact sound judgment, such that a person suffering in this way is liable to do things that when not sick, he or she would never consider. (§6)

Although the document draws upon the *Catechism* to argue that "suicide is contrary to the will of God who gave us life," the *Catechism*'s grounds for condemning suicide are mentioned only in a footnote (n. 12). The main text quotes the *Catechism* directly regarding the impact of psychological disturbances upon responsibility for suicide and the church's enduring hope and prayers for the salvation of those who have taken their lives. The section then discusses the grief of persons who have lost someone to suicide—a grief that can be complicated by mixed emotions, second-guessing, guilt, and isolation. Catholics must be willing to "walk this long road" with the bereaved, remembering the merciful heart of Christ, to whom we entrust "all who have died as a result of a mental illness" (California Catholic Conference 2018, §6).

Finally, a variation of this approach appears in materials for a novena celebrated during the USCCB's 2023 Catholic Mental Health Campaign. In its section on "suicide awareness," the document provides links to the CDC, suicide prevention resources, and books and videos available through the Association of Catholic Mental Health Ministers website (2023, 16–17). Its ethical instruction begins with the admission that there are "unfortunate but common misperceptions of the beliefs of the Catholic Church with respect to people who tragically take their own lives." However, "developments in the behavioral sciences" and pastoral experience in working with bereaved families have helped the church, under the "guidance of the Holy Spirit," to gain "a more mature and complete understanding of suicide" (17).

The document's short moral analysis of suicide relies exclusively on the *Catechism*, with no references to *Evangelium Vitae* or any other document from CST. Yet the materials reshape the *Catechism*'s argument by reordering it. Here, the analysis begins by quoting the *Catechism*'s statements about psychological disturbances and diminished responsibility (*CCC* §2282). It explains that "suicide is always considered *a* grave matter" [emphasis added]—a phrase perhaps less obvious in its technical significance than *Evangelium Vitae*'s reference to suicide as "objectively . . . a gravely immoral act"—before repeating the *Catechism*'s description of human beings as stewards of their lives (*EV* §66; *CCC* §2280). There is no explicit discussion of suicide as a violation of justice or charity. This section of the text concludes by quoting the *Catechism* regarding the possibility of salvation for those who have died in this way and the church's prayers on their behalf (USCCB 2023, 17).

In some ways, the impact of the tragic-consequence model is less evident in this material, which does not refer to "victims" of suicide or compare it to a terminal disease. Yet the text clearly focuses upon mental illness to explain suicide. Not only does it refer to the role of the behavioral sciences in developing the church's understanding of suicide, but it also reorganizes the *Catechism*'s argument to bring the impact of psychological disturbance to the fore. The text urges readers to learn how to encourage people considering suicide to "find the care they need" (USCCB 2023, 17). Yet perhaps the clearest evidence of this medical model appears within the novena prayer itself, which asks God to inspire community leaders to recognize the need for "effective mental health care and suicide prevention programs." For those who have taken their lives, the prayer asks: "May Mother Mary carry them into the loving arms of her son Jesus, asking him to grant them complete joy, without the pain of heart and mind that led to suicide" (16). By contrast, the characterization of suicide as "a grave matter" is quite brief (17). The central ethical problem is not the act of suicide but the response to persons in danger of suicide and to the families of the dead.

As these texts illustrate, the unjust-act model and the tragic-consequence models are not mutually exclusive, yet their emphases are quite distinct, especially regarding the role of mental illness. While the first treats mental illness as a possible mitigating factor, the second regards mental illness as the primary impetus of a tragic event.

Suicide as a Symptom of Social/Communal Dysfunction or Injustice

Scholarship on suicide has addressed the issue from sociological as well as psychological perspectives, and social historians have highlighted the ways in which suicide is shaped by culture (Watt 2004, 2–4, 8; Barbagli 2015). Social pressures that encourage suicide do not fall evenly across populations, and persons marginalized in other areas may also face disproportionate suicide risks (Antus 2020, 398, 399–400; McCarthy 2018, 117). Thus, it is possible to approach suicide as a symptom of the health of societies/cultures/institutions. While this model acknowledges the significance of psychological disorders, its focus is upon the social and historical circumstances that can encourage suicide.

In CST as broadly construed, this perspective interprets suicide as a sign of social dysfunction or injustice. Although assisted suicide lies beyond the scope of the present discussion, this approach can be an important argument in such analyses, as illustrated, for example, in the Congregation for the Doctrine of the Faith's *Samaritanus Bonus* (2020, §IV). Yet CST also employs this lens for interpreting suicide in other contexts.

CST references to youth suicide often associate it with social inequity or malaise. John Paul II warned that young people with no hope of employment were taking their lives—a point emphasized later by Pope Francis (John Paul II 2001, §27; Francis 2018). Other papal addresses associate suicide in this demographic with the deceptive glamour of secular culture, or its failure to provide "spiritual capital" for young people (Benedict XVI 2007; Francis 2022). Young people vulnerable to suicide include those dismissed as "losers" by society, bullied, or exposed to the trauma of war (Francis 2023a, §8; 2023b). Similarly, in *Listen, Teach, Send*, the USCCB acknowledges that many young people have been touched by suicide, and that they are particularly at risk when family crises (including divorce, unemployment, domestic abuse, poverty, incarceration, and immigration status) are compounded by "loneliness, social isolation, anxiety, stress, insecurity, or clinical depression"

(2024b, 19). This last example highlights the impact of social status upon psychological health.

Moreover, CST sometimes explicitly connects suicide with marginalization. The USCCB's *Keeping Christ's Sacred Promise* repeatedly emphasizes the heightened suicide rates of indigenous people, explaining this as a consequence of historical and contemporary forces, including "socioeconomic systems that perpetuate poverty on the reservations" (2024a, 10, 22, 38). Prisoners enduring extreme isolation in high-security prisons, argues Pope Francis, are at increased risk for suicide (2014b, §IIc). In many societies, persons with leprosy suffer, not only from the disease, but also from social rejection, which can influence depression and suicidal thoughts (Czerny 2022).

Finally, CST occasionally mentions suicide to demonstrate the devastating impact of a situation or state-of-affairs. In "Responses to the Plague of Gun Violence," Bishop Frank Dewane, Chairman of the USCCB's Committee on Domestic Justice and Human Development, includes statistics on gun suicides, and discusses the possible efficacy of various control measures in reducing such deaths (2019, 1, 2, 3, 5, 6). During his homily at a mass in Rome with clergy sex abuse victims, Pope Francis acknowledged that for some, their "wounds" culminated in the "terrible tragedy" of suicide. "The deaths of these so beloved children of God," he said, "weigh upon the heart and my conscience and that of the whole church" (2014a). In both cases, suicide confirms the terrible consequences of the social or ecclesial situation that occasioned it. It is a symptom of dysfunctions or injustices even if psychological disorders magnify their effects.

Suicide as Reminder of Shared Humanity and Finitude

Thus, despite its relative inattention to suicide beyond the health care context, CST already reflects different lenses for interpreting it, one focused on the act, another on the mental health of those who die, and the third, upon the social circumstances in which it occurs. I would like to suggest a fourth heuristic approach, drawing upon the opening lines of *Gaudium et Spes*: "The joys and the hopes, the griefs and the anxieties of the men of this age, especially those who are poor or in any way afflicted, these are the joys and hopes, the griefs and anxieties of the followers of Christ. Indeed, nothing genuinely human fails to raise an echo in their hearts" (Vatican Council II 1965, §1). Although these sentences include no direct reference to suicide, they offer a starting point for considering it as a reminder of shared human finitude or limitation, especially as made evident in the stories of those touched by another's death.

At first glance, *Gaudium et Spes* is not an obvious resource for reconsidering suicide, not least because its clearest reference to the topic includes "willful self-destruction" within a long list of "infamies" that "poison human society," harm the agents more than the victims, and represent "supreme dishonor to the Creator." This approach that seems to anticipate the account in *Evangelium Vitae* 66, even though not all suicides qualify as "willful," that is, voluntary (*GS* §27). Yet if one turns instead to the Pastoral Constitution's opening sentences, one finds a useful lens for interpreting the significance of suicide's experiential legacy.

For anyone familiar with *Gaudium et Spes*, is difficult to read the autobiographical accounts of those touched by suicide without viewing many of them and those they have lost as buffeted by "griefs and anxieties" that lasted for years or even decades (see, for example, in Shoener and Dolan 2020, xvi, 5–8, 14–17, 19–20, 30–1, 33–4, 102–5, 137; in Rohlheiser 2018, 59–63). Some struggled to make sense of a catastrophe that fell without warning, while others had been bracing themselves for the bad news for years. Many searched desperately for answers unattainable on this side of the grave (McKinless 2018, 21–2; Pope 2020, 14–17; Zimmerman 2024, 22, 41–2, 89–90). Compounding such sufferings are the stigma and the sense of isolation associated with suicide (Rubey 2020, 138; Antus 2020, 403; Rohlheiser 2018, 32–7). If, as *Gaudium et Spes* proclaims, Christians share in the "griefs and anxieties" of the afflicted, then certainly the church is called to stand at the foot of this cross.

Without drawing explicitly on *Gaudium et Spes*, some Catholic authors have invoked Pope Francis's theology of accompaniment, or his image of the church as a "field hospital" as foundations for a pastoral response to suicide (Shoener and Dolan 2020, 77, 161; McKinless 2018, 22). Elizabeth Antus movingly emphasizes the importance of recognizing those who have taken their lives within the communion of the saints (2020). Moreover, an accompaniment approach to suicide already appears in CST in the call from "Hope and Healing" for the church to "walk this long road" with the bereaved (§6). Thus, *Gaudium et Spes*'s specific contribution to a shared humanity perspective on suicide emerges from its second sentence, which indicates that Christians share the joys and sorrows of the afflicted because "nothing genuinely human fails to raise an echo in their hearts" (§1).

How do the experiences of those touched by suicide reveal something "genuinely human"? If suicide is a tragedy that only God can heal, then suicide as such is not the sign of true humanity. One of Aquinas's objections to suicide is its inconsistency with the natural inclination to preserve one's life (II-II, q. 64, art. 5). Instead, the experiences of those touched by suicide are signs of human finitude or limitation—our vulnerability to wounds beyond our control. Unlike sin, which distorts human nature, finitude reflects our status as creatures. Through the incarnation, Jesus shared this vulnerability.

To think of suicide as reminder of finitude, it is helpful first to consider the breadth of its impact. In 2014, an article in the American Association of Suicidology's official journal suggested a continuum of terms for those touched by suicide, differentiating those "exposed" and "affected" from the "short-term" and "long-term bereaved" (Cerel et al. 2014). Examples of the first include persons whose only contact with the deceased came through news reports (fans of celebrities), strangers who discovered the body, first responders and health care workers, and those with limited connections to the person who died through work, school, organizations, place-of-residence, and so on. However, some *exposed* persons experience significant post-traumatic symptoms, so that they also qualify as *affected*. The impact of exposure to suicide can be deep, even if the original personal connection was remote (594–5, 597).

This range of such exposure, already sobering, expands even further if we consider the impact of suicide over time. Suicide can alter the dynamics of a family, affecting children born after the death occurred. It can also shape the lore of a place, drawing those considering suicide to a site where persons have taken their lives in the past. Exposure to suicide seems to cross boundaries of time and space. It illustrates our common vulnerability through social connection.

Suicide as a revelation of finitude appears even more directly in the reflections of some bereaved families. The death of their daughter Karla, Tom and Fran Smith acknowledge, pushed them into "the world of powerlessness." Despite their love and support, they could not break through her isolation. These parents' journey of "assimilation" required not only adjusting to the loss of their daughter but also accepting that they could not prevent her death. This process has reminded them, the Smiths explain, that "we are powerless in other areas of life as well" (2020, 159). Such powerlessness could also be described as finitude.

Accepting such finitude requires a special kind of courage and compassion. A world where there is always someone to blame for terrible events—even if we blame ourselves—is a safer world, a more intelligible world. Guilt provides an explanation, a motive for righteous anger, the promise that self-awareness can protect us from repeating our mistakes. Acknowledging finitude means recognizing our vulnerability in a world without easy answers for many instances of terrible suffering. To experience finitude as relief, we must learn to live with mystery.

A third illustration of finitude in connection with suicide comes from experts in the behavioral sciences. Psychologist and clinical suicidologist David Jobes explains that current data about risk factors does not allow professionals to make reliable predictions about who will die by suicide, and that there are similar deficiencies in data about the efficacy of common treatments (2020, 85, 88). Despite long-standing clinical and research interest, scientific understanding of suicide is still limited (see Franklin et al. 2017, 188–9, 217). While the behavioral sciences have facilitated the development of church teaching on suicide, that scientific understanding itself is by no means complete.

Ironically, the failure to recognize this finitude can exacerbate the sufferings of the bereaved. The range of risk factors that have been associated with suicide is quite broad, so that many people experience one, and often more, at any given time (Franklin et al. 2017, 188). After the fact, when those mourning a suicide try to make sense of their tragedy, the significance of such factors may seem painfully self-evident. Yet such clarity was not present in advance (see Zimmerman 2024, 105–10). As Jobes points out, for example, millions of people suffer from mental illness without succumbing to suicide (2020, 85). Even for experts in the field, hindsight can be better than foresight (see in Zimmerman 2024, 89–90; Jobes 2020, 93).

We are all affected by the finitude of time and place—the knowledge available in our own period of history. Current knowledge shapes our capacity to respond to our experiences. At present, suicide is often a painful reminder of such finitude. There is no magic pill to protect us from exposure to suicide, no vaccine to create immunity from suicidal ideation, no antiseptic to wipe away the dangers for those already struggling. Honest acknowledgment of what we do not yet know about suicide encourages us to recognize our finitude—a finitude that will always remain "genuinely human," even if research improves our prospects for preventing suicide.

Finally, for CST and Catholic social thought, suicide can be a salutary reminder of what we have failed to see—an illustration of institutional and disciplinary finitude. In a homily described in *L'Osservatore Romano*, Pope Francis drew a remarkable lesson from the story of Judas's suicide in Mt. 27:3-10. Not only did the religious leaders and learned authorities have hearts closed to a "poor, penitent man who didn't know what to do," but after his suicide, they focused upon protecting the purity of the Temple from profanation by blood money (Francis 2016). The National Catholic Mental Health Campaign's reference to "unfortunate but common misperceptions" among church members suggests that Catholics can have similar blind spots today (USCCB 2023, 17). Recognizing our finitude and escaping from this narrow vision can reshape our understanding of divine mercy and of the church itself. Elizabeth Antus writes, "Catholics can learn from God's preferential love for those who are brought down by the agony of mental illness and suicidality that God does not want an exclusive club of heroes" (2020, 413).

Catholic social ethics, moreover, should ask whether an emphasis upon assisted suicide has perhaps sucked a good deal of oxygen from the room, in terms of the disciplinary energy we devote to suicide in other contexts. What does suicide have to tell us about the preferential option for the poor, marginalization, or distributive justice? Acknowledging our disciplinary finitude may not only prepare us to accompany those touched by suicide more effectively but also enable them to accompany us.

Conclusion

Selected documents from universal and US documents in CST (broadly interpreted) already provide three models for interpreting suicide outside of a medical context. To these models, focused respectively upon suicide as an unjust taking of innocent human life, a tragic consequence of mental illness, and a symptom of social/communal dysfunction or injustice, the opening lines of *Gaudium et Spes* suggest a fourth perspective: suicide as a reminder of shared humanity and finitude. Our vulnerability to suicide exposure and suicidal ideation, our inability to save others from themselves, and even the state of our current scientific knowledge and theological reflections, all reflect the limits of the human condition. Recognizing this may strengthen Christian resolve to support and learn from suicide survivors and those we have lost.[6]

Notes

1 Note that all four references to *suicide* in Lysaught and McCarthy's selected review of the literature applying CST to bioethics concern assisted suicide (2018, 112, 113, 115, 120).

2 Ironically, someone searching for the site's resources on suicide outside the medical context at that time could more easily find them by searching for *mental health*, since a search using the term "suicide" produced more than 500 results, many of them focused on assisted suicide.
3 In the United States, deaths from medically assisted aid in dying are not included within official suicide statistics (see Antus 2020, 398).
4 "Quia 'non sunt facienda mala ut veniant bona,' vel ut vitentur mala, praesertim minor et minus certa." The translation is my own.
5 On the relevance of Donatist practice for Augustine's position, see also Adamiak and Dohnalik (2023, 3823–5); Barry (1995, 471–3).
6 I would like to thank my students in THL 565 for honestly sharing their insights and reactions regarding this topic.

Bibliography

Adamiak, Stanislaw, and Jan Dohnalik. 2023. "The Prohibition of Suicide and Its Theological Rationale in Catholic Moral and Canonical Tradition: Origins and Development." *Journal of Religion and Health* 62: 3820–33. https://doi.org/10.1007/s10943-023-01900-w.

Antus, Elizabeth L. 2020. "'The Silence of the Dead': Remembering Suicide Victims and Reimagining the Communion of the Saints." *Theological Studies* 81 (2): 394–413. https://doi.org/10.1177/0040563920929653.

Aquinas, Thomas. 1963. *Summa Theologiae*. Cura fratrum eiusdem ordinis. Biblioteca de Autores Cristianos. 5 vols.

Augustine of Hippo. 1972. *Concerning the City of God against the Pagans*. Translated by Henry Bettenson, with an introduction by David Knowles. Penguin Books.

Barbagli, Marzio. 2015. *Farewell to the World: A History of Suicide*. Translated by Lucinda Byatt. Polity Press.

Barry, Robert. 1995. "The Development of Roman Catholic Teachings on Suicide." *Notre Dame Journal of Law, Ethics, and Public Policy* 9 (2): 449–501. https://scholarship.law.nd.edu/ndjlepp/vol9/iss2/4.

Benedict XVI. 2007. "Address of His Holiness Benedict XVI to the Bishops of Japan on their 'Ad Limina' Visit." December 15, 2007. https://www.vatican.va/content/benedict-xvi/en/speeches/2007/december/documents/hf_ben-xvi_spe_20071215_japan.html.

California Catholic Conference. 2018. "Hope and Healing: A Pastoral Letter from the Bishops of California on Caring for Those Who Suffer from Mental Illness and Addressed to All Catholics and People of Good Will." May 1. https://cacatholic.org/resources/mental-health/hope-and-healing/.

Caramuel, Juan. 1664. *Theologiae Praeterintentionalis*. Borde, Arnaud, Borde, and Barbier.

Catechism of the Catholic Church (CCC). 2003. Libreria Editrice Vaticana. https://www.vatican.va/archive/ENG0015/__P7Z.HTM.

Centers for Disease Control and Prevention. 2024a. National Center for Health Statistics. National Vital Statistics System, Mortality 2018–2022 on CDC WONDER Online Database Data are from the Multiple Cause of Death Files, 2018–2022, as compiled from data provided by the 57 vital statistics jurisdictions through the Vital Statistics Cooperative Program. https://wonder.cdc.gov/controller/saved/D158/D389F360.

Centers for Disease Control and Prevention. 2024b. *Suicide Data and Statistics.* April 24. https://www.cdc.gov/suicide/facts/data.html.

Cerel, Julie, John L. McIntosh, Robert A. Neimeyer, et al. 2014. "The Continuum of 'Survivorship': Definitional Issues in the Aftermath of Suicide." *Suicide and Life-Threatening Behavior* 44 (6): 591600. https://doi.org/10.1111/sltb.12093.

Congregation for the Doctrine of the Faith. 2020. *Samaritanus Bonus*: Letter on the Care of Persons in the Critical and Terminal Phases of Life, July 14. https://www.vatican.va/roman_curia/congregations/cfaith/documents/rc_con_cfaith_doc_20200714_samaritanus-bonus_en.html.

Czerny, Cardinal Michael, S.J. 2022. "Message from the Interim Prefect of the Dicastery for Promoting Integral Human Development for the 69th World Leprosy Day." January 30. https://www.humandevelopment.va/en/news/2022/messaggiogiornatamondialemalatidilebbra.html#:~:text=Message%20from%20the%20Interim%20Prefect,2022&text=Leprosy%20(Hansen's%20Disease)%20is%20a,in%20decline%20for%20several%20decades.

Dewane, Bishop Frank J. 2019. "Responses to the Plague of Gun Violence." November 11. https://www.usccb.org/issues-and-action/human-life-and-dignity/violence/upload/Remarks-Bishop-Dewane-Responses-to-the-Plague-of-Gun-Violence-11-11-2019.pdf.

Ehlman, Daniel C., Ellen Yard, Deborah M. Stone, Christopher M. Jones, and Karin A. Mack. 2022. "Changes in Suicide Rates: United States, 2019 and 2020." *Morbidity and Mortality Weekly Report* 71 (8): 306–12. http://dx.doi.org/10.15585/mmwr.mm7108a5.

Fleming, Julia. 2008. "When 'Meats are like Medicines': Vitoria and Lessius on the Role of Food in the Duty to Preserve Life." *Theological Studies* 69 (1): 99–115. https://doi.org/10.1177/004056390806900105.

Francis, Pope. 2014a. "Homily of Pope Francis. Holy Mass in the Chapel of the Domus Sanctae Marthae with a Group of Clergy Sex Abuse Victims." July 7. https://www.vatican.va/content/francesco/en/homilies/2014/documents/papa-francesco_20140707_omelia-vittime-abusi.html.

Francis, Pope. 2014b. "Address of Pope Francis to the Delegates of the International Association of Penal Law." October 23. https://www.vatican.va/content/francesco/en/speeches/2014/october/documents/papa-francesco_20141023_associazione-internazionale-diritto-penale.html.

Francis, Pope. 2016. "Clinging to the Written Word: Morning Meditation in the Chapel of the Domus Sanctae Marthae." April 11. https://www.vatican.va/content/francesco/en/cotidie/2016/documents/papa-francesco-cotidie_20160411_clinging-to-the-written-word.html.

Francis, Pope. 2018. "Address of His Holiness Pope Francis to Participants in the Meeting: 'European Jesuits in Formation.'" August 1. https://www.vatican.va/content/francesco/en/speeches/2018/august/documents/papa-francesco_20180801_gesuiti-europei.html.

Francis, Pope. 2021. "Angelus." Saint Peter's Square, October 10. https://www.vatican.va/content/francesco/en/angelus/2021/documents/papa-francesco_angelus_20211010.html.

Francis, Pope. 2022. "Address of His Holiness Pope Francis: Visit to Assisi for the Event 'Economy of Francesco.'" September 24. https://www.vatican.va/content/francesco/en/speeches/2022/september/documents/20220924-visita-assisi.html.

Francis, Pope. 2023a. "Message of His Holiness Pope Francis for the 2023 World Day of the Poor." November 19. https://www.vatican.va/content/francesco/en/messages/poveri/documents/20230613-messaggio-vii-giornatamondiale-poveri-2023.html.

Francis, Pope. 2023b. "Message of His Holiness Pope Francis for the XXXVIII World Youth Day." November 26. https://www.vatican.va/content/francesco/en/messages/youth/documents/papa-francesco_20231109_messaggio-giovani_2023.html.

Franklin, Joseph C., Jessica D. Ribeiro, Kate H. Bentley, Xieyining Huang, Katherine M. Musacchio, Bernard P. Chang, Kathryn R. Fox, Evan M. Kleiman, Adam C. Jaroszewski, and Matthew K. Nock. 2017. "Risk Factors for Suicidal Thoughts and Behaviors: A Meta-Analysis of 50 Years of Research." *Psychological Bulletin* 143 (2): 187–232. http://dx.doi.org/10.1037/bul0000084.

Griffin, Carter. 2020. "Moral Theology and Church Teaching on Suicide." In *Responding to Suicide: A Pastoral Handbook for Catholic Leaders*, edited by Ed Shoener and John P. Dolan, 63–69. Ave Maria.

Himes, Kenneth, R., O.F.M., eds., et al. 2005. *Modern Catholic Social Teaching: Commentaries and Interpretations.* Georgetown University.

Jobes, David, with Ed Shoener. 2020. "Suicide Assessment, Treatment and Prevention." In *Responding to Suicide: A Pastoral Handbook for Catholic Leaders*, edited by Ed Shoener and John P. Dolan, 83–96. Ave Maria.

John Paul II. 1995. *Evangelium Vitae* [Encyclical Letter on the Value and Inviolability of Human Life]. The Holy See, March 25, 1995. https://www.vatican.va/content/john-paul-ii/en/encyclicals/documents/hf_jp-ii_enc_25031995_evangelium-vitae.html.

John Paul II. 2001. Post-Synodal Apostolic Exhortation, *Ecclesia in Oceania*, November 22. Libreria Editrice Vaticana. https://www.vatican.va/content/john-paul-ii/en/apost_exhortations/documents/hf_jp-ii_exh_20011122_ecclesia-in-oceania.html.

Koslov, Elissa, Molly Nowels, Michael Gusmano, Muhammed Habib, and Paul Duberstein. 2022. "Aggregating 23 Years of Data on Medical Aid in Dying in the United States." *Journal of the American Geriatrics Society* 70 (10): 3040–4. https://doi.org/10.1111/jgs.17925.

Lysaught, M. Therese, and Michael McCarthy. 2018. "A Social Praxis for US Health Care: Revisioning Catholic Bioethics via Catholic Social Thought." *Journal of the Society of Christian Ethics* 38 (2): 111–30. https://www.jstor.org/stable/44987794.

McCarthy, Michael. 2018. "Bewildering Accompaniment: The Ethics of Caring for Gender Non-Conforming Children and Adolescents." In *Catholic Bioethics and Social Justice: The Praxis of US Health Care in a Globalized World*, edited by M. Therese Lysaught and Michael McCarthy, 113–27. Liturgical Press.

McKinless, Ashley. 2018. "Life After Suicide: How One Catholic Ministry Is Helping Families Deal with Devastating Loss." *America* 218 (6): 18–25. https://www.americamagazine.org/faith/2018/03/06/how-one-catholic-ministry-helping-families-deal-devastating-aftermath-suicide.

Nussbaum, Abraham. 2018. "Far from Disadvantaged: Encountering Persons with Mental Illness." In *Catholic Bioethics and Social Justice: The Praxis of US Health Care in a Globalized World*, edited by M. Therese Lysaught and Michael McCarthy, 63–76. Liturgical Press.

Pope, Charles. 2020. "A Grief Revealed and Redeemed: The Death of My Sister, Mary Anne Pope." In *Responding to Suicide: A Pastoral Handbook for Catholic Leaders*, edited by Ed Shoener and John P. Dolan. Ave Maria.

Rohlheiser, Ronald. 2018. *Bruised and Wounded: Struggling to Understand Suicide.* Paraclete.

Rubey, Charles T. 2020. "Loving Outreach to Survivors of Suicide." In *Responding to Suicide: A Pastoral Handbook for Catholic Leaders*, edited by Ed Shoener and John P. Dolan, 135–42 Ave Maria.

Shoener, Ed. 2020. "The Suicide Death of My Daughter, Katie." In *Responding to Suicide: A Pastoral Handbook for Catholic Leaders*, edited by Ed Shoener and John P. Dolan,19–28.Ave Maria.

Shoener, Ed, and John P. Dolan. 2020. *Responding to Suicide: A Pastoral Handbook for Catholic Leaders.* Ave Maria.

Slater, Thomas, S.J. 1908. *A Manual of Moral Theology for English-Speaking Countries.* 2 vols. Benziger Brothers.

Smith, Tom, and Fran. 2020. "Journey from Suicide Loss to Assimilation." In *Responding to Suicide: A Pastoral Handbook for Catholic Leaders*, edited by Ed Shoener and John P. Dolan, 155–60. Ave Maria.

United States Conference of Catholic Bishops. 2017. "Secretariat of Pro-Life Activities: 'Suicide and Assisted Suicide: The Role of Depression.'" https://www.usccb.org/issues-and-action/human-life-and-dignity/end-of-life/euthanasia/upload/Suicide-and-Assisted-Suicide-The-Role-of-Depression.pdf.

United States Conference of Catholic Bishops. 2023. "National Catholic Mental Health Campaign: Novena for Mental Health." October 10, 2023. https://www.usccb.org/resources/Novena%20for%20Mental%20Health%209-Days_5.pdf.

United States Conference of Catholic Bishops. 2024a. *Keeping Christ's Sacred Promise: A Pastoral Framework for Indigenous Ministry.* https://www.usccb.org/resources/Indigenous%20Pastoral%20Framework%20-June%202024-Final%20Text.pdf.

United States Conference of Catholic Bishops. 2024b. *Listen, Teach, Send: A National Pastoral Framework for Ministries with Youth and Young Adults.* https://www.usccb.org/resources/National%20Pastoral%20Framework%20YYA%20APPROVED3.pdf.

Vatican Council II. 1965. *Gaudium et Spes,* December 7. https://www.vatican.va/archive/hist_councils/ii_vatican_council/documents/vat-ii_const_19651207_gaudium-et-spes_en.html.

Watt, Jeffrey R., ed. 2004. *From Sin to Insanity: Suicide in Early Modern Europe.* Cornell University Press.

Zimmerman, Rachel. 2024. *Us, After: A Memoir of Love and Suicide.* SFWP e-Book.

12

The Lost Disciple?

The Life and Death of Judas Iscariot according to Early Christian Witnesses

Tabea Pelzmann

Who was Judas Iscariot?[1] In modern times, his name has become synonymous with betrayal and the "Judas kiss" with treason. In the Bible, Judas Iscariot appears in all four gospels as the one of the twelve disciples who will hand Jesus over to the authorities (Mk 3:19; Mt. 10:4; Lk. 6:16; Jn 6:71). And, at least according to Matthew, he hanged himself afterward (27:5), making him the only suicide in the NT. It seems like a legitimate question to ask what message the author might have wanted to send with his portrayal of Judas and how it might have affected an ancient audience. Taking a closer look at the Gospel of Matthew as well as at historical events and attitudes and the reception of Judas in early Christianity can shed light on the person of Judas. Assessing the character and role of Judas has never been an easy task and there is no universal image of him. The gravity of his deed and the many gaps left by the evangelists regarding his character have contributed to the colorful interpretations offered since the earliest church.

The main point of this article is to emphasize that Judas' actions in the Gospel of Matthew do not necessitate his eternal damnation. Based on biblical and cultural contexts, neither his betrayal nor his suicide requires such a conclusion. Moreover, Judas' suicide was not the main element of the final biblical passage that mentions him (Mt. 27:3-10). Consequently, there is no reason to give up hope for Judas.

What Do We Know about Judas Iscariot according to the Four Gospels?

Elements regarding Judas recur in all four NT gospels. In addition to being one of the Twelve, Judas' betrayal of Jesus is the first time he is mentioned in them (Mt. 10:4; Mk 3:19; Lk. 6:16; Jn 6:70-71) and is predicted by Jesus during the Last Supper (Mt. 26:21; Mk 14:18; Lk. 22:21; Jn 6:70). However, the nuance of Judas' image differs with each gospel. Only in the synoptic Matthew, Mark, and Luke does Judas receive money for his deed and the motif of the Judas kiss is found (Mt. 26:15, 49; Mk 14:11, 45; Lk. 22:5, 47-48). In addition, Satan plays a prominent role in the description of the betrayal in Luke and John (Lk. 22:3; Jn 13:27), but not in Mark and Matthew. Furthermore, Judas' suicide is found only in Matthew (Mt. 27:3-5). Mark and John do not mention his fate, while Luke, who is also the author of the Acts of the Apostles, presents his death as one that was not intended by Judas: "falling headlong, he burst open in the middle, and all his bowels gushed out" (Acts 1:18).[2]

Considering the differences between the two accounts of Judas' death, we must remember how the evangelists composed their good news. They "were not writing history as we tend to think of it (a journalistic relaying of facts and events that happened in the past), and yet, in their theologically driven narratives, they did aim to include historically reliable information about people who really lived" (Carey 2011, 250). It is, therefore, not surprising that there are distinctions in their stories. In fact, these differences are far more interesting and ever more important when seeking the theological message that each author intended to convey. The narration of Judas' suicide is one such example for the Gospel of Matthew.

Matthew's Narration of Judas in Its Literary and Historical Context

In order to understand the portrayal of Judas in the Gospel of Matthew, we must follow the gospel narrative and explore the places where Judas appears. Judas Iscariot is first introduced as one of the twelve apostles in Mt. 10:4, characterized from the beginning as "the one who betrayed him." By describing him in this way, Judas' character is never neutral but always already connected to Jesus' Passion and his role in it. Readers therefore never perceive Judas as just one apostle among the others, and it might seem as if he is the black sheep from the very beginning. However, the verb form in the original ancient Greek text that refers to his act of betrayal (the aorist) suggests otherwise. It makes clear that Judas did not always betray Jesus, but only punctually at a certain point in time. This indicates that Judas was a genuine follower of Jesus at the beginning and during the narrative when he is not specifically mentioned. This assumption would also apply, for example, to the mission of the twelve, when Jesus sends them out to the "lost sheep of the house of Israel" to "[c]ure the sick; raise the dead; cleanse those with a skin disease; cast out demons" and not to take payment for it (10:6, 8). This may seem surprising at first, since Judas following these instructions does not fit with the stereotypical image of him as someone focused on monetary greed.

Simply counted among the Twelve after this first appearance, Judas' name reappears in 26:14-16 when he bargains with the chief priests to betray Jesus in exchange for thirty pieces of silver. This leaves readers with questions: What has happened to Judas in the meantime? Why is he doing this? These are questions for which no easy answer can be found. However, this passage is preceded by an unnamed woman in Bethany anointing Jesus' head with costly perfumed oil (26:6-13), so it is possible (though not necessary) that the two encounters are related since money and the death of Jesus are relevant elements in both (Most 2008, 73–4).

In the first story, Jesus' disciples object to the anointing because they think it would have been better to sell the oil and give the money to the poor. Contrary to the account of the same event in John 12:4, it is not Judas but all the disciples in general who protest against the act (26:8-9). Consequently, there is no mention of a dishonest motive behind the criticism. Instead, it must be read as a genuine lack of understanding on the part of the disciples. Indeed, as Jesus explains, their feeling is not wrong in general, but they simply do not grasp the uniqueness of Jesus' presence among them and her anointing him prior to his burial. The disciples' reaction to Jesus' explanation is not narrated, although as mentioned above, Judas' action can be interpreted as such.

Judas' subsequent encounter with the chief priests gives little information about his motive, although the thirty pieces of silver point to monetary interest. However, Matthew's reason for emphasizing the monetary element may not relate primarily to Judas as a greedy person, but to something else entirely. Throughout the narrative, Matthew specifically mentions the thirty pieces of silver three times (26:15; 27:3, 9; unlike Mark, who does not give the exact amount) and money in general an additional five times (including references to the thirty pieces of silver as "them": 27:5-6, 7, 10). The motive is especially prominent in Mt. 27:9, though Judas has already died four verses earlier: "And they took the thirty pieces of silver, the *price* of the one on whom a *price* had been set, on whom some of the people of Israel had set a *price*" (Blomberg 1992, 409, emphasis mine). Therefore, such attention to money is not simply synonymous with the focus on Judas' greed since by now the lens has shifted to the chief priests and their actions. This does not mean, however, that the monetary element is irrelevant to understanding Judas. The amount of money he receives is not arbitrary. Rather, it is a reference to Exodus 21:32 and Zechariah 11:12 (Evans 2012, 427). Exodus 21:32 mentions a payment of thirty silver shekels that the owner of an ox must make if it gores another person's slave. Zechariah, who acts as a good shepherd and thereby represents God, is paid the same amount for his service. This amount is used to criticize the little value that is attributed to the prophet and to God's shepherding of his people (11:7-14) (Klein 2008, 388).[3] The reappearance of the same amount in the gospel can therefore be interpreted as a criticism of Judas, who apparently does not appreciate Jesus enough.

During Jesus' Last Supper with his disciples, before Jesus blesses the bread and wine, Judas is mentioned again (26:20-25). Jesus predicts the betrayal, including the woe that "[i]t would have been better for that one not to have been born" (26:24). This statement is often used to prove Judas' eternal damnation (Davies and Allison 1997, 463–4);[4] however, it is not that simple. In the NT, a woe can be both an expression of compassion (24:19) and a judgment (23:13-14). The same is true for the OT, where the woe can lament someone, including oneself, as being pitiable (1 Sam. 4:8; Ps. 120:5; Jer. 15:10), or it can serve as a threat (Jer. 13:27; Ezek. 24:6, 9).[5] In addition, both Jeremiah and Job say that it would have been better for them not to have been born (Jer. 15:10; 20:14-18; Job. 3:1-19).[6] In both cases, the phrase expresses the experience of great hardship. Differences to the situation of Judas are, however, that the statements describe a current emotional situation rather than a prediction about the future, and that they are both talking about themselves and not about someone else. Moreover—and this may be the primary difference—Jeremiah and Job suffer because they follow God, while Judas will experience great sorrow because he strays from that path.

These considerations show that Jesus' words regarding Judas are not necessarily condemnatory. Rather, they can be understood as a warning that hardship will follow for the one who betrays him, and at the same time—since this is not necessarily mutually exclusive—as having compassion on that person. Judas responds to Jesus' words by asking if it is surely not him who will do this. Because this scene follows his bargain with the chief priests, Judas' statement attracts attention and seems hypocritical (26:14-16) (Evans 2012, 429; Gundry 2010, 117). Considering that he could claim innocence in this direct confrontation, his response suggests that whatever his motives, at this point Judas is acting out of conviction and is certain of what he is doing.

Even before Judas' appearance at Jesus' arrest in the Garden of Gethsemane, one might recognize a possible reference to him when Jesus says: "My soul is sorrowful even to death" (26:38).[7] When interpreted as a parallel to Ben Sira: "Does not sorrow draw near to death when a companion and friend turns into an enemy?" (Sir. 37:2), it sheds new light on the agony in the Garden (Evans 2012, 434).[8] Jesus is then not only moved by his impending fate but also by Judas turning against him (Garland 1993, 250).

The following betrayal and arrest of Jesus is initiated by the arrival of Judas with "a large crowd with swords and clubs, from the chief priests and the elders of the people" (26:47, 47-56). A kiss from Judas is the mark of recognition for the arresting party. While Judas calls Jesus "Rabbi," Jesus calls him a friend and tells him to do what he has come to do (26:49-50). This is a seemingly inappropriate title for Judas in this situation. However, the Greek word for friend (*hetairos* / ἑταῖρος) that is used by Jesus appears only two other times in the NT—both times in Matthew—and can be understood to refer to a relationship between the speaker and the person addressed that is ignored and disrespected by the other (Rengstorf 1935, 698). The first of the two episodes is the parable of the workers in the vineyard (20:1-16), where the landowner says to one of the grumbling laborers, who is unhappy about the fact that they all receive the same pay at the end of the day, regardless of the time they have spent in the vineyard: "Friend, I am doing you no wrong; did you not agree with me for a denarius?" (20:13). The second is also a parable that narrates a wedding banquet where a guest is not properly dressed (22:1-14) and is therefore approached by the hosting king with the question: "Friend, how did you get in here without a wedding robe?" (22:12). A comparison with related rabbinic parables suggests that the guest must have either rejected or soiled the garment (Rengstorf 1935, 698). These parallels point to interpreting the use of "friend" (*hetairos* / ἑταῖρος) in this context to indicate that Judas also failed to honor the relationship he had with Jesus by leading the crowd into the Garden of Gethsemane. This is the second time that Judas' lack of appreciation for Jesus is indicated, after the motive behind the thirty pieces of silver.

Judas' story continues after Peter denied knowing Jesus three times under duress in the high priest's courtyard and "wept bitterly" at the realization that Jesus had foretold his weakness (26:69-75). Jesus was then handed over to Pilate, the Roman governor over Judea (27:2). This central episode with Judas (27:3-10) is not related in any other gospel and exhibits Matthew's particular theology with its Jewish imprint. In this gospel, not only does Jesus emphasize the persistence of the Jewish law (5:17-19), but his life and death are—more than in the other gospels—punctuated by references to the OT and the fulfillment of its prophecies (see e.g., 1:22-23; 4:14-16; 26:56) (Ehrman 2006, 24). That said, this gospel is also critical of the Jewish leaders, holding them fully responsible for the death of Jesus, in contrast to Pilate who declares him innocent (Ehrman 2006, 25). These characteristics are particularly prominent in the gospel's final episode with Judas. In contrast to earlier references (26:14, 20-21, 47), Judas is not referred to as one of the twelve disciples, signifying his alienation from the group (Bergler 2022, 626). He seeks out the chief priests and elders at the temple (27:5), while the surrounding episode—Jesus' condemnation—occurs in front of Pilate's bench (27:19).

At this point in the narrative, Judas realizes Jesus' condemnation and repents by saying "I have sinned" (*hēmarton / ἥμαρτον*; 27:3-4).[9] Judas thereby uses "the standard language of confession" (Davies and Allison 1997, 563), his emotion punctuated by his attempt to return the money (Vortisch 2022, 128). If one takes Judas' remorse seriously, the question of his motive becomes even more pressing. What did he expect to happen? What was he thinking? Did he just see the money and not think about the consequences? Or did he expect it to play out differently altogether (Vortisch 2022, 124)? Did he expect, for example, that Jesus would call on the "more than twelve legions of angels" that his Father would have sent him if he had asked for them (26:53)? The fact that he had to come to terms with Jesus' conviction may seem surprising or even unrealistic, considering that Judas, like all the apostles, had heard Jesus' predictions of his Passion (16:21-23; 17:22-23; 20:17-19) (Vortisch 2022, 126). However, one might draw a parallel with Peter, to whom Jesus foretold that he would deny him three times, which did not prevent him from doing so. Jesus' words only unfolded their meaning to Peter in retrospect (Vortisch 2022, 127). In both cases Jesus would have been able to say: "I told you so."

But there is more to Judas' confession before the chief priests and the elders: "I have sinned by betraying innocent blood" (27:4). Judas thus becomes the first person in the course of the Passion narrative to attest to Jesus' innocence, followed by Pilate's wife and ultimately Pilate himself (27:18-19, 24) (Bergler 2022, 622). In addition, the emphasis on Jesus' innocence allows readers to draw a reference to Deuteronomy 27:25: "Cursed be anyone who takes a bribe to shed innocent blood" (Vortisch 2022, 130–1). Although Judas merely speaks of betrayal, or literally of handing over Jesus, in this context it can be interpreted as being synonymous with killing. This is true for Judas, whose statement clarifies that he already considers himself a sinner, even before Jesus has actually died. Rejected by the chief priests, Judas throws the money down in the temple and hangs himself in an unspecified place (27:5).

The way chosen by Judas—hanging himself—has a specific connotation. The Greco-Roman world in which Matthew wrote his gospel linked this method with desperation (Hooff 1990, 68). Although a common way to take one's life, it was associated with the lower classes, lacking prestige and considered vulgar, especially in the Roman world (Hooff 1990, 69–71; Vortisch 2022, 144). Therefore, it would not have been chosen by someone who, for example, cared "for his reputation" (Hooff 1990, 71, 69–71; Vortisch 2022, 144). The motive of *dolor* (pain, anguish, sorrow), on the other hand, is overrepresented when it comes to this way of ending one's life (Hooff 1990, 71),[10] a motive that seems to match Judas' situation.

Because the Gospel of Matthew was likely written by an ethnically Jewish Christian author who valued the Jewish Scriptures (Schnelle 2024, 345–6), these texts must be considered crucial sources. The sole account of a suicide by hanging in those Jewish Scriptures that became the OT is of Ahithophel, whose action is not condemned (2 Sam. 17:23). Ahithophel was David's counselor, but when the king's son rebelled against David, he changed sides and counseled Absalom (2 Sam. 15-16). When Absalom did not follow his (good) advice on how to continue the rebellion, Ahithophel returned home, put his household in order, and hanged himself (2 Sam. 17:14-23).

Interpreters differ on the extent to which the story of Ahithophel's death is an antetype to that of Judas.[11] One similarity is the choice of words, as the Septuagint, the ancient Greek translation of the Hebrew Bible, describes the suicide with the same words used by Matthew: Both Judas and Ahithophel went away (*apelthōn* / ἀπελθὼν) and hanged themselves (*apēnxato* / ἀπήγξατο) (Harris 1900, 504). They are the only ones in the biblical texts who hang themselves after both had become traitors—one to David and one to the son of David (Bergler 2022, 632–3). However, their respective motivations are different. While Ahithophel kills himself seemingly without remorse following his unheeded advice and tainted honor and/or his predicted failure of the rebellion and thus his own death sentence,[12] Judas regrets his deed, which was successfully executed (Bergler 2022, 632–3). Both deaths are left without comment and therefore free of judgment.

Later rabbinic texts do not give a unanimous verdict on Ahithophel's fate (*b. Sanh.* 104b/105a; *m. Sanh.* 10.2) (Bergler 2022, 634; Brown 1994, 644), information that may also give hope for Judas' eternal fate. In addition, there is a rabbinic text, *Genesis Rabbah* 27:27, in which suicide brings atonement (Davies and Allison 1997, 562–3). Yakim of Serurot—who can be identified with Alcimus, a person appearing in the Bible who killed sixty Hasideans in violation of an agreement and an oath in 1 Maccabees 7:12-18 (Freedman and Simon 1951, 599; Davies and Allison 1997, 563)—mocks his uncle, R. Yose b. Yoezer, who is about to be crucified. His uncle, a firm believer in God's justice, warns Yakim of his future fate since he is not doing God's will: Even if Yakim is doing well now, how much better will he himself do? And if crucifixion is what happens to him as a man doing God's will, how much more will happen to Yakim? The words of his uncle "penetrated into his heart like the venom of a snake, and he went and applied to himself the four modes of the death penalty applied by a court, namely, stoning, burning, decapitation, and strangulation" (Neusner 1985, 401). After the suicide of his nephew, his uncle dies as well (Freedman and Simon 1951, 600), and seeing the bier of Yakim "flying through the air, he said, 'By a brief interval he reached the Garden of Eden before me'" (Neusner 1985, 401).

In sum, we cannot claim that the ancient world perceived suicide as either completely positive or negative (Vortisch 2022, 136–44). Both positions are found, and the Bible does not render a judgment. Christian culture developed a clear rejection of suicide only over time, with Augustine (354–430 CE) and his reception at its center (Vortisch 2022, 137–8). Judas' action can be interpreted both as an emotional expression of his deep grief as well as an attempt at atonement, self-enforcement of justice (Num. 35:33; 2 Sam. 21:1-6) (Vortisch 2022, 136; Garland 1993, 254), or self-punishment (Most 2008, 75).

This is, however, not the end of the narrative. Instead, when Judas dies, not even half of the episode (27:3-10) has been narrated, which now focuses on the chief priests and their handling of the thirty pieces of silver that Judas threw down in the temple. This striking fact shows that the death of Judas was not the central element of this narrative. Instead, the chief priests take counsel for the second time in this chapter (the first instance being their decision-making about Jesus). Matthew even uses the same phrase both times (Bergler 2022, 637).[13] The chief priests take Judas' surrendered money and use it to buy the potter's field as a place to bury foreigners (27:6-7).[14] Judas' money as the price of blood is given as the reason why the field is called Field of Blood (27:6-8). By calling the pieces of silver "blood money" (27:6), the chief priests again demonstrate their awareness of their own actions (Bergler 2022, 637).[15] At the same time they continue to practice the legalistic interpretation of Jewish law for which Jesus had criticized them (5:17-20; 12:1-14; 15:1-20) by refusing to deposit the money in the temple treasury (Bergler 2022, 637). In keeping with Matthew's presentation of the Passion narrative, their actions are interpreted as the fulfillment of a prophecy, in this case by Jeremiah: "Then was fulfilled what had been spoken through the prophet Jeremiah, 'And they took the thirty pieces of silver, the price of the one on whom a price had been set, on whom some of the people of Israel had set a price, and they gave them for the potter's field, as the Lord commanded me'" (Mt. 27:9-10; cf. Jer. 18-19; 32:6-15). Although Matthew only mentions Jeremiah, it is reasonable to suggest that he also thought of Zechariah, but "follows a standard literary convention of his day by referring only to one source" (Blomberg 1992, 409).[16] Zechariah's narrative, in the context of the thirty pieces of silver, of the prophet working as a good shepherd (Zech. 11:4-17) ends with the contrasting image of a worthless shepherd following after a good one, a worthless shepherd "who does not care for the perishing, or seek the wandering, or heal the maimed, or nourish the healthy, but devours the flesh of the fat ones, tearing off even their hoofs" (11:16). The actions of the chief priests, not caring for the fate of Judas, make it possible to identify them with this bad shepherd in contrast to Jesus, who is the good shepherd (Mt. 2:6; 25:32). This can be seen as the fulfillment of Scripture.

As for the book of Jeremiah, several motifs also appear in Matthew's scene. Jeremiah 19:1-13 constitutes a thematic parallel: "Jeremiah prophesies that a locality associated with potters (v. 1) will be renamed with a phrase connoting violence (v. 6) and used as a burial place (v. 11), as a token of God's judgment upon Jerusalem (and in particular, upon the Jewish leaders (v. 1)" (Moo 1983, 159). Furthermore, the book of Jeremiah as a whole tells of a prophet who warns his people to change their sinful ways lest God judge them by delivering them into the hands of the Babylonian Empire, a judgment that will result in deportation and exile from out of their land (Jer. 25:21b). In addition to worshiping other gods, two of the sinful ways resulting in the destruction of the city and its Temple are the shedding of innocent blood (Jer. 7:6-15; 19:4) and the lack of repentance (Jer. 8:6). Both elements are relevant in this passage from Matthew, since innocent blood is being shed, and the chief priests show no remorse.

To better understand the parallels, it is important to remember that all the gospels were written in particular historical contexts. During the years between the composition of the Gospel of Matthew (*c.* 90 CE)—likely by an ethnically Jewish Christian living in the Diaspora in Syria whose community had by then separated from the synagogue (7:29; 23:34)—and the life and ministry of Jesus, the first Jewish revolt against Rome was launched. Its failure, which resulted in the destruction of the Second Temple in or around 70 CE), was a devastating experience for the Jewish community (Schnelle 2024, 345–7). Because the early Christian community was a movement within Judaism (Boyarin 2004, 2), these events were similarly traumatic.

The Gospel of Matthew witnesses to the shift away from the ritual authority of chief priests (e.g., 4:20; 5:6; 19:22), who could no longer offer atoning sacrifices, and the Temple as the place of atonement, to Jesus as the new embodiment of atonement (26:28) (Weaver 2014, 2, 8). By knowingly putting to death an innocent and just person the priests have themselves become guilty. They show their knowledge of their own actions; for example, by deliberately seeking false testimony (*pseudomartyrian* / ψευδομαρτυρίαν) (26:59-60) (Bergler 2022, 626). Moreover, instead of fulfilling their duty and preventing that "the guilt of innocent blood remain[s] in the midst of [. . .] Israel" (Deut. 21:8), as they could do in the case of an untraced murder (Deut. 21:8-9), they persuade the crowd to demand the death of Jesus (Mt. 27:20) and thus actively bring innocent blood into the midst of Israel.

Consequently, it is possible that the description of Judas in the Gospel of Matthew is a means of exposing and highlighting the sinfulness of the chief priests in order to explain and deal with the fact that God allowed the destruction of the Second Temple to happen. "In an act of profound and unintended irony the chief priests, even before the death of Jesus, have already pronounced the judgement of God on themselves and their leadership role within the Jewish community" (Weaver 2014, 7).

Thus, for Matthew and his audience, God's judgment for the deeds of the chief priests and elders has already taken place. According to the gospel, this judgment includes all the other "righteous blood shed on earth" (23:35), as well as the deed of the persuaded crowds who demanded Jesus' death (27:20-26) (Berger 2020, 124). Jeremiah is an example of how throughout the scriptures, the welfare of the nation always depends on the people's obedience to God's commandments (Deut. 6:1-3), and just like the exile and the destruction of the First Temple (2 Kgs. 24:3-4; 25:8-12; Ps. 106:38-42) (Barton 2014, 206), the destruction of the

Second Temple could be interpreted as the result of the people's sinful behavior, including the shedding of innocent blood.

But Jeremiah, to whom we now return, does not stop there. His prophecy is not only negative but also hopeful, promising that the people will be allowed to return from exile and painting a picture of a faithful people living in the land afterward. For example, when Jeremiah is told by God to buy a field from his cousin for *seventeen shekels of silver*, knowing at the same time of the coming defeat of his people, he gives a strong sign of this hope for the future and for the return of the people to the land (32:36-40).

Closer analysis of Matthew's gospel therefore suggests that this episode contains more information and interpretive possibilities than evident on first reading. Additionally, the chief priests appear to be more present than Judas, who only actively shapes the situation in Mt. 27:3-5 (Bergler 2022, 621, 626). Generally, Matthew portrays Judas as one who does not appreciate the good shepherd he had in Jesus (2:6), which leads him to alternate authorities, resulting in an experience of hardship that led him to end his life. The story of Judas' death, while meaningful in itself, is also a prelude to the criticism of the still-inner Jewish leadership of its time (Bergler 2022, 626), and a coming to terms of the Jewish Christian movement (Schnelle 2024, 344–7)[17] with the destruction of the Second Temple.

Early Non-Biblical Christian Witnesses to the Character and Role of Judas

As with the NT, no uniform picture of Judas' life and death exists in other early Christian witnesses. To sample this diversity, we must explore the Fragment of Papias, the Gospel of Judas and the Acts of Peter, three apocryphal writings of the second and third centuries.

Apollinaris of Laodicea, who lived *c.* 310–390 CE, explicitly rejects the theory that Judas performed suicide (Smith 2016, 309, 311). Instead, he purports that Judas tried to hang himself but was cut down in time and survived (Smith 2016, 309, 311). He then goes on to quote Papias (*c.* 60–140 CE), a church leader from Hierapolis in Asia Minor, to whom two different versions of Judas' death are attributed (Smith 2016, 309). It is impossible to say for sure which of the two versions is original, but both of them attempt to demonstrate the death of Judas as a typological fulfillment of Scripture, for example by using a phrase or image that links Judas to the wandering Cain (Gen. 4:14; Ps. 109:10) (Smith 2016, 311, 313).

According to the short version, "Judas walked about in this world as a weighty example of impiety. He was so inflamed in the flesh that he could not pass where a wagon could easily pass. When the wagon struck him, his bowels emptied out" (Smith 2016, 313). The longer version has Judas swelling up as well but goes into much more detail, for example by adding pus and worms to the description. In the end, "[a]fter many tortures and punishments," he dies "in his own land" (Smith 2016, 313). In this case, there is no detailed description of his death, but the focus is on the suffering he must endure beforehand. In both versions, it is clear that he is being punished for what he has done.

Not all texts that mention Judas are as negative. A lesser-known work is the Greek Gospel of Judas (GJd), thought to have been written *c.* 150–170 CE (Nagel 2014, 268). Irenaeus of Lyon is the first to mention it in his collected works, generally cited as *Adversus Haereses* (c. 180 CE) (Nagel 2014, 261). The Gospel of Judas is not often cited, with a total of three references from the second to the fifth centuries (Nagel 2014, 262). The Greek word for gospel (*euangelion* / εὐαγγέλιον) means good news, something most would not associate with Judas. However, it is questionable whether there is actually good news for Judas in this work. After all, the main subject of the text is the secret Gnostic doctrine that is revealed to Judas, not Judas himself and his fate (Gathercole 2007, 29).

Gnosticism describes a stream of thought that differs from the theological tradition of the official church, for example, by asserting the material world as something bad from which the spirit must be saved (Rudolph 2009). In the Gospel of Judas, as is common for a so-called dialogue gospel, "Jesus appears to one or more of his disciples and engages in extended conversations with them without much, if any, narrated plot" (Layton 2021, 64). A Coptic translation from the early fourth century CE contains about 95 percent of the original text (Nagel 2014, 263–4). The remaining five percent, however, leave a lot of room for speculation (Bergler 2022, 933–4; Nagel 2014, 264). The gospel portrays the other disciples as erring in practicing their faith and contrasts this with Gnostic doctrine.[18] The Gnostic perspective is reflected in word choice and content for both the person and mission of Jesus as fully divine as well as the role of Judas and other disciples. The content of the gospel is highly unusual: on the one hand, Judas surpasses the other disciples because he is the bravest of them all and thinks further than the others (GJd 35),[19] receives special teaching (35:24-36:4), will be a ruler in the end times (46:19-23), and will outdo all other because he will sacrifice the human that carries the pneumatic Jesus (56:19-20) (Thomassen 2008, 169–70). On the other hand, he is predicted to grieve much and will not be part of the holy generation (46:11-13; 46:25-47:1) (Thomassen 2008, 169–70). "Judas is set apart from either of the two realms and generations. He will become 'the thirteenth,' a position which is, as it were, 'betwixt and between' the two realms" (Thomassen 2008, 163). It is difficult to decide to what extent the image and fate of Judas in this text is to be understood positively or negatively.

Another source is the Acts of Peter,[20] a Greek work from the second or third century CE, which is only available in a fourth-century Latin translation preserved in a seventh-century codex called *Actus Vercellensis* (Döhler 2017, 1–2). This narrative revolves around a competition between the apostle Peter and Simon Magus (Acts 8:9-24) (Stoops 2012, 13), a Gnostic (Rudolph 2009), who is defeated in the end and dies. Judas is mentioned only once in a speech given by Peter on the temptations of Satan. Like the gospels of Luke and John, this author associates Judas' betrayal with Satan's work. However, he shifts responsibility away from Judas—something the evangelists do not do—when Peter blames Satan: "You forced Judas, my fellow disciple and fellow apostle, to act ungodly, so that he betrayed our Lord Jesus Christ, who must demand expiation from you" (Döhler 2017, 78–9, translation mine). According to this text it is, therefore, Satan who is at fault and who deserves punishment for the betrayal, not Judas.

These sources present a variety of early Christian interpretations of the role and character of Judas and show the range of ways in which he can be understood. It is far from clear who the historical Judas really was, what to think of him, and how he might have died. Did he deserve and suffer divine punishment, or was he chosen to make a sacrifice, for better or/and worse, as in the Gospel of Judas, or was he, after all, a helpless victim of Satan's temptations? Or perhaps something else entirely?

Conclusion: How Can We Read Judas in a New Light?

In conclusion, the biblical texts and other early Christian witnesses do not give a clear answer about Judas and his death. There is no definitive condemnation of Judas in the Gospel according to Matthew or in early Christianity in general, neither of him as a person nor of his suicide. Matthew does criticize Judas, but the criticism is not for how he ended his life, but for the choices and actions he made in life by not valuing Jesus as he should have. The suicide itself is not condemned but is "a statement of fact. To insist that Matthew was condemning suicide because the betrayer of Jesus died in this way is to read into the story an attitude that did not become basic Christian teaching until some three hundred years after the gospels were written" (Clemons 1990, 23). Moreover, Matthew is the evangelist who also knows of Judas' regret. For him, therefore, Judas is not a one-dimensional character who is simply evil; rather, he is a complex individual who, to an extent, must remain a question for readers. Reading Judas in a new light, then, cannot mean understanding everything about him, but accepting the shadowy parts of the story about him that simply cannot be illuminated.

Although Judas' suicide is merely stated and not judged, this does not mean that it is meaningless. It may show the depth of his regret and sorrow for what he had done. It may be understood as Judas trying to right the wrong himself after the chief priests failed to help him in any way. It may have been his way of trying to atone for what he had done. In any case, the story can and should be a reminder to those in positions of responsibility to take their roles seriously and not to leave people alone in their desperation when they are in a position to help: "From everyone to whom much has been given, much will be required, and from the one to whom much has been entrusted, even more will be demanded" (Lk. 12:48). Judas' fate shows the importance of a good shepherd, but also that those who are good shepherds, like Jesus, should be valued accordingly. Judas, on the other hand, becomes the epitome of the lost sheep while Jesus, arrested by his enemies, is unable "to go after the one that is ost until he finds it" (Lk. 15:4). The chief priests, however, could care for him, but they do not. Instead, they fail to live up to their responsibility—which Matthew considers to have dire historical consequences.

Does this mean that Judas is lost forever? That no one will ever go after him to find him? Not necessarily, since Christian faith is based on the resurrection of Jesus, the true Good Shepherd (Jn 10:1-21). In a medieval basilica in France, St. Mary Magdalene in Vézelay, there is a capital of a column that expresses exactly this hope for Judas.[21] It shows Jesus carrying Judas on his shoulders like a lost sheep, thus catching up with the search for the one lost sheep he could not seek during his time on earth. The question of Judas' salvation cannot be answered with certainty by reading the Bible and the early non-biblical Christian witnesses but must remain a question of faith and hope beyond exegetical work. Therefore, there is reason to hope—just as the sculptor of this capital seems to have done.

Notes

1 I would like to thank Sherri Brown for her support and guidance during the conceptualization and process of writing this article.

2 This article uses the NRSVue translation for direct quotations unless otherwise noted.

3 It should be noted, however, that some authors argue that the amount paid to Zechariah is indeed a large sum (Meyers and Meyers 1993, 276–9).

4 See, e.g., Wilson (2022, 345) and Brown (1994, 637–44).

5 I thank Prof. Gordon Brubacher for sharing his insights.

6 This phrase can also be found in 1 Enoch 38:2; 1 Clement 46:8; Hermas, *The Visions* 4:2; *Mishnah Chagigah* 2:1 (Davies and Allison 1997, 463).

7 To illustrate the use of the same vocabulary, the NABRE translation is used here.

8 The translation "companion and friend" follows the ancient Greek version (Septuagint) of Sirach (*hetairos kai philos* / ἑταῖρος καὶ φίλος). The Hebrew version of these words (כנפשך רע) chooses an even stronger image: "a companion like your very self" (Rey and Reymond 2024, 104–5). If the connection is intended, it would emphasize the closeness that once existed between Jesus and Judas as his disciple.

9 To what extent Judas' remorse is true and valid is debated among scholars, as some argue that Matthew purposefully does not use the typical word *metanoein* (μετανοεῖν), but *metamelesthai* (μεταμέλεσθαι) to mark the faultiness of Judas' remorse. However, it can be argued that Jesus uses the same word in his Parable of the Two Sons (Mt. 21:28-32), which tells of two sons who are to work in the vineyard but do not go initially, to describe a positive change of heart on the part of one of the sons (21:29) (Bergler 2022, 628).

10 It should be noted, however, that because of the sources available, this view represents mostly the opinion of the upper class and may not reflect the opinion of the general public (Vortisch 2022, 148).

11 While Bergler identifies 2 Samuel 17:23 as the antetype (Bergler 2022, 632), Harris argues for a connection, that is, however, not the basis of the NT story (Harris 1900, 530).

12 This latter interpretation can already be found in *Jewish Antiquities* 7.9.7 (229) by the ancient Jewish historian Flavius Josephus.

13 While NRSVue reproduces this parallel, NABRE and NIV, for example, use two different verbs to describe the Greek phrase.

14 According to ancient tradition, this place is located at "a site at the east end of the Valley of Hinnom, just south of Jerusalem (cf. Jer 19:7)" (Blomberg 1992, 408).

15 Bergler argues that the phrase could not be used by the chief priests at that time because Jesus was not yet dead (Bergler 2022, 638). However, it seems to be clear to

all observers at this point how the story will turn out, so this does not seem to be a contradiction. Nevertheless, given the different versions of Judas' death and the clear presence of Matthean influence, it seems plausible that this scene was shaped by the community's polemic against the Jewish leadership (Bergler 2022, 638), with whom they had ongoing conflicts. Berger notes that if this scene is historical, it must have taken place after Easter, since the day of Jesus' death was part of the Jewish Feast of Unleavened Bread and it seems unlikely that the priests would have purchased a field on that day (Bergler 2022, 638).

16 See also, for example, Mk 1:2 which only quotes Isaiah but also draws on Malachi 3:1 (Blomberg 1992, 409).

17 For an overview of the discussion, see Schnelle (2024, 344–50, 362–8).

18 For more information on this see, for example, Turner (2009, 95–133).

19 The quotation follows the page numbers and lines of the discovered document as used by Kasser and Wurst (2007).

20 For an English translation, see Stoops (2012).

21 The capital can be seen on the cover of a book by Christoph Wrembek, S.J., who meditates on it (Wrembek 2021).

Bibliography

Barton, John. 2014. *Ethics in Ancient Israel*. Oxford University Press.

Berger, Klaus. 2020. *Kommentar Zum Neuen Testament*. 4th ed. Gütersloher Verlagshaus.

Bergler, Siegfried. 2022. *Judas: Einer Der Nachösterlichen Zwölf*. Vol. 2. Wissenschaftliche Monographien Zum Alten Und Neuen Testament 168. Vandenhoeck & Ruprecht.

Blomberg, Craig L. 1992. *Matthew*. The New American Commentary 22. Broadman Press.

Boyarin, Daniel. 2004. *Border Lines: The Partition of Judaeo-Christianity*. Divinations: Rereading Late Ancient Religion. University of Pennsylvania Press.

Brown, Raymond E. 1994. *The Death of the Messiah. From Gethsemane to the Grave: A Commentary on the Passion Narratives in the Four Gospels*. Vol. 1. The Anchor Bible Reference Library. Doubleday.

Carey, Holly J. 2011. "Judas Iscariot. The Betrayer of Jesus." In *Jesus Among Friends and Enemies. A Historical and Literary Introduction to Jesus in the Gospels*, edited by Chris Keith and Larry W. Hurtado249–67. Baker Academic.

Clemons, James T. 1990. *What Does the Bible Say about Suicide?* Fortress Press.

Davies, W. D., and Dale C. Allison. 1997. *A Critical and Exegetical Commentary on the Gospel According to Saint Matthew. Commentary on Matthew XIX-XXVIII*. Vol. 3.

The International Critical Commentary on the Holy Scriptures of the Old and New Testaments. T&T Clark.

Döhler, Marietheres, ed. 2017. *Acta Petri. Text, Übersetzung Und Kommentar Zu Den Actus Vercellenses*. Texte Und Untersuchungen Zur Geschichte Der Altchristlichen Literatur 171. De Gruyter.

Ehrman, Bart D. 2006. *The Lost Gospel of Judas Iscariot: A New Look at Betrayer and Betrayed*. Oxford University Press.

Evans, Craig A. 2012. *Matthew*. Cambridge University Press.

Freedman, H., and Maurice Simon, eds. 1951. *Midrash Rabbah. Genesis*. Translated by H. Freedman. Vol. 2. 2 vols. Soncino Press.

Garland, David E. 1993. *Reading Matthew. A Literary and Theological Commentary on the First Gospel*. Reading the New Testament Series. Crossroad.

Gathercole, Simon J. 2007. *The Gospel of Judas: Rewriting Early Christianity*. Oxford University Press.

Gundry, Robert H. 2010. *Commentary on the New Testament. Verse-by-Verse Explanations with a Literal Translation*. Hendrickson Publishers.

Harris, J. Rendel. 1900. "Did Judas Really Commit Suicide?" *The American Journal of Theology* 4 (3): 490–513. https://doi.org/10.1086/477430.

Hooff, Anton J. L. van. 1990. *From Autothanasia to Suicide: Self-Killing in Classical Antiquity*. Routledge.

Josephus, Flavius. 2005. *Josephus Flavius. Translation and Commentary. Volume 4: Judean Antiquities, Books 5–7*. Edited by Christopher T. Begg. Brill.

Kasser, Rodolphe, and Gregor Wurst, eds. 2007. *The Gospel of Judas. Together with the Letter of Peter to Philip, James and a Book of Allogenes from Codex Tchacos. Critical Edition*. National Geographic Society.

Klein, George L. 2008. *Zechariah*. The New American Commentary 21B. B&H Publishing Group.

Layton, Bentley, ed. 2021. *The Gnostic Scriptures*. 2nd ed. Yale University Press.

Meyers, Carol L., and Eric M. Meyers, eds. 1993. *Zechariah 9-14. A New Translation with Introduction and Commentary*. Anchor Bible. Doubleday.

Moo, Douglas J. 1983. "Tradition and Old Testament in Matt. 27:3-10." In *Gospel Perspectives. Studies in Midrash and Historiography*, edited by R. T. France and David Wenham, Vol. 3, 157–75. JSOT Press.

Most, Glenn W. 2008. "The Judas of the Gospels and the Gospel of Judas." In *The Gospel of Judas in Context. Proceedings of the First International Conference on the Gospel of Judas, Paris, Sorbonne, October 27th–28th, 2006*, edited by Maddalena Scopello. Nag Hammadi and Manichaean Studies 62, 69–80. Brill.

Nagel, Peter. 2014. *Codex apocryphus gnosticus Novi Testamenti*. Wissenschaftliche Untersuchungen zum Neuen Testament 326. Mohr Siebeck.

National Council of Churches, ed. 2024. *NRSVue Holy Bible. New Revised Standard Version Updated Edition*. SPCK Publishing.

Neusner, Jacob, ed. 1985. *Genesis Rabbah. The Judaic Commentary to the Book of Genesis. A New American Translation. Vol. II. Parashiyyot Thirty-Four through Sixty-Seven on Genesis 8:15 to 28:9*. Vol. 2. Brown Judaic Studies 105. Scholars Press.

Rahlfs, Alfred, ed. 2006. *Septuaginta. Id est Vetus Testamentum Graece Iuxta LXX Interpretes*. Ed. altera, quam Recogn. et emendavit Robert Hanhart. Deutsche Bibelgesellschaft.

Rengstorf, Karl Heinrich. 1935. "Εταῖρος." In *Theologisches Wörterbuch Zum Neuen Testament,* 2. Kohlhammer.

Rey, Frédérique Michèle, and Eric D. Reymond. 2024. *A Critical Edition of the Hebrew Manuscripts of Ben Sira. With Translations and Philological Notes*. Supplements to the Journal for the Study of Judaism 217. Brill.

Rudolph, Kurt. 2009. "Gnosis, Gnostics, Gnosticism." In *Brill's New Pauly Online*. Brill. https://doi.org/10.1163/1574-9347_bnp_e425720.

Schnelle, Udo. 2024. *Einleitung in das Neue Testament*. 10th ed. UTB Religion, Theologie 1830. UTB.

Smith, Geoffrey S. 2016. "The Death of Judas According to Papias." In *New Testament Apocrypha. More Noncanonical Scriptures*, edited by Tony Burke and Brent Landau, 1. William B. Eerdmans Publishing Company.

Stoops, Robert F., ed. 2012. *The Acts of Peter*. Early Christian Apocrypha 4. Polebridge Press.

Thomassen, Einar. 2008. "Is Judas Really the Hero of the Gospel of Judas?" In *The Gospel of Judas in Context. Proceedings of the First International Conference on the Gospel of Judas, Paris, Sorbonne, October 27th–28th, 2006*. Nag Hammadi and Manichaean Studies 62,57–70. Brill.

Turner, John D. 2009. "The Sethian Myth in the *Gospel of Judas*. Soteriology or Demonology?" In *The Codex Judas Papers*, edited by April D. DeConick. Brill, 95–133.

Vortisch, Johannes. 2022. *Das unschuldige Blut im Matthäusevangelium: zur geschichtstheologischen Deutung des Todes Jesu*. Wissenschaftliche Untersuchungen zum Neuen Testament 2. Reihe 578. Mohr Siebeck.

Weaver, Dorothy Jean. 2014. "'What Is That to Us? See to It Yourself' (Mt 27:4): Making Atonement and the Matthean Portrait of the Jewish Chief Priests." *HTS Teologiese Studies / Theological Studies* 70 (1): 1–8. https://doi.org/10.4102/hts.v70i1.2703.

Wilson, Walter T. 2022. *The Gospel of Matthew. Matthew 14-28*. Vol. 2. Eerdmans Critical Commentary. William B. Eerdmans Publishing Company.

Wrembek, Christoph, S.J. 2021. *Hope for Judas? God's Boundless Mercy for Us All*. New City Press.

Index

About the Contributors

Elizabeth Antus is a Catholic feminist theologian and Assistant Professor in the Department of Theology and Religious Studies at Georgetown University. She researches the theological dimensions of sexual violence, mental health, suicidality, and disability. Her work has appeared in *Theological Studies*; *Journal of Religious Ethics*; *Journal of Religion, Disability, & Health*; *Political Theology*; and *Concilium*. She is currently completing a book entitled *The Tender Gift of Self-Love: A Feminist Theological Engagement with Augustine*. Notably, her *Theological Studies* article is entitled "'The Silence of the Dead': Remembering Suicide Victims and Reimagining the Communion of Saints."

Amy Badura-Brack is Professor of Psychological Science at Creighton University, where she teaches courses in Psychopathology, Health Psychology, and Introductory Psychology and directs the department's undergraduate internship program. She also serves as Chair of Creighton's Social and Behavioral Institutional Review Board. Badura-Brack has published forty-eight professional papers on topics including the effects of trauma exposure, PTSD, depression, anxiety, and suicide. Her work integrates clinical insight with empirical data, often bridging the divide between psychological science and practice. Her contribution to this volume is coauthored by research assistant **Ryan Fabry.**

Gordon Brubacher is Resident Assistant Professor of Scripture and Social Justice at Creighton University, teaching courses on peace and justice in the Older Testament; Christian ethics of war and peacebuilding; and social justice in Islam. Special experiences include teaching Hebrew Bible and Ancient Near Eastern Studies at the Ecumenical Institute of Theological Studies at Tantur, Jerusalem, working with the Bethsaida Archaeology Project by the Sea of Galilee and with the Cave of Letters Exploration Project near the Dead Sea; and working alongside peace teams in that region. His most recent publication is the commentary on Hosea in the *Anabaptist Community Bible* (2025).

Jamall A. Calloway is an Assistant Professor of Theology and Religious studies at Georgetown University, where he teaches courses in religion, philosophy, literature, and black liberation theology. He is also currently an honorary research lecturer in the School of Religion, Philosophy, and Classics at the University of KwaZulu-Natal, Pietermaritzburg Campus, in South Africa. He is the author of *Imagining Eden: Black Theology and the Search for Paradise* (2025).

Christina Jones Davis is Assistant Professor of Pastoral Theology and Marriage and Family Therapy at Christian Theological Seminary (CTS). An ordained minister in the Progressive National Baptist Church, Davis holds a ThD in Pastoral Care and Counseling from the Emory University Candler School of Theology, where she received the *W.E.B. DuBois Noomo Award for Academic Excellence*. Her research and teaching interests focus on spiritually integrated counseling, substance abuse and addiction treatment, and relational psychoanalytic theory and self-state multiplicity among women of color. Davis teaches courses in Crisis Care, Foundations of Pastoral Care, Theological Perspectives on Pastoral and Spiritual Care, Social & Cultural Dimensions of Counseling, and Psychodynamic Family Therapy.

Julia Fleming, Professor of Theology at Creighton University, focuses her research upon the historical development of Roman Catholic moral theology and Catholic social thought. Her most recent publications address capital punishment, ecclesiastical immunity, and nineteenth-century Jesuit responses to lynching.

LaRyssa D. Herrington is a recent graduate of the University of Notre Dame where she completed her doctorate in systematic theology and liturgical studies. Her research works at the intersection of Black and womanist theologies, political and liberation theologies, ritual studies, and sacramental theology. Notable publications include "Baptism as *Mystical-Political Engagement*? Exploring the Rite of Baptism in African American Slave Narratives during the Antebellum Period" in *Black Theology: An International Journal*, and "Do you hear what I hear?": Karl Barth, the *sensus fidelium*, and Theologies of Proclamation as Tools for Engaging Contemporary Social Movements in *Liturgy*.

Christopher J. Krall, S.J., is a priest of the Society of Jesus and an assistant professor of Theology and Neuroscience at Creighton University. He teaches courses in Systematic Theology, Science-engaged Theology, the Spiritual Exercises, and the Christian Tradition. Krall serves as a reserve chaplain in the United States Navy and has been deployed to Eastern Africa. His publications focus on human flourishing and are found in *The Journal of Religion and Society*, *The Journal of Moral Theology*, and *Lumen et Vita*. His PhD is from Marquette University, with other graduate degrees from Boston College, University of Toronto, and Oxford University.

Michael G. Lawler is Amelia and Emil Graff Professor Emeritus of Catholic theology at Creighton University, where he taught courses on sacraments, marriage, and sexuality at Creighton, as well as in Ireland, England, Italy, and Australia. Lawler has authored 29 books and some 200 scholarly essays. In addition to his contribution to the present volume, Lawler has coauthored several books with **Todd A. Salzman**, including *The Sexual Person: Toward a Renewed Catholic Anthropology* (2008), winner of the 2009 Catholic Press Association's Book of the Year award. Their most recent coauthored book is *Sexual and Gender Doctrinal Language: A Source of Pain and Trauma in the Catholic Church* (2025).

Tabea Pelzmann, Mag. Theol. (Magister Theologiae), BA, is a pastoral worker in the Diocese of Rottenburg-Stuttgart, Germany. She has studied Education and Theology at the Catholic University of Eichstätt-Ingolstadt, Creighton University in the United States, and the Eberhard Karls University of Tübingen.

Kimberly L. Penner holds a PhD in Theology from the University of Toronto. She is Associate Teaching Faculty for the University of Alberta, St. Stephen's College, and full-time Pastor at Stirling Avenue Mennonite Church, Kitchener, Ontario. Her research focuses on the contextual and embodied nature of ethics, theories of power, Christian feminist approaches to peace and violence, and life-giving sexual ethics.

Nicolae Roddy is Professor of Theology at Creighton University, where he teaches courses in Hebrew Bible and Christian Traditions. A former Fulbright scholar to Romania, Roddy authored the *Romanian Version of the Testament of Abraham: Text, Translation, and Cultural Context* (Society of Biblical Literature, 2001). For over twenty years, he taught biblical archaeology for the Jewish Studies Center in the Faculty of Letters at the University of Bucharest, Romania. Between 1996 and 2016, Roddy served as codirector and area supervisor for the Bethsaida Archaeology Project, located near the northern shore of the Sea of Galilee. Following upon several publications, his most recent book is *Roots of Scripture: The Prophetically Influenced Priestly Scribal Critique of Human Institutions and Its Relevance for Today* (2024).

Todd A. Salzman is Amelia and Emil Graff Chair Professor of Catholic Theology at Creighton University. Besides the present contribution, he and coauthor **Michael G. Lawler** have published the award-winning *The Sexual Person: Toward a Renewed Catholic Anthropology* (2008); *Sexual Ethics: A Theological Introduction* (2012); *Virtue and Theological Ethics: Toward a Renewed Ethical Method* (2018); *Introduction to Theological Ethics: Foundations and Applications* (2019); *Pope Francis and the Transformation of Catholic Health Care Ethics* (2021); and *Sexual and Gender Doctrinal Language: A Source of Pain and Trauma in the Catholic Church* (2025). Their scholarly articles have appeared in *Theological Studies, Louvain Studies, Horizons, Heythrop Journal, Irish Theological Quarterly, Commonweal,* and *America.*

www.ingramcontent.com/pod-product-compliance
Ingram Content Group UK Ltd.
Pitfield, Milton Keynes, MK11 3LW, UK
UKHW020216290926
15470UKWH00001B/213

9 781666 977547